Pioneers of
Irregular Warfare

Pioneers of Irregular Warfare

Secrets of the Military Intelligence Research Department in the Second World War

Malcolm Atkin

Pen & Sword
MILITARY

First published in Great Britain in 2021 by
PEN & SWORD MILITARY
An imprint of Pen & Sword Books Ltd
Yorkshire – Philadelphia

Copyright © Malcolm Atkin, 2021

ISBN 978-1-52676-600-7

Typeset by Concept, Huddersfield, West Yorkshire, HD4 5JL.
Printed and bound by CPI Group (UK) Ltd, Croydon CR0 4YY

Pen & Sword Books Ltd incorporates the Imprints of Aviation, Atlas,
Family History, Fiction, Maritime, Military, Discovery, Politics, History,
Archaeology, Select, Wharncliffe Local History, Wharncliffe True Crime,
Military Classics, Wharncliffe Transport, Leo Cooper, The Praetorian Press,
Remember When, White Owl, Seaforth Publishing and Frontline Publishing.

For a complete list of Pen & Sword titles please contact
PEN & SWORD BOOKS LTD
47 Church Street, Barnsley, South Yorkshire, S70 2AS, England
E-mail: enquiries@pen-and-sword.co.uk
Website: www.pen-and-sword.co.uk
or
PEN & SWORD BOOKS
1950 Lawrence Rd, Havertown, PA 19083, USA
E-mail: uspen-and-sword@casematepublishers.com
Website: www.penandswordbooks.com

Contents

List of Plates

List of Figures

Abbreviations

BEF – British Expeditionary Force
CIGS – Chief of the Imperial General Staff
DCIGS – Deputy Chief of the Imperial General Staff
DDMI(I) – Deputy Director, Military Intelligence (Intelligence)
DDMI(O) – Deputy Director, Military Intelligence (Operations)
DDMI(R) – Deputy Director, Military Intelligence (Research)
D/M – Unofficial title briefly replacing GS(R) in April 1939
DMI – Director of Military Intelligence
DMT – Directorate of Military Training
DSR – Directorate of Scientific Research
GC&CS – Government Code and Cypher School
GHQ – General Headquarters
G(R) – formal name of MI(R) Middle East
GSO – General Staff Officer (in Grades 1–3)
GS(R) – General Services (Research). The research unit from which MI(R) was formed
HDS – Home Defence Scheme of Section D
ISPB – Inter-Services Project Board
ISSB – Inter-Services Security Board
IWM – Imperial War Museum
LDV – Local Defence Volunteers (original name of the Home Guard
LRDG – Long Range Desert Group
MD1 – The designation of MI(R)c after its transfer to the Ministry of Defence
MI1(a) – Distribution of reports and intelligence records
MI1(c) – The designation for SIS within the War Office
MI1(R) – Official title of what is usually known as MI(R) or MIR in June 1939 to formally replace GS(R)
MI3 – Geographical information
MI5 – Security Service
MI6 – Popular name of SIS
MI7 – Propaganda and Censorship
MI9 – Escape and Evasion organization
MI10 – Weapons and Technical Intelligence
MI11 – Field Security

MIL – Liaison, Arms traffic and Law
MIR – Alternative form of MI(R) in contemporary documents from June 1940
MI(R) – Military Intelligence Research department from June 1940
MI(R)a – Coordination of Projects and Services section of MI(R)
MI(R)b – Special Operations and Political Action section of MI(R)
MI(R)c – Technical section of MI(R), later transferred to the Ministry of Defence as MD1
MO9 – Military Operations department created to manage the Commandos
NID – Naval Intelligence Department
NWEF – North Western Expeditionary Force (Norway campaign)
OCTU – Officer Cadet Training Unit
OER – Officers Emergency Reserve
PUS – Permanent Under-Secretary of State
RARO – Regular Army Reserve of Officers
SAS – Special Air Service
Section D – Sabotage section of SIS, which worked closely with MI(R)
SIME – Security Intelligence, Middle East
SIS – Secret Intelligence Service, popularly known as MI6
SOE – Special Operations Executive
SPD – German Social Democratic Party (*Sozialdemokratische Partei*)
STS – Special Training School (of SOE)
TA – Territorial Army
TARO – Territorial Army Reserve of Officers
TNA – The National Archives
VCIGS – Vice Chief of the Imperial General Staff

Acknowledgements

Especial thanks go to Elizabeth Holland, who shared her memories of her father Jo Holland, the founder of MI(R), and revealed the family connections to other MI(R) officers. Thanks are also owed to Darron Wadey for discussion on the operations of MI(R) in the Netherlands and to Gerard Murphy for providing sources relating to Jo Holland's service in Ireland. As with previous publications, the assistance of Lee Richards of ARCRE in copying documents in The National Archives has been invaluable and we thank the staff of The National Archives and Imperial War Museum for their kind attention. I am particularly grateful to David Gordon and David Sampson for making photographs of their remarkable collections available for reproduction. Thanks also to Kate Atkin for additional photography. The cooperation of the copyright holders is acknowledged in the individual captions. As ever, thanks to my wife Susanne for her support and patience, correcting my grammar and for compiling the Index. Rupert Harding and Sarah Cook of Pen & Sword steered the completed text through the publication process with their customary skill and patience.

Preface

This study grew out of earlier research on Section D of SIS (Atkin, 2017) and began on the false premise that Section D and MI(R) could be directly compared. It became clear that they had very different remits but should have been complementary in their pioneering approach to irregular warfare. This holistic vision was hindered by War Office and personal politics, mixed with a good deal of what, with hindsight, appears as naivety and nationalistic arrogance. It was a frustrating experience for many of its officers as its initiatives often never quite fulfilled their promise, not least because of repeated lapses in security and an inherent requirement to reveal their plans to foreign General Staffs whose loyalty to the Allied cause could be questionable. Their efforts in field operations were often failures, but the founder of MI(R), Jo Holland, argued that this was a role forced upon them and operational failures should not devalue the contribution of MI(R) as a 'think tank' which made major contributions to the development of clandestine warfare. Post-war, the history of MI(R) tended to be seen mainly as the preface to Colin Gubbins' career in the Special Operations Executive (SOE), frequently distorted to place him in the best possible light. Unfortunately Jo Holland died before he felt able to offer his own interpretation of events. Wherever possible, I have tried to go back to the contemporary records and this has led both to a revised interpretation of MI(R) as a whole and particularly of the contribution of Colin Gubbins.

In an environment driven by acronyms, the Military Intelligence (Research) department of the War Office went through a remarkable number of name changes in its short life between 1938 and 1940. It was known at various times as GS(R), D/M, D/MIR, MI1(R), MI(R) or simply MIR and had subdivisions as MIR(a) to (c). In this book it is generally referred to as MI(R). The head of MI(R), and the focus of its story, was Lieutenant Colonel (later Major General) J.C.F. Holland, known in the army as Jo or Joe and to his family as Jack. In publications he is most commonly named as Jo and this practice is followed here.

In general, ranks are not used in the text due to the frequency with which they changed and the confusing use of temporary and acting ranks. For further information on the career progression of many MI(R) officers see the online Appendix 1 (https://independent.academia.edu/MalcolmAtkin).

Introduction

British Intelligence in the inter-war period was greatly under-resourced after the Military Intelligence Directorate was abolished in 1922 and merged with Military Operations. The Intelligence branch within the combined directorate dealt with matters of strategy but operational formations were expected to assign their own Intelligence staff from regimental officers, often with little specialist training. Major General Frederick 'Paddy' Beaumont-Nesbitt, head of the Intelligence branch, became head of a re-established Directorate of Military Intelligence in September 1939 and played a key role in overhauling Military Intelligence, including championing a small research unit in the War Office which originated as GS(R) and eventually became MI(R). It had been created in late 1938 as a small think-tank for irregular warfare but was dissolved in October 1940. The short history of MI(R) was intertwined with that of Section D of SIS and the two leaders, Jo Holland and Laurence Grand, worked in close partnership.[1] In March 1939 these pioneers conceived an integrated plan of military and civilian guerrilla warfare and subversion which set the agenda for irregular warfare until the creation of SOE in July 1940. A Middle East equivalent, G(R), was formed in April 1940 under the general oversight of MI(R) but had a more operational focus. G(R) survived until September 1941 when it was finally absorbed by SOE. In the Far East elements survived until 1942, by which time former members of MI(R) were scattered amongst the new generation of special forces.

Lieutenant Colonel Jo Holland was a visionary who created a blueprint for many aspects of clandestine warfare and was a key source of advice to the War Office during 1940. His imagination raced far ahead of the immediate crisis and in August 1940 Holland tried to persuade the Director of Military Intelligence that MI(R), re-orientated on research rather than operations in the field, should focus on developing the technology and tactics for STOL (short take off/landing) and helicopter-borne operations. Holland saw the role of MI(R) as being essentially one of research and was philosophical about the use made of its work which was more famously developed by others. He commented, 'As you know, MI(R) has done a very considerable amount of work and has seen one idea after another evolved and taken away.'[2] These ideas included the escape and evasion service (MI9) and the Commandos. MI(R) officer Quintin Hogg (Lord Hailsham) described it as 'a clearing house for bright ideas'.[3] Not all were happy with this altruistic attitude and there was a tension with Colin Gubbins, recruited in April 1939 as a major, who wanted a more active role. Gubbins was not given the chance in Norway to use the MI(R)-inspired Independent Companies in the guerrilla role for which they were intended but more surprisingly, given the reputation he was already acquiring as an expert in guerrilla warfare, he struggled to find a format for the GHQ Auxiliary Units in Britain.

MI(R) was not structurally incorporated into SOE in the same way as Section D, although many former officers soon drifted into the new organization. Instead its sections were incorporated into other parts of Military Intelligence with the technical section MI(R)c most famously becoming 'Churchill's Toyshop' in the new Ministry of Defence. Colin Gubbins became head of SOE in 1943 and one of his most significant contributions was to draw SOE back towards the original para-military concept preached by MI(R). His own 'back story', and that of MI(R), was then partially rewritten to suit his post-war legend. In 1948 Gubbins falsely claimed that 'in 1940 when British forces were evacuated from Western Europe there was not a single contact of any kind with occupied Western Europe until somebody was dropped back there'.[4] He exaggerated when maintaining, in regard to training, 'there was ... practically nothing existing, just one explosives school and a dozen officers and civilians'. Thus 'all had to be built up from scratch.'[5]

Where antecedents to SOE were acknowledged by later historians they would frequently focus on Gubbins' personal contribution to MI(R). Biographer A.R.B. Linderman unfairly maintained 'Holland was thinking up clever projects and the men of Section D were chasing ghosts', while it was Gubbins who was presented as having the more practical role.[6] It was Gubbins who, in 1945, commissioned the first official history of SOE, although Mackenzie's opus, completed in 1947, was not released for publication until 2000. This contained an extensive description of MI(R) but was completed shortly after SOE had been abolished and Gubbins, by now an acting major general, had been unceremoniously cast aside and retired on the pension of his substantive rank of colonel. Mackenzie blended official archives and oral testimony from key figures in SOE, dismayed by the treatment of their former leader, but it is not clear if he interviewed Laurence Grand of Section D and Jo Holland of MI(R); neither of them ever told their story in public. Unlike Gubbins, both retired with the substantive rank of major general. For Mackenzie, 'MI(R) was successful as a research department largely because it was allowed to assume some executive responsibility. Its job (as construed by Colonel Holland) was not only to think up new schemes, but to drive them through the clogging medium of War Office discussion till they worked and stood on their own legs.'[7] This was only partly true. Although firmly maintaining MI(R) was superior to Section D, both in technique and with its schemes having a 'harder and more practical air' (an aspect that the present study will question), Mackenzie also had to admit 'It is impossible to claim that it [MI(R)] achieved much subversion, or that it left much organization on which SOE could build.'[8]

The driver in these early assessments was that, if SOE had any antecedents it had to be MI(R), in which Gubbins played a major role, and little credit was given to any branch of SIS, not helped by the fierce secrecy with which SIS surrounded any aspect of its work. In fact, it can be argued that MI(R) was less successful when it tried to compete with Section D in covert field operations, but this was not its intended role. Holland was trying to build a principle that irregular warfare should be driven by military strategy and led by soldiers, in contrast to the use of civilian agents and economic sabotage championed by Section D and the early SOE. Holland's perspective was arguably the most successful in the long term, once Allied resources improved, but in 1940 MI(R)'s reliance on the cooperation of foreign General Staffs (on the naïve assumption that they would automatically welcome British advice) was a fatal flaw.

The distortion in presentation was continued by M.R.D. Foot, who in his Preface to *SOE in France* (1966) acknowledged the influence of Gubbins 'who enabled me to call on his unrivalled recollections of what went on'.[9] Sadly, by then Holland was already dead and Grand followed the SIS tradition of silence. There was no equivalent memorial to Holland or Grand as that to Gubbins published in 1993 by his devoted followers, Peter Wilkinson and Joan Bright Astley, as *Gubbins and SOE* (1993), which established the tone for more modern, near hagiographical, studies. It was only in 2005 that Simon Anglim provided a more considered modern summary of the work of MI(R) and the present work is able to offer a more in-depth analysis of this pioneer of irregular warfare.[10]

Chapter One

The Formation of MI(R)

Inspired by the success of the Arab Revolt and its attached British officers, in January 1918 the War Office had created a prototype special forces unit under Major General Lionel Dunsterville (Dunsterforce). Its task was to unify the disparate anti-Bolshevik and anti-Turkish groups fighting in Persia (Iran) and the Caucasus, to secure the important oil installations at Baku and protect the strategically important Trans-Caucasian railway. Success would also secure the exposed eastern flank of the British troops in Mesopotamia, previously protected by the Czarist forces. Dunsterforce comprised up to a thousand men who were required to be of 'strong character and adventurous spirit, especially good stamina, capable of organizing, training and eventually leading, irregular troops'.[1] The project had only limited success but set an important precedent.

In the 1920s and 1930s Britain faced guerrilla warfare at the hands of the IRA, Indian nationalists and the Arab Revolt in Palestine. Together with the operations of Chinese guerrillas opposing the Japanese invasion of 1937, such attacks emphasized the need to better counter guerrilla tactics and for the War Office to incorporate irregular warfare into its own planning. Orde Wingate's Special Night Squads were formed in Palestine in June 1938 from British personnel, Jewish police and members of the paramilitary Haganah, using guerrilla tactics to contain the Arab insurgents, but brought accusations of acting as 'death squads'. A new urgency came from the Germans' successful use of the *Sudetendeutsche Freikorps* (which became the basis of the Brandenburg special forces regiment) to carry out subversion in Bohemia and Moravia during the dismemberment of Czechoslovakia from 1938. Fear of enemy guerrilla operations and 'fifth column' activities (first given a name in the Spanish Civil War of 1936–1939) increasingly took hold of the military and diplomatic psyche and seemed to threaten the conventional approach to fighting a war.

The War Office needed a strategy for both countering and developing these 'ungentlemanly' tactics for its own ends. In 1936 it had formed a small research section innocuously titled General Service (Research) under the Deputy Chief of the Imperial General Staff (DCIGS) to provide a fellowship for an officer to carry out a period of undisturbed research into a topic that was outside the scope of everyday War Office responsibilities. Its charter was to research into problems of tactics and organization, consulting with other branches of the War Office and Commands in order to collect new ideas, and to liaise with technical research branches.[2] The DCIGS explained: 'This section must be small, almost anonymous, go where they like, talk to whom they like, but be kept from files, correspondence and telephone calls.'[3] The existence of GS(R) was belatedly made public on 10 March 1938 when, in a statement to the House of Commons, the Secretary of State for War (Hore-Belisha) announced 'When so much instruction is to be gained from present events the absence of any branch exclusively concerned with pure military research is noticeable, and a small section to study the practice and lessons of actual warfare will be established.'[4] GS(R) was not secret *per se* but it was to maintain a low profile so as to keep it free from interruption and interference within the War Office.

The reports produced by the early incumbents were considered useful but had little practical impact (Fig. 1). This changed when, in December 1938, the post was offered to Major Jo Holland, a Royal Engineer staff officer in the War Office, then recovering from a bout of recurring illness arising out of his First World War service in Salonika.

J.C.F. 'Jo' Holland (Plates 1 and 35) was born in India, the son of a noted geologist, and was universally described as being intelligent, imaginative and practical. Full of humour, he also had a ruthless streak. His obituary by Major General William Broomhall recalled:

> Being able to see the solution to a difficult problem more quickly than most people, he would at once initiate a course of action to achieve that solution. Thereafter, he would ensure that nobody impeded the achievement of the object ... Persons less able than himself (of whom there were many) who could not see so clearly how the result was being achieved were apt to resent the ruthless way he pursued the object and he inevitably made some enemies.[5]

Figure 1. GS(R) Reports 1936–1939. *(TNA HS 8/258)*

No. 1	The Reorganization of the War Office
No. 2	Employment of Historians by the War Office in a consultative capacity
No. 3	Reorganization of the General Staff
No. 4	Army Requirements from the RAF in modern warfare
No. 5	Organization of Armoured and Mobile Units and Formations
No. 6	Training of the Army
No. 7	Considerations from the Wars in Spain and China with regard to certain aspects of Army policy
No. 8	Investigation of the possibilities of Guerrilla Activities

His frustration with ponderous War Office procedures was expressed in bursts of fiery temper and Holland's secretary in MI(R), Joan Bright, remembered how 'I can feel now the quick downward movement by which I ducked the impact of a book flung at my head one day on opening the door of his office'.[6] But Holland soon recovered and he inspired great respect and affection. For Joan Bright: 'The engine which drove us was Colonel Holland. We admired him, feared him. Loved him.'[7] He was more relaxed outside his work environment, and his daughter Elizabeth remembers him as effervescent, a skilled raconteur and the automatic centre of attention at parties, but in common with the other tight-lipped pioneers of Intelligence work at the time, he never spoke of his work in MI(R)!

Holland had been commissioned into the Royal Engineers in 1914 and developed a speciality in Wireless Signals (until 1920 the Royal Engineers were responsible for all military communications). He served in Salonika with Divisional Signals and was then seconded to the Royal Flying Corps as an aerial observer. In October 1918 he was awarded the DFC after having completed over 200 hours of long-distance reconnaissance and contact patrols but there is no basis in the myth that he served with Lawrence of Arabia on aerial reconnaissance.[8] During service in the gruelling Salonika campaign, he contracted amoebic dysentery, leading to recurring bouts of illness which significantly impaired his career. His RAF squadron moved to Ireland in 1919 but he then transferred back to the Royal Engineers and served in the Special Signal Company as a temporary major. It is uncertain if he was officially connected with any Intelligence work but he certainly had direct experience of the IRA.

On the night of 9 January 1921, aged 24, he was shot in the right chest during a mysterious confrontation in a Cork public house.[9] He had been posted to Chatham in October 1920 on a signals course but during the Christmas vacation it is claimed in his Royal Engineers obituary that he had unofficially returned to Ireland to take revenge after the IRA had killed a friend. The obituary maintained he waited in a public house for the killer to appear, indicating he knew the identity of the IRA man and that this was, therefore, likely to be a sanctioned operation. Whilst waiting, the barmaid reputedly urged him to leave but he refused, which begs the question how she knew that Holland was a British officer and the nature of his mission.[10] Shots were fired and Holland staggered out of the pub wounded and was rescued by a conveniently passing armoured car. The *Cork Constitution* of Monday, 10 January reported an 'Exciting City Incident' in which, on the previous night at around 8.00pm in the South Mall/Anglesea Street area, 'five revolver shots in quick succession' were heard but there were no signs of an ambush. When the police arrived they failed to elicit any information on the shooting.[11] Holland subsequently received £125 compensation for 'gunshot wounds through body', and £5 for expenses in making the claim.[12] This may have been a semi-official Intelligence mission (not unknown in Ireland at the time), with the story as recounted in the Royal Engineers obituary being a long-surviving cover story. The incident does not appear in his service record and, despite Holland's reputation as a raconteur, the story was never told to his family.

After his eventful time in Ireland, Holland served in a succession of divisional staff posts before being posted in 1928 to India, where he served on the North West frontier and attended Quetta Staff College. Promoted major in 1933, Holland returned to England and became a staff officer in Southern and then Northern Command. He worked at the War Office from April 1936 in the wide-ranging Staff Duties Directorate, first in SD2 (War Organization) and from September 1937 in SD7 (organization and equipment of armoured vehicles). There he would have met another Royal Engineer, Laurence Grand (Plate 4), who from 1935 to 1938 was Deputy Assistant Director of Mechanization. In 1938 Holland was due for posting overseas but in October he was declared unfit after being diagnosed with a duodenal ulcer. As a consequence, in December he accepted the opportunity given by the VCIGS to take up the vacant research post in GS(R) and carry out a piece of research exploring the methodology for a future war with Germany. The specific topic was to be irregular warfare, focused initially on defensive counter-measures to protect the Empire from the threat of German-inspired subversion and insurrection. This followed long-running efforts by the War Office to establish clear guidelines for dealing with guerrilla warfare, beginning with *Notes on Guerrilla Warfare in Ireland* (1921) which morphed into *Imperial Policing and Irregular Warfare* (1933).[13] Holland's lack of formal Intelligence expertise was symptomatic of the ad hoc nature of recruitment to Military Intelligence at the time. This was considered only a temporary posting, probably with low expectation, but Holland (with the considerable assistance of Laurence Grand, now on secondment to SIS as head of Section D), managed to establish a radical new field of study in the War Office. Section D had been formed a few months earlier in April 1938 to progress plans for clandestine civilian sabotage and subversion from within SIS. The topic chosen for Holland may reflect a concern of the War Office not to be left behind, and wanting to explore the use of guerrillas on a military (more respectable) basis.

Both Holland and Grand believed that guerrilla warfare was likely to be important in any coming war, capable of diverting large numbers of troops from attacking conventional forces and contributing to the expected implosion of the Nazi state by economic disruption. Holland wanted to establish a doctrinal approach to organizing irregular warfare on a para-military basis but rather than managing an executive arm like Section D, Holland believed the role of GS(R)/MI(R) 'was to produce ideas, work them up to a practical stage and then cast them off to grow under their own steam under whomever in MI(R) he had brought up for the purpose'.[14] In accepting this limitation, fellow MI(R) officer Colin Gubbins saw Holland as 'completely unselfish ... [and] had no intention of building an empire for himself'.[15] Similarly, for Joan Bright Holland 'never sought personal aggrandisement'.[16] M.R.D. Foot interpreted such comments as representing 'an unusually modest and self-effacing member of a traditionally self-effacing caste'.[17] Holland did not lack ambition, but instead of building an empire for himself, he firmly believed that irregular operations should be the responsibility of the existing operational departments of the War Office, modernized to incorporate this new form of warfare, rather than create ad hoc new structures: 'I have always thought that each appropriate branch of the General Staff ought to deal with the various activities which we have undertaken, except for the fact that it is probably useful to have a branch with a certain amount of freedom and contact with unusual sources of information and possibilities of action.'[18]

The concept of guerrilla warfare was popular at the time, greatly inspired by the posthumous publication of T.E. Lawrence's *Seven Pillars of Wisdom* in 1935. In that year Second Lieutenant Harry Fox-Davies of the Durham Light Infantry (who later assisted in raising the Middle East Commandos) had promoted guerrilla warfare to his then divisional commander, Archibald Wavell. Fox-Davies pointed out that 'a handful of men at the heart of the enemy's communications could do damage out of all proportion to their numbers'. In response Wavell, an admirer of Lawrence, maintained that a 'trained guerrilla' was impossible but believed it would be possible to train specialist uniformed troops to operate behind enemy lines and that 'guerrilla warfare ... is well worth reading and thinking about'.[19] During army manoeuvres in 1936 Wavell had Fox-Davies mount an unscheduled raid on the rear of the opponent's forces to capture the enemy HQ, causing a premature end to the exercise. Wavell's concept of regular troops operating in an irregular manner was at the heart of what became Holland's vision for MI(R) and would have a major impact on MI(R)'s later operations in the Middle East and the broader development of Special Forces.

In gathering together historical precedents, Holland referred back to the use of the Cossacks against Napoleon's army and the French *francs-tireur* who disrupted German lines of communication after the battle of Sedan in 1871, the more recent hit-and-run tactics of guerrillas in South Africa, China and Spain, and particularly British experience in Ireland.[20] He explained that 'there is little doubt that the Irish made guerrilla warfare into a science, which has been followed since ... It is proposed to base this present study on such information as can be obtained of Irish principles and their application by other revolutionaries subsequently.'[21] He argued that if guerrilla organizations could be established in countries likely to be invaded by a shared enemy then this could divert enemy forces from the main battle; he was less hopeful of prospects for action in countries already occupied. Czechoslovakia had already been invaded, Poland, Romania and Yugoslavia seemed at particular risk from the Germans, and Libya, Ethiopia and Albania from the Italians. Holland began a 'desk-top' study of the wide range of available literature on the subject, including the Boer War (with *Kommando* by Denys Reitz, published in 1932, having become required reading for army officers), T.E. Lawrence's popular accounts of the First World War Arab Revolt, accounts of Russian experiences in the Caucasus and Central Asia, Trotsky's writings on the Russian Civil War and the memoirs of guerrilla warfare by General von Lettow-Vorbeck in East Africa and Jósef Pilsudski in Poland. More recent were the instructions issued to Sinn Fein in its journal *An t'Oglach* (*The Volunteer*), Edgar Snow's *Red Star Over China* (1937) and the Grand Mufti's instructions to the Arab rebels in Palestine. The most recent contribution was Mao Tse Tung's *On Guerrilla Warfare*, published in 1937 and probably privately translated by SIS before its first official translation into English in 1940. Although stressing political education, the basic tactics of guerrilla warfare described by Mao Tse Tung followed the now well-established canon that was later synthesized for MI(R) by Colin Gubbins. Holland's sources also included the training instructions of the First World War Home Guard (Volunteer Training Corps), with the official history of the VTC claiming that 'the force was to take the form of bands of irregulars, and its duty in case of invasion was to carry on a form of guerrilla warfare'.[22] The *VTC Regulations* of 1916 explained:

> The object will be to constantly harass, annoy, and tire out the enemy, and to impede his progress, till a sufficient force can be assembled to smash him ... They must therefore be prepared to move in the lightest manner without baggage of any kind; they must live in temporary shelters, and for this the country is amply suitable.

The British Army's first manual on the topic had been *Notes on Guerrilla Warfare in Ireland* (1921), expanded as *Imperial Policing and Irregular Warfare* in 1933 (*see below*, p. 53 and Appendix 2). T.E. Lawrence also provided a definition of 'Guerrilla Warfare' in the 1929 edition of *Encyclopaedia Britannica*. This maintained 'Guerrilla war is far more intellectual than a bayonet charge' and concluded:

> Rebellions can be made by 2% active in a striking force, and 98% passively sympathetic. The few active rebels must have the qualities of speed and endurance, ubiquity and independence of arteries of supply. They must have the technical equipment to destroy or paralyze the enemy's organized communications, for irregular war is fairly Willisen's definition of strategy, 'the study of communication,' in its extreme degree, of attack where the enemy is not. In fifty words: Granted mobility, security (in the form of denying targets to the enemy), time, and doctrine (the

idea to convert every subject to friendliness), victory will rest with the insurgents, for the algebraical factors are in the end decisive, and against them perfections of means and spirit struggle quite in vain.[23]

After Lawrence's death in 1935 came the best-selling *Seven Pillars of Wisdom*. Lawrence stressed the fundamental guerrilla tactics of mobility, attacking communication lines rather than direct frontal assault and the need to operate within a generally sympathetic population. With this weight of material, Gubbins' later claim that 'there was not a single book to be found in any library in any language which dealt with this subject' – was part of the hyperbole he created around his own contribution in writing the pamphlets *Art of Guerrilla Warfare* and *Partisan Leader's Handbook* for MI(R) (*see below*, p. 53).[24]

Scheme D, March 1939

While Jo Holland worked in lonely isolation in the War Office on his desk-based studies and was tied by the need to be publicly accountable for his budget, in SIS Laurence Grand rapidly expanded Section D and secretly prepared to take to the field on a very different basis.[25] Grand had begun work a few months earlier to research the potential of unavowable clandestine warfare against Germany, using sabotage, subversion and black propaganda and focused on a pre-emptive war against German economic assets from bases in neutral countries, using civilian agents. Holland found the obsessive security of Section D amusing. Staff were not supposed to acknowledge each other in the street and he would go up behind them and shout 'boo' in their car, but together Grand and Holland created 'Scheme D'.[26] This both authorized Section D to immediately go to war and also provided a mechanism for the expansion of GS(R) by allowing it to tap into the secret budget of SIS. Together, they would offer 'an alternative method of defence ... to organised armed resistance ... based on the experience we have had in India, Iraq, Ireland and Russia, i.e. the development of a combination of guerrilla and IRA [Irish Republican Army] tactics'.[27]

Holland and Grand had been near-contemporaries (Grand being nine months younger) at both Rugby School and the Royal Military Academy Woolwich, and latterly had both been staff officers at the War Office, involved in plans for the mechanization of the army. Both were witty and charming but while Grand was very tall and elegant, his mind constantly racing with new ideas and eager for action, by comparison Holland was 'short and burly', a chain-smoker with a sometimes explosive temper but who took a more calculating and long-term approach in his thinking. According to Holland's secretary/personal assistant, Joan Bright, 'Grand was a volatile dreamer, Holland an unsmiling visionary' but despite their different characters 'he [Holland] and Grand got on well together' and they remained close friends after the war.[28] This is contrary to the opinion expressed by Gubbins when claiming to speak for Holland after the latter's death, saying Holland 'had no faith in "D" [Grand], with his wild cat and fantastical schemes, never getting down to brass tacks and specific achievements'.[29] This was a projection of Gubbins' views and was by no means an accurate assessment, but has tended to be accepted without question. The truth was far more complicated.

'Scheme D for Europe-wide sabotage and subversive operations' was first presented by Grand to Stewart Menzies, then head of Section II (Military) of SIS on 20 March 1939, just days after the Nazi occupation of Prague. This event clearly focused the minds of those attending the subsequent meetings. The proposal went first to SIS as it would be expected to fund the expansion of GS(R), providing the basis of Grand's later claim to have directed GS(R), or as it would become, MI(R). Mackenzie believed in 1947 that 'the basic ideas of this paper are recognizably those of Colonel Holland; its style and its unquenchable optimism are certainly Colonel Grand's' and the report was concocted by both men for mutual benefit, from Holland's perspective offering a clear pathway to expansion of GS(R).[30] Menzies advised that the scheme should next be submitted to the War Office in the form of the Deputy Director of Military Intelligence (DDMI), W.E. van Cutsem, and two days later it had reached the Chief of the Imperial General Staff (Lord Gort) and the Director of Military Operations and Intelligence (Sir Henry Pownall).[31] From there, it went to the Foreign Office, with the decisive meeting on 23 March attended by the Foreign Secretary (Lord Halifax) and the Colonial Secretary (Lord Cadogan), as well as by Lord Gort, Menzies and Grand. Holland was not present, either for reasons of military protocol or because he was content for Grand to present the scheme. Regarding occupied territories, Scheme D advocated

(a) creating the maximum of insecurity to occupying troops and occupying Gestapo;
(b) creating the maximum of insecurity on the lines of communication;
(c) encouragement of local desire for independence; and
(d) making any fresh adventure, and the most recent in Czechoslovakia and Austria, as expensive as possible.[32]

The plan was predicated on the prevalent government view that the Nazi state was brittle and would implode under pressure from an economic blockade. Such a collapse could be assisted by large-scale risings in already occupied countries and preparation for resistance in countries that might be over-run in the future. The overall aim was 'to ensure that no military effort could be made by the German Army without giving opportunity for such turmoil on its lines of communication as to render continued effort impossible'.[33] Based on the supposed fragility of Nazi Germany, Scheme D proposed being ready for a general uprising in German-occupied territories in just three or four months, whilst a 'combination of guerrilla and IRA tactics' could bring about a collapse of the strategically important oil-rich Romania, if occupied, in just three weeks.[34] The methodology drew on the practical experience of the British in confronting irregular warfare and it is clear that the IRA campaign in particular had seared its impact into the psyche of the War Office.

A series of country-by-country objectives was outlined: those neutral countries under the economic influence of Germany, the territories already occupied by Germany and Italy, and other countries thought to be at risk from future invasion. Scheme D was brutally honest about the methodology to be employed, including: 'Where possible they would endeavour to execute members of the Gestapo with as much show as possible, to produce in the minds of the local inhabitants that the guerrillas were more to be feared than the occupying secret police.'[35] This was said to be a lesson taken from the IRA. Arms would be supplied to Bohemia to enable the inhabitants 'to commence operations on the lines of the Irish Terror in 1920–21'. Anticipated guerrilla organizations in Denmark, Holland and Poland would be supplied, as would any resistance groups within Germany and Austria. Popular risings in Italian-held Libya and Ethiopia would also be encouraged. An uncomfortable Lord Halifax for the Foreign Office said that he agreed in principle with the scheme, 'which he now intended to forget'.[36] Foreign Office reluctance to engage with the practical consequences of subversion was to prove a major handicap over the coming months. Lord Gort (CIGS) gave formal War Office approval and Section D was authorized to begin preparing civilian operational activity against Germany while GS(R), now part-funded by SIS, would develop a more military-based concept.[37] The expansion of G(R) would be facilitated by the attachment of around twenty-six army officers to Section D, including Jo Holland, whose experience 'both on the North-West Frontier and in Ireland, will make him invaluable for planning in this connection'.[38] Grand explained: 'Jo Holland joined almost immediately and it was agreed that a new sub-section "DM" should be formed which would in general deal with all activities that could be carried out by uniformed troops.'[39] It would operate primarily through military missions, and ensure coordination with the War Office, offering a more respectable version of irregular warfare than Section D. An MI(R) summary report in June 1939 accepted its role as a part of Section D, describing 'Colonel Holland – then D/M of Section of D Organization'.[40] Joan Bright, who witnessed the, at times, mutual bewilderment of the Section D spies and military officers of MI(R) working alongside each other, summed up the distinction thus:

> Grand's Section D deeds would be done by undercover men, spies and saboteurs, who, if caught, would be neither acknowledged nor defended

by their government. Holland's MI(R) plans would be subject to proper strategic and tactical requirements and carried out by men in the uniform of the established Armed Services for whom the normal conventions of war would operate.[41]

This alliance should have meant that British Intelligence was able to cover the whole gamut of potential irregular operations but the partnership was blighted by the nervousness of the Foreign Office, a dismissive attitude in the War Office and the personal ambitions of Colin Gubbins. Holland later explained:

> Some explanation is needed of the respective spheres of MI(R) and the so-called 'D' organisation of the SIS. When a project is likely to involve military missions or to evolve into irregular military operations, or to require trained soldiers, it is within the sphere of MI(R). The 'D' orga- nisation should deal with individual agents, minor sabotage in enemy country, and contact with secret foreign organizations.[42]

The relationship between GS(R) and Section D was now too uncomfortably close for War Office liking. Holland formally reported to the Deputy Chief of the Imperial General Staff and the Director of Military Intelligence but Grand was clear that, until the outbreak of war, what became MI(R) was a functional element of Section D. Joan Bright simply stated: 'We became part of Section D.'[43] Even Colin Gubbins' account of his recruitment to MI(R) in April 1939 is ambiguous as to who was actually in charge. He says he was invited to a lunch by Holland but

> In a private room at St Ermin's Hotel I found that the real host, who was waiting for us there, was another sapper officer whom I also knew well. Over lunch he told us that he was the head of Section D and explained his charter.[44]

Within days of the agreement for Scheme D, on 3 April Holland produced a paper for the DCIGS and briefed him and the CIGS again on 13 April on what he casually called D/M.[45] The War Office was unhappy that one of its departments appeared subservient to SIS and in a high-powered meeting on 27 June between Holland and DCIGS, DMO&I, DDMO and DDMI, the original title of GS(R) was retained.[46] But the work was now moving from investigating the theory of irregular warfare to preparation for action and needed a more recognizable War Office status. It was agreed that the body was best placed under the then DDMI, Brigadier 'Freddy' Beaumont- Nesbitt, confirming its status as part of the Intelligence branch and GS(R) was formally rebranded as MI1(R), but was best known as MI(R) or MIR. The title was borrowed from a unit that had existed in 1918 to collect intelligence on Soviet Russia and this was in itself significant in light of one of its key target areas (*see below*, p. 149). The new MI(R) Charter of June 1939 took care to clearly distinguish between Section D and MI(R) with the role of MI(R) to earmark staff for training in sabotage and the theory of guerrilla warfare, but not necessarily to direct field operations.[47] Its tasks were

(a) the planning of para-military activities, under the direction of the DDMI;

(b) liaison with MO branches as regards coordination with War Plans; and

(c) preparatory action in peace in conjunction with other organizations.

The geographical priorities were agreed as being Poland and Romania, then Libya and Ethiopia, Czechoslovakia and Albania. SIS agreed to provide additional funding up to a level of around £10,000 p.a. for new staff and the development of sabotage devices in what became MI(R)c. Holland was conflicted by the opportunities offered by Scheme D, still believing that, even after the outbreak of war, the essential role of MI(R) would be in research and that responsibility for field operations should be passed on to existing service departments – whilst not being convinced that they were yet ready for the challenge. He also doubted that central control of guerrilla activities would be possible from within the War Office but assumed that management would devolve to special branches of military missions cooperating with local guerrilla activities. Consequently, he considered that a central staffing of three officers would be sufficient prior to the outbreak of war, with himself in charge, War Office staff officer Major Colin Gubbins responsible for the 'G.S. side' (general service and training), and Royal Engineer Major Millis Jefferis on technical developments. All three were initially only seconded until April 1940. The additional staff requested in Scheme D would be seconded to Section D or be directly managed by regular military missions, with Jefferis acting principally as an adviser to Section D's growing technical section. This minimalist vision soon changed, both because the War Office wanted to ensure the identity of MI(R) independent from Section D and through the practicalities of mounting the military missions. Staffing began to mushroom as MI(R) was given additional administrative responsibilities and, given the urgency of the situation, because the impatient Holland recruited officers in anticipation of formal agreement of projects that he hoped would eventually be managed elsewhere: 'To save time in implementing decisions by anticipating action in the selection of personnel and on technical matters.'[48] Once staff were gathered under its aegis, MI(R) then found itself under an assumption of responsibility for the projects and this began to overwhelm its research function.[49] Where possible, the careful Holland tried to economize. He tried to persuade George Larden, another former Rugby School pupil, then a regular Royal Artillery officer serving as adjutant to a London TA anti-aircraft regiment, to take two months' leave in May 1939 in order to go to Romania and make an unofficial unpaid survey of their railway system on behalf of MI(R).[50] He also resisted employing Stuart Macrae on a permanent basis for as long as possible, although placing increasing demands on his time with Oldham's Press (*see below*, p. 33).

In acknowledgement of their new joint agenda, Section D moved out of the shabby basement of SIS HQ at 54 Broadway in London and moved around the corner to the 6th floor of a Victorian mansion block at 2 Caxton Street, where it was joined by the expanded MI(R). Eric Maschwitz described the early premises in Caxton Street as a cramped little office where the security was somewhat weakened by the staff cars and uniformed dispatch riders that were constantly parked outside it.[51] Sharing resources, the distinction between Section D and MI(R) could blur in practice. They jointly organized pre-war training courses at the adjacent Caxton Hall and Peter Wilkinson admitted that in later months 'as much of my time was spent at the headquarters of Section D in Caxton Street as in MI(R). I was given a desk in their Balkan section and allotted the secret symbol DH/M'.[52] In February 1940 he was spending three hours a day working under George Taylor.[53] Some staff, such as Kavan Elliott, moved from Section D to MI(R) while R.T. Cripps moved the other way.

The legality of what was proposed under Scheme D continued to worry Lord Gort (CIGS), who was keen to distance the work of MI(R) from the War Office by insisting that the MI(R) contribution should be based upon Reserve or Territorial rather than Regular officers and that any of the latter should not participate 'too openly' or become involved in anything that, if discovered, might cause embarrassment.[54] The CIGS also insisted on having the final responsibility for implementing any future action. MI(R) would only become operational in circumstances when British military action was imminent, meaning that during the 'phoney war' MI(R) was characterized by position statements and desk-based studies, rather than activity in the field. This was of little concern to Holland, who saw the role of MI(R) as an advisory think-tank and was prepared to let Section D get on with the dirtier aspects of irregular warfare, operating without official sanction. By contrast, the assumption that MI(R) would work largely at an official level in partnership with the General Staffs of threatened countries proved naïve in a period of German ascendency. The perceptive CIGS also warned against any appearance of forcing advice on foreign General Staffs (the Belgians were already showing signs of irritation with the British and French in this respect).[55]

With his small core team of Gubbins and Jefferis in place during April 1939, Holland provided an internal memo to clarify their basic objectives:

(a) to study guerrilla methods and produce a guerrilla Field Service Regulations manual;
(b) to evolve destructive devices suitable for the use of guerrillas; and
(c) to evolve procedure and machinery for operating guerrilla activities.[56]

Holland also sent a letter on 19 April 1939 to the military attachés in Warsaw, Bucharest, Athens and Belgrade asking for their opinion on his proposals to delay an enemy advance, asking what types of explosives were in standard use and specifically what railway or road bridges should be considered for demolition. He particularly wanted to know whether there were any existing plans for guerrilla or para-military action in their countries and raised the touchy matter of the likely reaction to Britain giving advice on the subject.[57]

The first task was to produce a field service manual, in line with British Army tradition which demanded a documented regulation for each and every eventuality. Holland originally envisaged this as being substantial, with an introduction explaining the principles and tactics of guerrilla warfare, followed by chapters dealing with their detailed application in each country.[58] This had to be scaled back to three simple pamphlets that could at least establish the credentials of MI(R) in its dealings with foreign General Staffs and then might be used as the basis for further expansion. Majors Gubbins and Jefferis were recruited to complete these pamphlets. Royal Artillery and War Office staff officer Colin Gubbins (Plate 2) had an awareness of guerrilla warfare from service in Russia and Ireland but more importantly had specialisms in linguistics, recruitment and training from the policy-making section of the Military Training Directorate (MT1). He also had an established interest in Russia, Poland and Czechoslovakia which suited the immediate priorities of MI(R). Millis Jefferis (Plate 3) came from a field company of the Royal Engineers (who MI(R) relied on for implementing many of its plans) with a reputation as an inventive explosives expert, to write an explosives guide and then to develop explosive devices for the use of MI(R) and the wider military. Keeping these quick-thinking individuals grounded was Joan Bright, recruited by John Walter (a Royal Engineer officer, then of Section D and later MI(R)) as a secretary, who established a wider reputation as an efficient office organizer. Gubbins regarded Joan Bright as 'a woman of considerable culture and great verve, working really as a GSO2 not as a Secretary ... We shared some tough times.'[59] Eric Mockler-Ferryman, who worked in the DMI, recalled his impressions: 'I can well imagine that you ruled visiting generals and admirals with an iron hand in a velvet glove.'[60] According to

Macrae, Bright kept the 'bag of gold' (the secret funding from SIS) with the account book, and 'more or less ran the show'.[61] She was later responsible for compiling the MI(R) War Diary.[62] Women with such a role were unusual within the War Office at the time and therefore attracted attention but Holland would have noted that Section D was prepared to place women in positions of responsibility (and SIS already had female intelligence officers). Lesley Wauchope joined as another secretary and was described by Bright as having 'the face of an untroubled Madonna' but with a wicked wit and no respecter of other's pretensions. Together they 'giggled at the same things as we typed our way through the hectic months of reality and idiocy' preceding the outbreak of war.[63]

Gubbins explained how he was recruited. Holland came up to his desk at the War Office and said 'You are to lunch with me; the CIGS says so.'[64] They went to a private room at the St Ermin's Hotel where they met Laurence Grand. All three men had attended the Royal Military Academy Woolwich where Gubbins was senior to both Holland and Grand. The three officers later came across each other in the War Office on various aspects of mechanization (Gubbins was in MT1, Holland in SD7 and Grand was Deputy Assistant Director of Mechanization). Holland may also have met Gubbins during service in Ireland, although there is no evidence that they served together there or were particular friends. Gubbins had served in the Soviet and Polish section of the DMI and was a qualified interpreter in Russian, Urdu and French; he also spoke Japanese (having been born in Japan). He had also visited Czechoslovakia in October 1938 as part of the team monitoring the withdrawal of Czech troops from the Sudetenland. Gubbins was no expert on guerrilla warfare but his expertise in training from MT1 was urgently required. Joan Bright described Gubbins as 'quiet-mannered, quiet-spoken, energetic, efficient and charming. He was a "still waters running deep" sort of man, he had just enough of the buccaneer in him to make lesser men underrate his gifts of leadership, courage and integrity'.[65] He cultivated a devil-may-care attitude and according to Peter Wilkinson, his close colleague and biographer, 'I have seldom met a man more vigorous and a more inspiring soldier.'[66] Like Grand and Holland, he inspired great loyalty among his subordinates but there was also a darker side to his character with a reputation for ambition and ruthlessness. Writing in May 1941, Robert Bruce Lockhart (Director-General of the Political Warfare Executive) commented 'Jebb had said the other day that Gubbins was the most ambitious man he knew. If that is Jebb's verdict, you know what Gubbins must be!'[67] Jo Hollis, Secretary to the Chiefs of Staff Committee, went further and later declared that Gubbins was 'evil'.[68] Even Wilkinson had to admit 'he was not much liked by his contemporaries … they thought him a little pushy and ambitious'.[69] This aspect of his character would have a major impact on MI(R) and its relationship to Section D of SIS.

It was a prolific few months. In the midst of exploratory visits to Poland, the Baltic and the Balkans (*see below*, p. 68), Gubbins quickly produced *The Partisan Leader's Handbook* (40pp) and, with Holland, the *Art of Guerrilla Warfare* (22pp), distilling key points from existing publications and Holland's philosophy on the subject into a concise, practical outline of strategy and field guide. At the same time Millis Jefferis produced *How to Use High Explosives* (16pp) as a guide to service explosives and devices. The three pamphlets were important statements of MI(R)'s credibility and were subsequently translated into more than sixteen languages and widely circulated, printed pocket-sized on thin paper between plain brown covers. Some were produced on edible rice paper.[70] At a more strategic level, on 1 June 1939 Holland produced his second report in the GS(R) series, *Report No. 8: Investigation of the possibilities of Guerrilla Activities* (*see* Appendix 2) for the DCIGS, which summarized their progress to date.[71] This stressed Holland's core belief that irregular warfare had to be coordinated and used as a tactic to support conventional warfare. If so, 'it should, in favourable circumstances, cause such a diversion of enemy strength as eventually to present decisive opportunities to the main forces of his opponent. It is therefore an auxiliary method of war of which we have not yet sufficiently exploited the possibilities.'[72] Annexed to the report was a summary of Gubbins' visits to Poland, the Baltic and the Balkans, together with reports by Jefferis on the initial work in creating sabotage devices and a report on the progress made in training and recruitment. The potential demonstrated by these publications was sufficient, on 19 July, for Holland's deferred posting to Malta to be cancelled.[73]

The main strategy of the expanding MI(R) was to dispatch military missions to neutral and Allied governments and supply material to foreign resistance organizations (Fig. 2). With war considered likely within four months, Holland wanted to establish the widest possible range of introductions, hence Gubbins' whistle-stop tours across Europe. Officially, the development of new sabotage devices was also put on temporary hold in favour of arranging the supply of existing materials to the target countries, although this was ignored by the ever-inventive Millis Jefferis. The overall priority was to provide Poland with as much of MI(R)'s specialist munitions as possible but an assessment of the resources needed to sabotage the Romanian oil wells was also considered urgent.[74]

Military missions had been used extensively from 1917 in many parts of the world to first combat German intrigue and later to try to limit the post-war chaos, as well as trying to exert a British influence on world events. Now MI(R) 'Active' missions were intended to advise allied General Staffs and guerrilla forces in on-going theatres of war with the *Art of Guerrilla Warfare*

Figure 2. Summary list of MI(R) missions September 1939–October 1940. (TNA HS 8/263)

Mission	Country	Aims	Commanding Officer	Date of Despatch
No. 4	Poland	Liaise with General Staff over plans for guerrilla warfare.	Lt Col. C. Gubbins (MI(R) component)	August 1939
Gubbins Mission	Poland and Czechoslovakia	Liaise with General Staffs over organization of resistance.	Lt Col. C. Gubbins	September 1939
Romanian Mission	Romania	Liaise with General Staff over plans to demolish oil wells.	Lt Commander D. Watson	August 1939
No. 10	Namsos, Norway	Establish wireless station to guide in British landings.	Captain P. Fleming	April 1940
No. 13	Norway	Liaise with Norwegian forces and encourage guerrilla warfare.	Major A. Brown	April 1940
'Shadow' Missions	Greece and Yugoslavia	Assist in preparations against enemy invasion.	Major L.G. Barbrook (Greece)	June 1940
No. 19	Belgian Congo	To carry out reconnaissance of possible lines of enemy infiltration and, if necessary, prepare for allied invasion.	Lt Col. F. McKenzie	July 1940
No. 101	Ethiopia	Organize local tribes against the Italians.	Colonel D. Sandford	March 1940
No. 102	Libya	Distributing funds for subversive activities by the Senussi tribes.	Lt Col. D. Bromilow	September 1939
No. 103	Central and South America	To report into the organization of British communities.	Lt Col. C.G. Vickers	August 1940
No. 105	Atlantic Islands	Covert reconnaissance in Azores and Canaries and distribute British propaganda.	Walford, Fisher	July, August and September 1940
No. 106	Aden	Harass Italians across the Straits and stop contraband trade with East Africa.	Lt Col. R.A.B. Hamilton (Lord Belhaven)	October 1940
No. 104	Australia and New Zealand	Organize and train Australian Independent Companies.	Lt Col. J.C. Mahwood	October 1940
No. 107	Kenya	To carry out anti-Italian activities in Southern Ethiopia.	Lt Col. H.C. Brocklehurst	October 1940
Rodd Mission	Nigeria	Advise Governor on para-military activities.	Captain F. Rodd (Lord Rennell)	June 1940

(*see* Appendix 2) anticipated the attachment of military missions to partisan forces (first achieved with Mission 101 in Ethiopia):

> In cases where the guerrillas are a nation in arms, or part thereof, fighting for their freedom in alliance with or assisted and instigated by a third power which is willing and anxious to render all assistance to them, it will usually be advisable for that third power to be represented by a mission at the headquarters of the guerrilla movement. The duties of such a mission would be to provide expert advice, to ensure liaison, to arrange the supply of arms, ammunition, money, etc., and to provide leaders and assistants to leaders, if such were found to be necessary.[75]

'Passive' missions to amenable neutral countries were intended to organize anti-'fifth column' activities in advance of any invasion, together with raising and training units of local troops trained in guerrilla warfare. But in 1940 neutral governments were reluctant to show overt support for the retreating Allies and so there were attempts to send undercover 'Shadow' missions as a preliminary to the subsequent dispatch of formal missions once allowed by a change in the political climate. Small 'Inspection' missions to neutral countries would also monitor the organization of British communities and try to improve their ability to counter German propaganda. Individual officers might also be sent as 'missionaries', which evolved into sending out officers as assistant military attachés.

It was the task of MI5 to identify enemy networks across the Empire but preparations for a military response to any 'fifth column' threat was a key purpose of MI(R). There was consequently a strong MI5 interest in some missions and MI(R) had a major role in creating the counter-espionage SIME (Security Intelligence Middle East: *see below*, p. 151). Although frequently descending into paranoia, concern over a Nazi 'fifth column' was well-founded. The pro-Nazi elements of the *Volksdeutsche* of the Sudetenland and Silesia steered the crises of 1937–1939 and there was concern over the *Ausland* and *Landesgruppen* organizations operating from German communities abroad. By 1940 the Germans had also developed the infiltration of military units to a level of which British exponents of irregular warfare at the time could only dream. The 800th Special Purpose Instruction Regiment, Brandenburg (the Brandenburg Regiment) was formed to operate in advance of the German main forces, often in civilian dress or Allied uniform, to seize and hold lines of communication or strategic assets, and proved very effective in the invasions of Denmark, the Low Countries and France.

The Foreign Office was suspicious and even hostile to pre-emptive Intelligence operations and some ambassadors refused to accept MI(R) missions into the country for fear of compromising their diplomatic activities. Holland shared the Foreign Office's righteous abhorrence at the start of the war of 'dabbling' in local politics but Section D had no such qualms and Laurence Grand may have influenced the implicit acceptance of this strategy in Gubbins' *Art of Guerrilla Warfare*.[76] In practice, interference could not be wholly avoided when trying to encourage a local population towards supporting the Allied cause and in Ethiopia MI(R) was drawn into internal politics with rival 'local experts' supporting different ethnic groupings. In the Belgian Congo an explicit aim of Military Mission No. 19 was to collect information on the sympathies of the army and business leaders in preparation for a possible British invasion.

The military missions proved difficult to organize and it was subsequently proposed to simply install MI(R) officers in legations as assistant military attachés. The latter could try to encourage foreign General Staffs to develop plans for guerrilla warfare but, perhaps more importantly, it was hoped they would also act as a contact point between the various British Intelligence agencies. The new AMAs were drawn from the list of suitable officers prepared by MI(R) but they had minimal training, dismissed as only the necessary 'low-grade' qualifications for MI(R) work. They had received just two weeks' training at the War Office and did not necessarily have the diplomatic skills of Commander Watson in Bucharest, who successfully worked between MI(R), Section D and NID (*see below*, p. 151 and Plate 24). Gubbins wanted them to go further and coordinate the work of the existing Intelligence agencies but in practice MI(R) had little to offer beyond the variable personal skills of the AMAs, and with no infrastructure to support them they could not fulfil Gubbins' dream of creating a new network independent of Section D.

There were also attempts to set up broader Intelligence Bureaux to investigate the possibilities for irregular activity in already occupied territories and the Caucasus. These were based on the precedent of the Arab Bureau of the GHQ Egyptian Expeditionary Force in the First World War, which encouraged the Arab Revolt. They were to be flexible, containing representation from Section D so that the appropriate outcome might be either an MI(R) military mission or a Section D sabotage and subversion project. A corollary of the Bureaux was to send out officers to collect intelligence and Holland bemoaned the fact that the collection of information no longer seemed to be a function of Military Intelligence and had been surrendered to SIS. But there was concern that MI(R) should not develop as a new intelligence-gathering agency and the concept was overtaken by the creation of SOE; a report in the MI(R) War Diary complained that the embryonic Bureaux were 'surrendered' to Dalton's SOE, 'thus allowing planning which should have been intimately connected with regular [War Office] plans to pass out of their hands.'[77]

With war expected imminently, Holland determined that MI(R) would focus its limited resources on assisting countries which remained unoccupied, rather than those which had already fallen to the Germans.[78] This approach would be soon tested with the fall of Poland. In June 1939 Holland explained that 'from now until the middle of August we must aim primarily at getting anything ready that we can in the time'.[79] Gubbins was at the forefront of this new phase of urgency and his series of foreign tours attempted to lay the groundwork for cooperation with foreign General Staffs. His work centred on Poland, as the likely spark to ignite the Second World War, where its General Staff already had a guerrilla organization. He made at least two visits in June and August, before returning with the official mission led by General Carton de Wiart (*see* Chapter Six). Gubbins worked almost exclusively on issues related to Poland until April 1940 and this diversion to operational matters away from the London office of MI(R) gave him a different perspective from Holland. Prior to the formal outbreak of war, the only way to disrupt the economy of Germany was by unavowable means but this placed MI(R) as the junior partner with Section D and caused great frustration to the ambitious Gubbins, who joined MI(R) after the division of responsibilities in Scheme D had already been agreed. Gubbins was aghast at what he saw as the amateurishness and extravagance of some of what were described as the 'wilder' projects of Section D, but at the same time he admitted being envious of its risk-taking in contrast to the ponderous nature of the War Office.[80]

Only three months after being empowered by Scheme D, MI(R)'s first progress report of 10 July 1939 unsurprisingly struggled to offer concrete results but importantly it pointed to having made contact with a large number of potential recruits for Military Intelligence work, drawn from a list compiled with the DMI, and noted that around seventy had already received preliminary training. The three pamphlets were now being printed into other languages and there was already some limited production of Jefferis' innovative sabotage devices (*see* Chapter Three).[81] A month later in August 1939 there were still no real plans for action, although Holland offered up the vague hope of future partnership with Poland, Romania and Czechoslovakia.[82] In Albania, conditions for a successful rebellion were said to be deteriorating and any action was increasingly hampered by the fear of antagonizing Italy and precipitating the latter's entry into the war. In Libya it was determined that any rebellion needed to be accompanied by successful military action and so MI(R) would provide a liaison officer between Wavell's new Middle East Command and the potential rebels (Lieutenant Colonel David Bromilow was dispatched a month later, *see below*, p. 168). The situation in Ethiopia was also thought to be deteriorating but in early July 1939 a conference at the Foreign Office had made MI(R) responsible for providing arms and funding to the rebels. It was also proposed to send Peter Fleming and Martin Lindsay on a reconnaissance mission to China (under cover of working for the Ministry of

Information), to establish what help the British could provide to the 1 million Chinese troops currently engaged in guerrilla warfare against the Japanese (*see below*, p. 178). Despite displaying considerable energy, the conclusions of the August 1939 progress report remained pessimistic, and its adherence to traditional War Office bureaucracy in the face of the imminent outbreak of war contrasted with Section D, which had already moved into direct action.

Chapter Two

The Outbreak of War

One of the most worrying admissions of the August MI(R) progress report was that 'Consideration has yet to be given to the scope of the organization after the outbreak of war.'[1] MI(R) was still heavily reliant on SIS and in Report No. 8 (June 1939) Holland made a veiled acknowledgement to their financial support when he said the expenses of those officers deployed abroad 'have generously been made available for us from another organization'.[2] The optimism surrounding the launch of Scheme D had dissipated and Holland believed substantial progress was not likely 'without something more assured in the way of financial arrangements' and for the War Office to take clear ownership of MI(R)'s work. He was characteristically blunt in his assessment that 'It is impossible to avoid the feeling that, on the present scale, the work is little more than busy-bodying.'[3] In response, the more diplomatic new DMI ('Freddy' Beaumont-Nesbitt, now a major-general) said 'in view of present circumstances' he was not inclined to pass on Holland's conclusion to CCIGS.[4]

Even as war was declared on 3 September, Holland wrote a report on 'The Organisation and Duties of MI(R)' to establish its war footing and emphasize MI(R)'s distinction from Section D. They were to undertake politico-military research to keep the General Staff informed of future possibilities but, taking a higher moral position than Section D, maintained 'We are, emphatically, not charged with political dabbling, but purely with military questions.'[5] Section D was already organizing small-scale sabotage in the Balkans, working secretly with opposition groups, but in most cases operations by MI(R) would have to rely on less covert, formal, military missions to nudge foreign allied and neutral military authorities into action.

> Development on the lines recommended in this report will be of little value unless Foreign General Staffs are prepared for guerrilla activities. It is submitted that authoritative action ought to be taken early with the object of bringing to their notice the possibilities.[6]

Holland stressed the need for continuing liaison with Section D but was clear on the division of responsibilities: 'it is for Section D when action must be subterranean, i.e. in countries which are in effective enemy occupation, and it is for us, when the action is a matter of military missions, whether regular or irregular'.[7] Holland later elaborated this fundamental distinction by explaining that MI(R) was responsible only for activities that could be discussed and planned with the authorities of the countries concerned, and carried out with their knowledge and cooperation, whereas Section D would operate without the knowledge, or even against the will, of those authorities.[8] The approaches were complementary and Holland proposed they should work together in joint bureaux (as proposed for China, *see below*, p. 179).

Despite Holland's belief in MI(R) remaining a small advisory unit, he swiftly recruited a new wave of staff in expectation of them being required for employment on military missions. Five officers from a mix of family members, existing acquaintances, and those from the Territorial Army Reserve of Officers (TARO) extracted from the list compiled by MI(R) and the DMI (*see below*, p. 50), were recruited on 25 August and retrospectively commissioned as soon as war broke out. They were John Walter, John Brunyate, William Allen, Ralph Greg and Michael Colefax.[9] Brunyate was a well-respected lawyer – and also Holland's brother-in-law; Greg was another well-travelled barrister who had lost a leg during a hunting accident in Africa in 1928 but had been placed on the Officers Emergency Reserve (OER). John Walter was a Royal Engineer already working in Section D; Allen was an expert on the Caucasus and Georgia (but was also under MI5 surveillance for his association with the British Union of Fascists: *see below*, p. 150). Colefax was a merchant banker with an interest in the oil industry.

The War Establishment of 8 September 1939 authorized an increase in numbers to a total of a GSO1 (Colonel Holland), two GSO2 (Gubbins and Jefferis), ten GSO3, a Quartermaster (A.F. Sutton) and a Clerk (Corporal Bidgood) and three shorthand typists.[10] Authority was also given to attach up to eight captains from the loose amalgam of the 'Intelligence Corps' comprising officers already on Intelligence duties.[11] Holland was almost apologetic in making this call on the pressured War Office budget but stressed that the core MI(R) staff remained small and that most officers envisaged for operational duties could be transferred to project budgets, including fourteen staff already quickly recruited for the Polish mission and seven for the Romanian mission, funded by SIS. Similarly, the practical implementation of demolition schemes, as in Romania, France and the Low Countries, was, as a first option, delegated to Royal Engineer Field Companies. Meanwhile, the small central MI(R) staff would act as a link between the various branches of the General Staff and SIS.

Majors Crockatt and Combe (both late Royal Scots) would collate information and project ideas as well as liaising with outside bodies (Crockatt focusing on Europe and Combe on Africa and Asia). The unfulfilled intention was that bureaux would then be established to act on their conclusions. With Gubbins now fully occupied with Poland, Crockatt and Combe were also responsible for supervising the rudimentary training of personnel. Walter, Greg and Colefax worked under Combe to form the nucleus of the anticipated Czech and Yugoslav bureau and also assisted on the training courses. John D. Kennedy, one of a number of senior staff of Courtaulds recruited by Section D and MI(R), was in charge of personnel and records, assisted by former solicitor John Brunyate. The latter was a brilliant scholar who had been awarded a Double First at Trinity College, Cambridge but his calm and patient manner, ideal for conducting interviews, concealed the fact that he was beginning to struggle with the early stages of muscular dystrophy.[12] Lieutenant A.F. Sutton was Quartermaster, providing liaison with other branches of the War Office concerning office administration and personnel. Millis Jefferis began to build the largely independent technical section, which would become MI(R)c.

A rush of new initiatives included a report on security operations in the Middle East in September 1939, plans for a group of 'toughs' to go to the Caucasus under the ever-eager Peter Fleming as the advance guard of a military mission, the dispatch of the Polish and Romanian missions, and the creation of the escape and evasion service MI9. The organization was particularly strengthened by the recruitment for the Polish mission of F.T. 'Tommy' Davies, who had briefly worked for SIS and who now became a workhorse of MI(R), and in October by Douglas Roberts, recommissioned from the OER but another SIS 'honourable correspondent' with expertise in Russian affairs. Roberts was first engaged on a study of the possibilities of action in Russia and the Caucasus but was then put in charge of training not only for MI(R) but also to report on training as a whole in the DMI (replacing Crockatt when the latter went to MI9: *see below*, p. 63). Roberts became the backroom lynchpin of MI(R), responsible for what became its 'Special Operations and Political Action' section (MI(R)b). When MI(R) Middle East was formed as G(R), he was sent to provide MI(R)'s expertise as its second in command before becoming head of Security Intelligence, Middle East (SIME). In 1946 he became head of the SIS anti-Soviet Section IX.

On 20 December 1939 Holland provided a new update on progress. He stressed again the strategic purpose of MI(R) was to seek out ways of increasing the effect of regular campaigns by devising an irregular component that would fall under the command of the theatre commanders, to 'try and foresee possibilities in the chaos which may be coming and to prepare for semi-military missions'.[13] Yet there was already a warning over MI(R) being diverted from its role as a 'think-tank' to managing operations directly:

> I have always thought that each appropriate branch of the General Staff ought to deal with the various activities which we have undertaken, except for the fact that it is probably useful to have a branch with a

certain amount of freedom and contact with unusual sources of information and possibilities of action.[14]

Despite this unselfish attitude, MI(R) began to ruffle feathers within the War
Office as its activities expanded and there was clearly some confusion as to its
purpose. The DMI acknowledged that the necessarily unorthodox methods
and procedures of MI(R) sometimes caused difficulties with other departments.[15] There were complaints about MI(R) appropriating staff from the
joint MI(R)/DMI index (*see below*, p. 50) without consultation. One case
involved Field Security personnel taken from their base at Mytchett when
MI(R) was recruiting on behalf of the Hopkinson mission (Phantom) in the
British Expeditionary Force (BEF). There were particular complaints from
the Ministry of Supply over MI(R)c developing its own munitions without
adequate consultation, although Holland insisted that it would be unreason-
able for the General Staff to have to go through normal procedures to
speedily develop specialist and ad hoc devices needed, for example, for the
destruction of Romanian oil wells, Danube barges or to sabotage railways.[16]
Brigadier Ronald Penney, DDMI(O), was not convinced:

> Some overlap is inevitable, but I consider that MI(R)'s difficulties are
> almost entirely of their own making. They know the War Office organi-
> zation, they know or should know who is concerned, and without undue
> sacrifice and secrecy they can and must keep either me or the DDMI(I)
> informed of what is going on when we are involved in any way at all.[17]

In an effort to bring MI(R) into the mainstream of the DMI and quieten
concern from other branches who saw MI(R) impinging on their spheres,
a revised charter was issued in February 1940, after MI(R) had proven its
worth in managing the supply of material to Finland and on the Inter-Services
Security Board (*see below*, p. 97). According to Joan Bright, this allowed MI(R)
to finally 'shake off the fluff' of SIS and come under proper military control.[18]
Four operational and one Intelligence roles were defined:

(a) general research as required by the DMI, including the examination
    and preparation of projects involving the employment of special or
    irregular forces to assist or increase the effect of normally conducted
    operations, directly or indirectly [under Roberts];
(b) technical research and production of appliances required for such
    projects [under Jefferis];
(c) operation of such projects as may be decided on in discussion
    between DMI and DMO&P and when such operation is not the
    function of any other branch of the War Office or other
    organization or headquarters at home or abroad [under Roberts];

(d) collection of information by special means outside the provinces of other sections of the Military Intelligence Directorate; and

(e) interviewing, training and recording of personnel possessing special qualifications likely to be required in conjunction with irregular activities.[19]

A level of secrecy was required but at the same time 'in order to avoid overlapping and confusion, the activities of MI(R) must be coordinated with other sections of the MI Directorate and branches of the War Office within their own spheres'.[20] In particular, it was not to develop an unwelcome independence as a new secret Intelligence service. Holland's original assertion that they had a role in the 'active collection of information of a specialised kind' was queried by the DDMI(O) and was consequently limited to that 'outside the province of other sections of the MI directorate' and only as necessary for particular projects. In April Beaumont-Nesbitt was able to conclude: 'We have found MI(R) in the War Office extraordinarily useful, though at times rather turbulent and unorthodox. The section has gradually evolved from being a sort of offshoot of the Secret Service into a regular section of the MI [Military Intelligence] Directorate.'[21] By then, its staff had established themselves as a useful secretariat and liaison body to other departments and the compilation of the index of potential Intelligence officers and provision of preparatory training through the Cambridge course (*see below*, p. 57) were viewed as being particularly useful.[22]

Within three weeks of the outbreak of war, MI(R) had symbolically moved out of its shared accommodation with Section D to offices on the third floor of the War Office.[23] There was a main workroom and an inner office for Holland, with a separate office for the secretaries. This cannot have helped the synergy with Scheme D but, nonetheless, Holland stressed in the December report that he and Grand 'have also been in very close touch'.[24] Grand made regular calls to Holland's new office to coordinate plans over equipment, manpower and facilities, and Douglas Dodds-Parker commented:

> In those early months I found nothing but the keenest wish to work together, in the face of extraordinary national danger and the understanding of the ill effects on those in the field of any quarrels at base. None were looking for a career, but only for the survival of our country, in freedom and, we hoped, of ourselves.[25]

There were many examples of good cooperation and even swapping of staff. In Romania the plans to destroy the oil wells was considered as primarily a military operation and therefore left to MI(R), whilst the on-going sabotage of the railway traffic into Germany was a responsibility of Section D. They shared a common explosives store in the legation under MI(R)'s Commander

Watson. In the Middle East, Section D and MI(R) trained together with the new limpet mines on the Bitter Lakes of the Suez Canal.[26] It is also likely that Section D supplied the novel explosives disguised as camel droppings that MI(R) later supplied to the Long Range Desert Group.[27] Nicholas Hammond moved back and forth between Section D and MI(R): originally recruited to Section D, he joined the attempt to send an MI(R) mission to Yugoslavia in June but then became assistant at the Section D training school on Mount Carmel in Palestine and served as Section D liaison to MI(R) in Cairo.[28] In August Hammond transferred back to MI(R), with subsequent confusion as to who had been previously responsible for paying his salary. In September he helped organize sabotage in Vichy Syria for the new SOE. In Greece Section D created a sabotage network of volunteers from the large British expatriate colony but their instructions included a warning that no sabotage was to be undertaken before any invasion as it might prejudice the work of the official MI(R) mission that was expected shortly.[29] In the end MI(R) could only provide Major L.G. Barbrook as an AMA in Athens and Section D then began secretly supplying sabotage equipment to the Greek Army but, wishing to preserve its anonymity, did so via the intermediary of Barbrook. An embryonic joint Section D/MI(R) was established on Crete by John Pendlebury, a former curator at Knossos who was given the cover of vice-consul at Canea. The idea was that Section D would establish supply dumps and recruit sabotage agents while Pendlebury would liaise with the Greek forces and operate openly in uniform. Captain Robert Cripps was loaned by MI(R) to Section D as a courier to Albania and Yugoslavia, and by contrast, Kavan Elliott began in Section D and then transferred to MI(R). The major exception to good cooperation was any matter concerning Poland and this resulted principally from the proprietorial attitude of Colin Gubbins, who saw this as his power base.

Gubbins was not happy with the division of labour as agreed in Scheme D and tested the boundaries of the working relationship in his dealings with Polish Intelligence, placing the blame for the resulting conflict on Laurence Grand. Gubbins had some support in the War Office as SIS tended to only share operational information when it suited its needs and on 5 April 1940 a report from MI(R)) noted that Section D '[has] various activities which are still more or less a mystery to us'.[30] The DMI, Beaumont-Nesbitt, wrote to Major General Ismay, Secretary to the Chiefs of Staff, in March, rueing that after six months of war the small MI(R) still remained an organization largely dealing only with the theory of irregular warfare. It was typical of War Office arrogance that Beaumont-Nesbitt's letter stressed the qualifications of MI(R), saying 'a section of MI (MI(R)) has made a special study of sabotage and guerrilla warfare', and by implication that Section D personnel were less well-qualified. Yet he grudgingly had to acknowledge that it was Section D that had been the most active in the field, the main problem being that this was outside War Office control:

> It has been left to SIS to put any projects into force. In many cases, too, such projects have been put forward and developed by SIS with little or no reference to Service Departments. To my mind this is fundamentally wrong and is not the way to secure maximum results.[31]

Despite such frustration, the existing demarcation of responsibilities was restated in the Hankey Inquiry of SIS in March 1940, establishing that MI(R) would only organize sabotage in arenas where regular British forces were directly involved, whilst Section D undertook operations in areas under enemy occupation or in neutral countries.[32] This could be read as a censure of Gubbins, who had tried to make MI(R) the controlling body for the Polish and Czech resistance and led to his removed as head of the 'Gubbins mission' (*see* Chapter Six). In his evidence to the Inquiry Beaumont-Nesbitt acknowledged,

> It had however now been arranged in principle that MI(R) ... should devote itself primarily to plans and research and that actual sabotage in enemy countries should be undertaken by the SIS. If, however, there was a possibility of our own troops acting in conjunction with the local Government, then the actual work of sabotage should more properly be entrusted to MI(R).[33]

An appreciation of the practical value of MI(R) was not helped by reports on MI(R) projects in April and June 1940 which still listed only the plan to destroy oil stocks in Holland and Belgium, and the Davies mission to Holland, as contributions in Western Europe (*see below*, pp. 132–3).[34] It is not surprising that there were increasing calls for a reorganization of irregular warfare.

The support of Beaumont-Nesbitt did not prevent MI(R)'s central establishment being progressively reduced as part of a rationalization of the Military Intelligence Directorate during March–June 1940, even as the perceived value of irregular warfare was increasing. Four Intelligence officers were lost in March 1940, prior to a radical reorganization in April when many responsibilities were transferred to other departments. On 11 April Combe, Walter and Brunyate were lost to MI11, which took over the Secretariat of the ISSB, and Kennedy and the clerk, Sergeant Bidgood, transferred to MI1 to continue to deal with personnel matters. Quartermaster Lieutenant Sutton transferred to the staff of the Assistants to the DMI when administration of all personnel in the Military Intelligence Directorate became the responsibility of AG17. The reduced MI(R) was then consolidated into three sections:

- **MI(R)a** – Coordination section for all projects, services and liaison with SIS (Lionel Kenyon, who joined 15 April 1940, assisted by Fleming and Davies);

- **MI(R)b** – Special Operations and Political Action section to investigate and execute certain projects; personnel; records of foreign personnel (records of British personnel passed to MI1x), liaison with MI(R) Middle East (briefly Douglas Roberts, assisted by Colefax and Greg); and
- **MI(R)c** – Technical section under Millis Jefferis, in liaison with the Directorate of Scientific Research, Ministry of Supply and Section D.[35]

By 24 April 1940 the central establishment was less than on the outbreak of war, whilst Section D had grown to around 300 staff.[36] On 3 June the strength was listed as Colonel Holland in Room 368, Majors Kenyon and Warren, Captains Kennedy, Davies, Greg and Walter in Room 367 and, at a safe distance, Major Jefferis and Captain Macrae in Room 173.[37] It was a tumultuous time for MI(R) but Holland was now arguing for a complete reorganization of irregular warfare within a new directorate under the DMI (*see* Chapter Twelve). Ironically, these cuts to the central Establishment took place at the same time as the workload was increasing substantially, with a large number of MI(R) project staff deployed on active service in the Norwegian campaign or transferred to build the new G(R) in the Middle East. Dodds-Parker described the atmosphere at the time in MI(R) as one of 'repressed frustration'.[38] For him, MI(R) should have come into its own after the invasion of France and the Low Countries, claiming 'Many who had doubted the para-military schemes of our middle-rank leaders became firm supporters. They seemed to welcome the presence of individuals who had ideas, had made some preparations, and were ready to carry out these projects themselves.'[39] Yet practical results remained limited, although the DMI valued the flexibility of MI(R)'s officers, in particular MI(R)c: 'The section is ready at any time to undertake anything and has means at its disposal of producing what is required at very short notice, and of a very high quality.'[40]

By 25 May and the imminent collapse of France, the economic blockade and 'spread of revolt' were seen as the best hope for victory, with a desperate War Office turning to Holland for fresh advice.[41] The situation worsened with the loss of heavy weapons at Dunkirk and now facing the threat of invasion, on 7 June the Director of Military Operations, Major General Sir John Kennedy, addressed the Chiefs of Staff, speaking from a brief prepared by Holland, and placed his faith on victory in irregular rather than conventional warfare:

We are certainly not going to win the war by offensives in mass and the only way of success is by undermining Germany internally and by action in the occupied territories. German aggression has in fact presented us with an opportunity never before equalled in history for bringing down a great aggressive power by irregular operations, propaganda and subversion enlarging into rebel activities ... It must be recognised as a principal that not only are these activities part of the grand strategy of the war, [but] probably the only hope of winning the war.[42]

A week later the Chiefs of Staff concluded that through 'economic pressure, by a combination of air attack on economic objectives in Germany and on German morale, and by the creation of widespread revolt in her conquered territories, the British Empire might still achieve the ultimate defeat of Germany'.[43] This analysis, harking back to Scheme D of March 1939, was the context for a renewed interest by government in providing better coordination for irregular warfare. The cuts to the MI(R) establishment were consequently reversed in late June, anticipating an agreement to a proposal of Holland and Beaumont-Nesbitt which would create a new department of irregular warfare in the War Office, with MI(R) at its heart. MI(R)'s John D. Kennedy optimistically explained the reversal of cuts was necessary due to 'the expansion of irregular warfare and because the supervision of hitherto entirely secret organisations which will now be the duty of MI(R)' (*see* Chapter Twelve).[44] On 2 July 1940 an expanded War Establishment was proposed, with one GSO1, four GSO2, nine GSO3 and a Warrant Officer (superintending clerk), and the responsibilities of the central HQ were listed in August 1940 (*see* Fig. 3).[45] As discussion of the role of the War Office in irregular warfare intensified during July 1940, under a new challenge from Hugh Dalton of the Ministry of Economic Warfare, Holland was finally obliged to accept the need for a more active operational role for MI(R) and raised with the Joint Intelligence Committee new aspirations for MI(R) to organize its own 'fifth column' and sabotage operations. Ever cautious, the Foreign Office suggested that this should be concealed under the heading of 'Welfare of British Communities Abroad'.[46] This proposal was too late in the day to have any impact and an unhappy Holland was increasingly concerned that the research function of MI(R) was being squeezed out by short-term operational needs and responsibility for irregular warfare might now be lost by the War Office. Such fears came even as Holland was suggesting a radical new approach to the development of future special forces and a vision diametrically opposed to that of Dalton for the new SOE (*see* Chapter Twelve).

With the realization that this was not going to be the short war of the earlier assessments, Holland's vision for resistance now firmly subordinated action to the strategic timetable for a large-scale Allied return to Europe, likely to be some years into the future. Local resisters were instructed to exercise restraint whilst they built up their capabilities, only becoming active on any large scale at the point when they could support an Allied invasion. Until then any small-scale sabotage should, as far as possible, be made to look

Figure 3. War Establishment of MI(R), August 1940. *(TNA HS 8/258)*

	GSO1	Colonel J.C.F. Holland	Overall command
	GSO2	Major L.F.R. Kenyon	General co-ordination; liaison with other bodies
MI(R)a	GSO2	Major F.T. Davies	Executive action for specific projects
	GSO3	Captain the Hon. Q. Hogg	Dominions and colonies; Missions to foreign countries
	GSO3	Captain J. Walker	Liaison with Lochailort training school
	Clerical	Miss J. Bright	
		Miss L. Wauchope	
		Miss M. Randall	
		Miss C. Binns	
MI(R)b	GSO2	Major J.D. Kennedy	Personnel
	GSO3	Major I.B. Greig	Personnel
	GSO3	Captain R.M. Greg	Personnel and Administration
	Clerical	Miss V. Long	
MI(R)c	GSO2	Major M.R. Jefferis	Technical
	GSO3	Captain R.S. Macrae	Technical
	Attached	Lieutenant Colonel Blacker	Technical
	Clerical	Miss Samuels	
		Miss Rees	

accidental. This careful strategy was confirmed by the Chiefs of Staff in September 1940, seeking that resistance forces should 'keep their powder dry' until they could act in support of an Allied offensive.[47] It was, however, an approach in direct conflict with Churchill's impatient desire to 'Set Europe Ablaze', exploited by Hugh Dalton's ambitions for the new SOE.

Holland believed the key to supporting national resistance movements would be the creation of specialist military units who could operate behind enemy lines. It was a principle at the heart of the creation of the Commandos, LRDG, SAS, Jedburgh teams and Chindits. The first rushed formation of Independent Companies in April 1940 (*see below*, p. 107), was followed by a more considered concept of specially-trained regular units for guerrilla operations. Dudley Clark, Military Assistant to the Chief of the Imperial General Staff, sketched out an idea for the Commandos to the CIGS on 5 June and this was approved three days later. The Commandos were to be an amphibious raiding and assault force, but Holland was thinking on more covert lines. On 7 June 1940 Holland produced 'An Appreciation of the Capabilities and Composition of a small force operating behind the enemy lines in the offensive'.[48] The object of this force would be 'to disrupt enemy L of C [Lines of Communication], destroy dumps and disorganise HQ', its methods being to travel fast, ... remain concealed ... avoid organised opposition as much as practicable ... attack the weak points in the enemy's organisation, make the sites untenable as long as possible and then, in most cases, depart'.[49] This far-sighted document became a blueprint for special forces, including the SAS. Such units, working with the local resistance, would operate in conjunction with the regular forces simultaneously attacking the enemy front. The troops would be infiltrated piecemeal or delivered by parachute drop, by sea or by raids through sparsely populated areas, with the principal targets being railways, roads, supply dumps and headquarters. The force would travel light and be supplied by air. Additional firepower would come from coordinated air attacks rather than having to provide their own heavy artillery. Operations would depend on effective portable wireless communications, although in 1940 the limit of imagination was for a set transported in a 'perambulator'. This vision was perhaps the most enduring legacy of Jo Holland's MI(R).

Chapter Three

The Technical Section

Jo Holland had a long-established interest in technical innovation in warfare, dating back to his service in the Wireless Signals and RFC, and in 1935 he wrote a ground-breaking article on the military potential of autogyros before his posting to the War Office for work on army mechanization.[1] Section D had formed a technical section in 1938 and as soon as the increased funding for MI(R) was secured in April 1939, Holland created a complementary version as MI(R)c, under Major Millis Jefferis, Royal Engineers (Plate 3). According to Joan Bright, Jefferis was 'red of face, kind of heart, he was an inventive genius'.[2] His deputy, Stuart Macrae, agreed – with the caveat that 'like most genii [he] was not a good organiser'.[3] With a brain 'like lightning', Jefferis 'seldom had to stop to think, and when he did he would scowl horribly. Then he would give an infectious little chuckle so that one could not help liking him.'[4] Jefferis shared Holland's vision of MI(R) as a think-tank, more interested in developing ideas for new weapons and devices than the engineering aspects of organizing their production, which was largely left to Macrae.[5] As a consequence, the section was 'apt to fly off at tangents' as Jefferis became side-tracked into some problem of pure mathematics.[6]

In post by 18 April, the first task for Jefferis was to produce a pamphlet on the use of explosives. Section D had just produced *Home Hints*, containing instructions on how to make explosives from everyday items and aimed at underground resistance groups. It was now complemented by Jefferis' *How To Use High Explosives*, which focused on the explosives, fuses and detonators as used by regular military forces and as would be supplied by MI(R). The booklet formed the basis of the later GHQ Auxiliary Units' explosives manuals. As well as instructions on blowing up buildings and railways, and the use of the camouflet, it also contained advice for disabling industrial machinery, including simply cracking the cast-iron base of machines with a large hammer (Plate 17). Although there was some overlap with the Section D technical section, the two bodies worked closely together, with MI(R)c focusing on devices with broad military application, to better appeal to the War Office. There was also symmetry in their products as they experimented with different approaches to the same issues. Thus MI(R)c's No. 9 L Delay switch (Plate 15) performed the same function as the Section D No. 10 Time Pencil, and the MI(R)c Blacker Bombard anti-tank weapon (Plate 10) matched the

Section D Northover projector. Stuart Macrae explained the distinction, describing Section D as the 'cloak and dagger boys' while MI(R)c 'was to run a more or less legitimate outfit which was to produce unusual but legitimate weapons, the gentlemen concerned all being in uniform and therefore not to be confused with saboteurs'.[7] The pressure, pull and release switches and the L Delay switch were consequently all classed as standard stores. Section D supplied MI(R)c with explosives and in the early days offered its facility at Bletchley Park for explosives testing, much to the annoyance of the code-breakers. Macrae recalled how he would telephone Section D and ask for 6lb of 'cheddar cheese', which would be collected on the next day at St James Park underground station from a gentleman wearing a bowler hat and a button-hole, and carrying a copy of *The Times* as well as a discreet brown paper parcel containing the explosives.[8] This was the sort of over-elaborate security in SIS that so frustrated Holland!

MI(R)c provided an alternative to SIS in allowing talented individuals to develop new ideas beyond the ponderous procedures of the Ordnance Board and Ministry of Supply. But in stark contrast to the Section D technical section hidden in utmost secrecy at Aston House, the work of MI(R)c was an open secret within the War Office and Macrae complained that work was disrupted by passing officers visiting the office out of pure curiosity, and that in the first half of 1940 'hardly a day passed without some general or other popping into Room 173 to inspect our bag of tricks and I soon came to be regarded as a professional conjurer'.[9] The success of the 'W' Mine brought increasing interest and Churchill, as First Lord of the Admiralty and then as Prime Minister, became entranced by their ability to produce prototypes for novel weaponry on demand. Churchill wrote to Ismay on 24 August 1940 regarding Jefferis: 'By whom is he employed? Who is he under? I regard this officer as a singularly capable and forceful man, who should be brought forward to a higher position.'[10] (By then Churchill had known Jefferis for nine months!) Such plaudits caused resentment in the Ministry of Supply and Ordnance Board over the independence of MI(R)c but even Jefferis and Macrae found it impossible to completely escape the delays that plagued British weapons development in 1940.

The section was first based with the rest of MI(R) and Section D in Caxton Street in London, sharing a cramped office with Gubbins, and then moved in September 1939 to a separate room at the War Office. Jefferis supplemented his limited resources by bringing unofficial contacts into the secret and using small outside contractors who could fulfil immediate requirements, avoiding the bureaucracy of the Ministry of Supply. Jefferis met Stuart Macrae in July 1939 and immediately they began working together unofficially on the development of a magnetic limpet mine, with the understanding that Macrae could recover his costs by making a profit from any manufacturing contract he was able to organize (or otherwise receive a financial commission payment). As an 18-year-old trainee engineer at the end of the First World War, Macrae had worked on a design to drop clusters of hand grenades from aircraft, but was now a magazine editor at Oldhams Press. Macrae had to balance his increasing part-time work for MI(R)c with existing commitments as the editor of the magazine *Armchair Science* until late September 1939, because Holland lacked funding to pay him on a full-time basis. Nonetheless, Holland rather testily expected Macrae to be additionally released by Oldhams Press as and when Jefferis had need of him.[11] In October 1939 Macrae was finally commissioned into the Territorial Army to work full-time as deputy to Jefferis. Macrae then also managed to secure the employment of Gordon Norwood, who had been his assistant at Oldhams Press. As well as having a major input to the inventions, Macrae was also in charge of the production processes as MI(R)c became responsible not only for experimental work but also for the packing and shipping of the material sent to Finland and the Balkans, and training in their use. Another key recruit was Cecil 'Nobby' Clarke, whom Macrae had first contacted whilst editor of *The Caravan & Trailer* regarding Clarke's innovative caravan designs. Macrae remembered: 'Clarke at once fascinated me. He was a very large man with rather hesitant speech who at first struck me as being amiable but not outstandingly bright. The second part of this impression did not last long.'[12] In July 1939 Clarke was again contacted by Macrae for help with designing powerful magnets for the limpet mine. Clarke was then appointed Assistant Director in the Naval Land Section of the Admiralty but while there he continued to help modify the limpet mine at Section D's Aston House. He eventually joined Section D and was made an instructor at the training base at Brickendonbury, Hertfordshire, becoming its commandant under SOE. In February 1942 Clarke rejoined Jefferis in MD1, where he invented the altimeter switch for sabotaging aeroplanes.

In a remarkable frenzy of invention, by the end of November 1939 the tiny MI(R)c, still only with a staff of four and working in one cramped office, had designed a portfolio including the Light Camouflet set and TV switch, 'U' Switch, Pressure Switch, Pull Switch and Limpet Mine. Work was also under way on the Sticky Bomb, the floating 'W' Mine and even a mini-submarine.[13] According to its charter, the role of the section was primarily to develop new devices and weapons and then turn them over to the Ministry of Supply for large-scale production but the latter did not necessarily see the relatively small production runs of MI(R)c's specialized equipment as a priority. So instead, the early production of MI(R)c's devices was put in the hands of small private companies who were not yet engaged in military production and therefore outside the control of the Ministry of Supply. They were, however, desperate for products to replace their no longer profitable pre-war production. Midgely Harmer Engineering at Park Royal produced the 'W' Mine; 'Nobby' Clarke's Low Loader Trailer Company in Bedford made the limpet mines; Tommasin made the TV switches; Hulburd Patents made the pressure switches; Bell's Asbestos made the Camouflet sets; and later the musical instrument makers Boosey & Hawkes in Edgware manufactured the 29mm spigot mortar ('Blacker Bombard').

By December 1939 Macrae began to consider how MI(R)c might begin production on a larger scale, although he maintained that Jefferis was opposed to this, in the spirit of MI(R) being a 'think-tank' rather than an executive arm.[14] In this instance, Holland was supportive of Macrae's idea and in June 1940 MI(R)c replaced their cramped office in the War Office with a suite of offices over well-equipped workshops at 35 Portland Place, HQ of the International Broadcasting Company (which was responsible for Radio Normandie and Radio Fécamp). IBC was enthusiastic and its chief engineer, Norman Angier, and other staff assisted with some of the experimental work. Macrae described Angier as a bohemian type of person who did not object to the presence of explosives on the premises but did object to the army uniforms. Macrae was so impressed that he engineered the enrolling of the whole staff of IBC as civilian workers of MI(R).[15]

The expansion brought MI(R)c into increasing conflict with the Ministry of Supply and in April it was admitted that a 'certain amount of professional jealousy and overlapping exists'.[16] In August 1940 MI(R)c was included in the wider review of MI(R) by Brigadier Wyndham (*see below*, p. 186), who believed that technical research should not be the responsibility of the army. Instead, he wanted the section transferred either to SOE, SIS or the Ministry of Supply. Macrae argued that they were carrying out vital work that could not easily be transferred elsewhere. To make the workshops at Portland Place seem more impressive during Wyndham's inspection, he acquired a supply of blue and white lab coats that allowed staff to dash through the building in front of their visitor, switching coats to make it appear that the place was far busier than it was in reality. Rooms were filled with impressive-looking meters and other electrical equipment to make the place look more like a modern test laboratory; completed devices were brought back from stores, disassembled and laid out on benches as if there were large assembly shops.[17] The deception worked and any transfer was delayed until a final decision on the disbandment of MI(R) as a whole in early October.

In September 1940, after its stores at Hendon were hit in an air raid, and a bomb destroyed the workshop in Portland Place, MI(R)c moved out of London to the Tudor mansion of The Firs, Whitchurch (north of Aylesbury, Buckinghamshire). Domestic and office accommodation were contained in the house (together with a bar) and the stables were converted to workshops, including a specialist facility for the manufacture of the precision components required for the L Delay. Surrounding fields were used as firing ranges. At last MI(R) had been able to catch up with the propensity of SIS to requisition country houses for its secret operations and the staff increased to around forty-five.

With the disbandment of MI(R) in October 1940, MI(R)c was about to be transferred to the Ministry of Supply but Churchill had been enthralled by the range of strange weapons that they had been able to demonstrate and his chief scientific advisor, Professor Lindemann, was able to convince Churchill that it would be useful to keep the genius of Jefferis and Macrae unfettered from the scrutiny and bureaucracy of the Ministry of Supply and Ordnance Board. In November 1940 there was a compromise whereby MI(R)c became MD1 under the control of the new Ministry of Defence, although administered by the Ministry of Supply. As Churchill was Minister of Defence as well as being Prime Minister, the legend was born of 'Churchill's Toyshop' (a somewhat trivializing term perpetuating the idea of eccentric mavericks under Churchill's direct control). Churchill minuted, 'As you know there is a feud running between Major Jefferis' inventions and the D of A's Department and I have had to take Jefferis under the protection of the Minister of Defence.'[18] At the end of the war MD1 finally came under the control of the Ministry of Supply and the Weapons Research Establishment at Fort Haldane before being finally disbanded.

Major Products of MI(R)c

Light Camouflet Set and TV Switch

A camouflet is an explosive charge dropped down a borehole into an underground chamber which magnifies the effect of the explosion, causing a massive crater, and is particularly useful for cutting roads and railway lines. The normal 3-inch (7.6cm) diameter camouflet as used by the Royal Engineers required a team of four men to put it in place but MI(R)c developed a lightweight version (albeit still weighing 80kg) with a switch to detonate the device once vibrations were picked up from a train or heavy vehicle passing overhead. The MI(R)c camouflet was only 2 inches (5cm) in diameter and could be managed by two men. Malcolm Munthe tried the equipment in Finland during February 1940, sinking the 2.4m-long iron tube vertically through the frozen ground, using a screw 'toecap' device like a large auger, cutting 1.2cm into the ground with each full turn. A small charge was then dropped into the tube and exploded, creating a small chamber at its base. Then 40lb of explosives were dropped down with a TV (Time Vibration) delay device. This electrical switch was made safe during installation by a large block of salt holding back the spring which, after the salt had been dissolved by releasing a small container of water set above it, would withdraw a strip of insulating material, leaving the device ready to complete its circuit on subsequent vibration. This arrangement did not work well in cold weather and was later replaced by a small bellows and an air leak valve. They were made in the decrepit workshop of the Kinematograph Engineering Company in Clerkenwell by Tommasin. Unfortunately, in Munthe's case a shell exploding nearby mimicked the vibrations of a passing train, setting off the TV switch and the mine exploded prematurely, but it successfully blew up a section of the railway tracks.[19] One insurmountable problem was that the camouflet could not easily be made safe once it was activated and the TV switch was soon abandoned.

Limpet Mine (Plate 8)

Jefferis remembered an idea of Professor Haldane from the First World War for a man to float down the River Meuse with a mine strapped to his chest, ready for it to be attached to the piers of a bridge. After reading an article entitled 'World's Most Powerful Magnet' in the July 1939 issue of *Armchair Science*, describing the small but incredibly strong Alnico magnet developed by GEC in New York, Jefferis contacted the editor, Stuart Macrae, and outlined the idea for what would become the limpet mine. This would magnetically attach a 4.5lb (2kg) explosive charge to a vessel below its water line. After what Macrae described as 'lunch, brandy and deep thought', Macrae offered to design a limpet mine for free, although Jefferis confided he had a 'private bag of gold' to pay expenses![20] Macrae in turn contacted 'Nobby' Clarke, who had impressed him by his unorthodox approach to mechanical problems in his design for caravans. Macrae visited Clarke at his home in Bedford, outlined the project and they started work the next day. Macrae bought the entire stock of small Alnico-type horseshoe magnets from his local ironmonger's shop and then ordered a gross from the manufacturer (James Neill & Co., Sheffield). Clarke also purchased some tin bowls from Woolworths and a local tinsmith made plates which could be screwed on as a watertight lid, incorporating grooves into which could be fixed the small horseshoe magnets. A metal plate attached to webbing straps allowed the mine to be held magnetically against the swimmer's waist, although experimentation was needed to adjust the width of the metal plate so that it was not impossible to detach the mine from the body. The first prototypes used porridge in lieu of high explosives and after flooding Clarke's bathroom several times, they were tested by Clarke and Macrae at Bedford Modern School's swimming baths, which was closed for the occasion; a metal griddle plate from Clarke's kitchen was propped up at one end of the baths to replicate the hull of a ship. Further tests were conducted on the River Ouse, with the mine attached to a motorboat which travelled at speeds of up to 15 knots before the mine was dislodged. In practice the Mk 1 version would stick to a reasonably clean hull at speeds of up to 10 knots. Explosives tests took place at the early Section D base at Bletchley Park, to the dismay of the codebreakers. One problem was to devise a suitable time delay and the first version used a spring-loaded striker, held back by an aniseed ball that slowly dissolved in the water. The delay could be adjusted by differing numbers of holes drilled in the aniseed ball. Before the mine was armed, the time delay device was protected from water by being stored in a condom. As a result of their experiments, which stripped the shops in Bedford of both aniseed balls and condoms, Macrae reported that he and Clarke had acquired 'the undeserved reputation for being sexual athletes.'[21] The mine could also be attached from the surface by a 1.5m-long placing rod. The initial production of several hundred was carried out in an improvised workshop at Clarke's Low Loader Trailer Company in Bedford at a price of £8 each (including a £2 commission to Macrae until he joined MI(R) full time). The first 200 were sent to Constanza and Alexandria in October 1939 with three crates addressed to 'The Romanian Government, Constanza' and two for 'Mustapha Barracks, Alexandria'. A smaller version (Type B), mushroom-shaped and with an improved magnet ring, carried just 3lb of explosives but would remain in position at speeds of up to 18 knots. The soluble pellets were also replaced by L Delay switches, protected in the water by a rubber sleeve. In all, around 260,000 limpet mines were made during the course of the war.[22]

Switch No. 1 Mk 1 Pull Switch (Plate 11)
This was designed by Macrae in late 1939 to replace the unsatisfactory use of the standard Mk III Igniter as a sabotage pull switch. He got the idea from a type of shirt stud which had a detachable head. It was designed in an hour, a prototype was made the next day and production began in just a fortnight. The pull switch was built around a brass tube threaded at both ends. To one end was screwed a standard fuse holder, linking the device to an explosive charge. The other end had a housing containing the release pin and spring. Attached to a trip wire, or similar, it was ignited when the pin on the switch was pulled out with a direct pull of about 4lb. This allowed the head of a split-headed spindle which carried the striker to pass through a plug under the tension of a powerful compression spring, and strike the small percussion cap which would in turn ignite a length of detonator cord, detonator and main charge. When set up correctly, a safety pin could easily be withdrawn but if there was too much tension on the trip wire then it jammed. Almost 3 million were made during the war at a cost of just *2s 6d* each!

Switch No. 2 Mk 1 Pressure Switch (Plate 12)
Designed by Jefferis in mid-1939, this switch entered service in October that year. It was originally intended to be used for blowing up railway lines and was set on a rectangular brass base, all designed to be hidden under camouflage. When trodden upon with a pressure of 50lb or more, the plunger

sheared off a brittle steel wire retainer, releasing the spring-loaded striker and triggering the attached explosive charge. Approximately 2.25 million of these switches were eventually made. As a safety device, the safety pin could not be withdrawn if the existing pressure on it was too high, preventing it from being tripped as the pin was withdrawn.

Switch No. 3 Mk 1 Release Switch (Plate 13)
This was designed by Macrae after the completion of the Pull and Pressure switches, and again, it went from design to production in just two weeks. It was a small sheet metal box (3in × 2in × ¾in) designed to be hidden inside or under suitable objects. When armed, a tapered tongue projecting from the underside of the lid bore down on a powerful leaf spring. The spring would remain in place as long as a weight of 1.5lb or more was pressing down on the device once the safety pin was withdrawn. When the pressure on the lid was removed, the spring, with a striker at one end, was released to strike a percussion cap and triggered the explosive charge. Nearly 2 million were produced, at a cost of 2*s* 3*d* each.

Switch No. 8, Anti-Personnel, Mk 1 (Plate 14)
This was designed in the spring of 1940 as a simple anti-personnel device that could be carried by all troops. Jefferis had first suggested basing such a device around a .303 cartridge with ICI in Ayrshire, who were already doing work with MI(R), and the design was then completed by Macrae. A modified .303 rifle cartridge (with a pointed steel bullet) was fired, using a pressure-sensitive trigger, from an 8in-long tube buried in the ground. The tip of the bullet lay 1.2cm above the ground and when trodden upon would release the compression spring and striker. The short delay in firing gave it the nickname 'the debollocker'. Some 1,439,450 were produced at a cost of 2*s* each plus 1*s* for the cartridge. This may be the device referred to in some Auxiliary Units lists as the 'Autumn Crocus'.

Switch No. 9, L Delay (Lead Delay) (Plate 15)
A new time delay switch was conceived by Jefferis as an alternative to the existing Section D No. 10 Time Pencil, which relied on an acid eating through a steel wire at a set rate, depending on the thickness of the wire and the strength of the acid. Macrae claimed that the No. 10 Time Pencil could not be calibrated accurately and could only give a broad timespan as to when they would fire of 'a few hours, a fair number of hours, or a lot of hours', and that they were susceptible to temperature variation. He exaggerated the limitations, although the standard advice was always to use two time pencils to avoid failure.[23] The MI(R) alternative was a more sturdy construction, better suited to general military use. It was based around a brass tube containing a time delay switch operating on the principle that a lead alloy wire

will stretch and break at a set time at a particular temperature. The research necessary to apply the principle was carried out by the British Non-Ferrous Metal Research Association and the time interval was then controlled by notching the wire to a set diameter. Once the safety pin was removed, the wire was held under tension – one end was fixed and the other attached to a spring-loaded striker. The wire would stretch and break, causing the striker pin to ignite a percussion cap, and thence an attached detonator and explosive charge. A tag attached to the safety pin stated the number of hours' delay of the device; once the tag was removed, any enemy discovering the device would have no idea of the time delay (as opposed to the different coloured bands painted around the early time pencils).

The methodology was, in theory, more reliable than the No. 10 Time Pencil but also suffered from temperature variation. Macrae did not believe that this was a serious problem as long as the users were 'good guessers' or carried a table of temperature variations.[24] The tag attached to the safety pin therefore identified the length of delay at a specified temperature, thus '1 HOUR AT 65°F'. The L delay also suffered from the handicap of ideally having to be set vertically (to allow gravity to take its course). Development and production were far more complex than for its rival, as a very precise lead alloy composition was required for the wire and the Ministry of Supply could find no commercial firm able to provide the lead wire or springs in the extremely narrow tolerances that were necessary. Although development began in February 1940, production did not commence until September, when the Ministry of Supply reluctantly had to agree that MI(R) would have to produce them in-house at its new workshops at The Firs, as it appeared only they could work to the fine tolerances required. Not appreciating the technical difficulties involved in the novel approach of the L Delay, on 26 August 1940 the VCIGS (Lieutenant General Sir Robert Haining) had erupted over the forthcoming expansion of MI(R) production facilities to make the L Delay, which seemed to encapsulate the independent spirit of MI(R)c. He complained: 'This is all quite unnecessary. There is nothing secret about a delay action fuse: this irregular channel acts in rivalry to the proper supply channel.' He went on to say that 'as MI(R) is to be done away with' (MI(R) then being under review by Wyndham), he wanted all its production activities tabulated and production arranged through proper channels. He went on: 'It has taken an infinity of pains to break down all the activities of this delay fuse: and the irregular methods involved in an unauthorised branch dealing with production can no longer be tolerated.'[25] The annoyance of the VCIGS was not least because he had not been briefed about the device and only learned of it through a Cabinet paper. Even Wyndham was obliged to point out that the work had been sanctioned by the production branches and had even been carried out at their request.[26] Once installed at The Firs, Whitchurch, a team under Norman Angier produced the switches on an assembly line 'in-house' and they maintained production until the end of the war, in all producing 1,320,000 L delays. Macrae felt justifiable pride in this technical achievement and seventy were included in each Mk 2 Aux Unit store for the GHQ Auxiliary Units. Nonetheless, in his autobiography he exaggerated the number produced and the simpler No. 10 Time Pencil remained the most commonly used device, with more than 12 million being produced.[27]

'W' Mine

On 10 November 1939 Holland and Jefferis returned in some excitement from a meeting with Winston Churchill, then First Lord of the Admiralty, and his scientific adviser, Professor Lindemann. They had been asked to develop a mine that could be dropped from aircraft or floated down the River Rhine to destroy bridges and river barge traffic. Holland and Jefferis saw this as a high-profile project that could seal their reputation with Churchill and save MI(R)c from being absorbed by the normal production systems of the War Office and Ministry of Supply. Jefferis wasted no time and sent an outline suggestion to Lindemann on the very next day, offering to produce a prototype in a week – just the sort of decisiveness that Churchill admired. Fortunately, Jefferis had already been working with the Midgley Harmer company on a floating fire mine which he could adapt and the first rough models of the 'W' Mine were presented to the Admiralty on 24 November. It worked by a chemical pellet (based on effervescing headache tablets that dissolved in five minutes) dissolving and releasing a lid on the cylindrical mine, freeing corks that then held the bomb 0.6 metres under the water, with horizontal antennae that would detonate the 20lb of explosives on contact. Jefferis decided to test the design by dropping one off Chiswick Bridge in London and then have Macrae follow its progress down the river in a rowing boat, courtesy of the local Sea Scouts. Unfortunately Jefferis forgot to remove the safety pin on the flotation device which meant that the mine simply sank immediately. The operation was observed by a mystified army guard post and a complaint found its way to Holland. His response was to 'misfile' the correspondence on the incident within an obscure file on the history of the bayonet (adding a half-eaten sandwich for good measure) and so ensuring that the matter was lost within the War Office filing system.[28] The design had to be coordinated with the Admiralty and Air Ministry but rapid progress was made. Not for the last time confusing the design and production processes, on 12 December it transpired that Churchill believed the mine was already in production. In a 'fool's paradise', according to Macrae, Churchill demanded 10,000 mines by 1 February.[29] Churchill called regular meetings after midnight (part of his notorious 'Midnight Follies') for progress reports and for poor Jefferis to give demonstrations, almost as a post-dinner entertainment. In early January Churchill tried to sell the idea of the project to the French, still convinced that production was under way and with no adviser prepared to disabuse him of this fact. Even as they crossed the channel to provide a demonstration, the ever-inventive Jefferis proposed modifying the design by replacing the electrical firing mechanism with a mechanical version. Horrified by the idea of Jefferis letting slip to potential French customers that he believed the existing design to be flawed, Macrae persuaded Jefferis to drop his proposed modification in the interests of speed but the French were not, in any case, enthusiastic. However, after the German invasion in May, 1,700 'W' Mines were successfully launched in *Operation Royal Marine*, causing river traffic between Karlsruhe and Mainz to be suspended and causing damage to the Karlsruhe barrage and a number of pontoon bridges.[30] The remaining mines were put at the disposal of the French to use as anti-tank mines. In all, 20,000 were produced during the war and it became a standard RAF store item. Having excited Churchill's interest in MI(R), the successful handling of this project was a major factor in the survival of MI(R) as MD1 in October 1940.

No. 74 ST Grenade (Sticky Bomb) (Plate 9)
The 'Sticky Bomb' (officially the No. 74 ST Grenade) was an anti-tank grenade consisting of a glass sphere containing 1.25lb (0.57kg) of nitro-glycerine and covered in a sticky stockinette, which was in turn encased in a protective sheet-metal casing. When the user pulled a pin on the handle of the grenade, its casing would fall away. Pulling another pin would arm the grenade and, upon being thrown, a mills grenade type lever was released on the handle that activated a five-second fuse. It was a short-range weapon best used from an ambush position, the idea being to smash the glass sphere against the target, squashing the explosive in order to increase the contact area for the 'poultice' effect, causing an inward blast to either punch a hole in the armour or at least produce deadly shrapnel from the inner face of the steel plate. One fear that the sticky cover could easily adhere to the thrower's clothing and cause an accident was claimed to be illusory as no confirmed cases could be found (which is not to say there were not near-misses before the safety lever was released).

Jefferis had come up with the basic idea before the outbreak of war and the early experiments were carried out with Dr Bauer and Dr Schulman of the Colloid Science Department of Cambridge University but had not gone well. Dummy grenades were made from lengths of bicycle tubing filled with plasticine and dipped in rubber solution to make them sticky, attached to wooden handles. The dummies proved uncontrollable in flight and would not adhere to the dustbins placed as targets in one of the Cambridge college quadrangles. Macrae took over the project in July 1939 and began experimenting with light bulbs wrapped in an old sock covered with glue. Fortunately, glass-blowers Hugo Wood of Leeds provided as many smashable glass flasks for experimentation as Macrae needed! Coaguline cement manufacturers Kaye Brothers Ltd of Stockport also began experimenting with adhesive from January 1940. In his autobiography Macrae, evidently still smarting over criticism about the grenade, maintained that successful tests had been held at Farnborough in January 1940 but this was not entirely accurate.[31]

On 31 May, in the midst of the Dunkirk crisis, Anthony Eden was inspired by a *Daily Mirror* article by Tom Wintringham, which claimed that 'Anyone who fought in Spain knows how to stop German tanks'. Eden asked the War Office to explain the methodology used in Spain and part of its response was that MI(R) was developing a 'sticky bomb' for use against tanks.[32] Eden stressed in terms approaching panic that new anti-tank grenades for Home Defence were 'vitally urgent and should be available in very large quantities. I don't mind where they come from as long as we get them, home or abroad.' Churchill characteristically leapt in to seek an explanation for the 'great sloth' completing the ST Bomb and demanded a report every three days.[33] To demonstrate progress, Jefferis ordered the production of 10,000 Sticky Bombs from MI(R) suppliers but on 17 June Major General Laurence Carr (Assistant Chief of the Imperial General Staff) informed the War Cabinet Office that the grenade 'was not very convincing'.[34] He went on, nonetheless, to unfairly criticize MI(R): 'They have wasted an enormous amount of time by not getting the Ministry of Supply to organize the production of the sticky bomb before awaiting the outcome of the trials.'[35] Despite the doubts, Ismay recommended to Churchill, in a rush to soothe him, that it was worth planning for production on a large scale in advance of the trials, because the Sticky Bomb was 'a very simple affair'.[36] As a consequence of such pressure, on 19 June the War Office Anti-Tank Committee decided to order a million.[37] The decision proved premature and a rushed trial on 22 June identified a fundamental problem in that the current adhesive would not stick to a wet or dirty tank![38] An irritated Churchill warned that 'any chortling by officials who have been slothful in pushing the bomb, over the fact that at present it has not succeeded will be met by great disfavour by me'.[39] There was a difference of opinion between the dismissive Anti-Tank Committee and the Director of Artillery (Ministry of Supply) whose simple argument was that there was no better alternative.[40] The Anti-Tank Committee recommended reducing the order to 100,000 but Carr requested the Ministry of Supply to press ahead with the existing order for a million.[41] As with the 'W' Mine, Churchill sowed further confusion and on 7 August wrote to Eden asking about the provision of training for troops in handling the Sticky Bomb 'which is now beginning to come through in quantity'.[42] In fact, they were still only being produced by MI(R)'s private contractors on a small scale for its missions abroad. By 22 August there was already puzzlement as to who had been responsible for placing the order and the Director of Artillery added to this by falsely claiming that production would shortly reach 40,000 per week. Carr became the scapegoat for acting 'more out of funk than anything else' by not daring to contradict Churchill.[43] Churchill was still frustrated by the delays and on 2 October 1940 tersely confirmed his original order. A handwritten note simply said: 'Sticky Bomb. Make one million. WSC.'[44] Macrae took this authority to the Ministry of Supply, who still refused to manufacture them on grounds of safety but were prepared to authorize MI(R) to do so itself. MI(R)c then took full responsibility for production and inspection while the Ministry of Supply issued the contracts. Kaye Brothers assembled the grenades from the components supplied from the other companies and they were then filled with nitro-glycerine by ICI at their Ardeer factory on the west coast of Scotland.

A consignment of 5,000 was due to be sent to Greece in November but after objections over the unsatisfactory method of packing devised by MI(R) the production was cancelled by the War Office.[45] Under protest from Churchill a consignment was eventually sent to Greece in December.[46] By 30 December, despite the earlier claims, just 65,935 had been completed and large-scale production did not finally begin until May 1941.[47] Most of the early production was sent to the 8th Army in North Africa but the Home Guard began to receive small quantities from July.[48] Between 1941 and 1943 approximately 2.5 million were produced and although the majority eventually came into Home Guard service, the Sticky Bomb continued to be used successfully in North Africa and Italy, and by the Australian Army during the New Guinea campaign. Despite the fears, the original version proved remarkably safe and effective but the detonator used initially on the Mk 2 version proved too sensitive and caused several fatalities before being replaced.

Darts
An anti-personnel device designed by Jefferis, the dart consisted of a cone-shaped device filled with high explosive, designed to be scattered from aircraft and embed itself in the ground, ready to explode when trodden upon. The 100m-high Battersea gasholder was hired to test it but before the dart could go into production it was supplanted by the simpler Switch No. 8 Anti-Personnel.[49]

29mm Spigot Mortar (Blacker Bombard) (Plate 10)
Colonel Stewart Blacker was a professional soldier in the Indian Army, with a reputation for eccentricity and a dislike of bureaucracy. He had served in the First World War as an aerial artillery spotter and in 1933 took part in an

expedition to fly over Mount Everest. Having retired to England he joined the Territorial Army but in 1940 he was considered too old for active service. He was, however, summoned to Woolwich in May 1940 to help with the organization of the Dunkirk evacuation. On arrival, his participation was cancelled, as was the next suggestion of him being placed in charge of troops on a ship bound for Shanghai. In some frustration, while at Woolwich he chanced upon his old friend, General Ismay, who suggested he go to see Jo Holland for a job. He went to MI(R) claiming to be the only privately established inventor of weapons in the country, was duly recruited, and then created a reputation for being charming and irritating to equal degree.[50]

Blacker quickly set to work to modify his earlier design for the 'Arbalest' spigot gun (which eventually became the PIAT) to produce the 29mm Spigot Mortar (aka Blacker Bombard). This was one of several types of 'sub-artillery' quickly designed in 1940 to meet the invasion crisis, but bedevilled by production delays that made it out of place by the time the mortar entered service. It was an anti-tank mortar, firing a 20lb anti-tank or 14lb high explosive round to a range of around 100–200 metres, using a 'squash head' or 'poultice' hollow-shaped charge.[51] The explosive was contained behind a cone of copper which squashed against the target and was then driven through the armour, along with accompanying shrapnel, by the force of the explosion. It was a muzzle-loading weapon, fired by a sprung steel rod (spigot) striking a black powder charge in the base of the bomb. Its short range and the cloud of smoke it produced made it advisable to ensure a direct hit on the target with the first round and from a well-concealed position. There was also a tendency for shrapnel from the exploding charge to fly back along its trajectory to the mortar position! The mortar weighed 360lb, requiring a five-man crew to operate and manoeuvre it and, although there was a mobile mount, GHQ stressed that it was primarily designed to be used from fixed positions.[52] This made it unpopular with those in the Home Guard who were chafing for a more mobile form of warfare but was of less concern to the War Office whose priority for the Home Guard was to defend 'nodal points'.

Following the tradition of MI(R) employing firms that were struggling to find wartime employment, the prototypes were made by the brass band instrument makers Boosey & Hawkes. The first test, using a derelict Matilda tank on Chobham Ridge firing range as a target, proved successful although it was then discovered that the Royal Armoured Corps had not actually given permission for their tank to be destroyed! The first demonstration was held in front of the Prime Minister at Chequers on August 1940. Ralph Farrant, previously deputy commandant at Lochailort Training School, had moved down to join MI(R)c as chief gunnery expert and had become very accurate at firing the spigot mortar but unfortunately the weapon fired prematurely while Norman Angier was setting it up and it almost struck General de Gaulle, who had not yet moved back from the line of fire. As the charge did hit its target tree, Churchill did not seem overly bothered.[53] Churchill immediately authorized £5,000 to develop the spigot mortar but there were the seemingly inevitable delays until the design was finalized. A test in February 1941 showed that a round could penetrate 7cm of armour but spirits were deflated when a test at Shoeburyness was a complete flop. The first three rounds missed the target tank and the fourth hit the wrong one. Adding to the embarrassment, a sticky bomb thrown for good measure also failed to do any damage. Churchill was insistent and on 26 March ordered 2,500 mortars to be completed without delay.[54] The C-in-C Home Forces was sufficiently impressed by a new demonstration in April 1941 to ask for production to be given as high a priority as possible and for it to be issued to anti-tank regiments, infantry brigades and airfield defence units as well as the Home Guard. According to GHQ Home Forces, the demonstration 'fully justified its adoption as an anti-tank weapon both by regular formations and the Home Guard'.[55] But increased production of the 2-pounder gun soon removed much of the urgency in producing such 'sub-artillery', although several spigot mortars were supplied to the 8th Army in the Western Desert and saw action at Tobruk and at El Alamein. In addition, 5,000 were supplied to the Soviet Union. The 29mm Spigot Mortar was not issued to the Home Guard until November 1941, partly due to bureaucratic concerns over having to provide storage facilities for the bombs, but there were 18,000 in service with the Home Guard by the end of 1942. The design was developed into the highly effective anti-submarine 'Hedgehog' mortar of the Royal Navy and the PIAT anti-tank weapon.

Mobile Land Mine (Beetle)
A small remote-controlled tracked vehicle carrying 120lbs (54.4kg) of explosives, it was designed by Metropolitan-Vickers with some input from Stuart Macrae in 1940 after a series of experiments dating back to 1935. It was wire-guided and powered by two electric motors, designed to stealthily approach and destroy concrete strongpoints or detonate minefields. The Beetle had an effective range of around 1,000 metres but the control wire could be broken under enemy fire or get trapped in the tracks, which did not have sufficient clearance over rough ground. Fifty were ordered for operational evaluation in August 1941 but in the end it was decided that they had no great operational value. The Germans later produced large numbers of the similar Goliath but it was equally not considered a success.

Autogyros and Helicopters (Plate 16)
Holland had been interested in the military potential of the autogyro since 1935 and in June 1940 he had the vision to identify the key role that helicopters and short take-off/landing (STOL) aircraft might play in the future

in supplying irregular forces behind enemy lines and to extract casualties.[56] Stewart Blacker, who was the director of several aircraft companies, was set to work with a number of aircraft designers and Holland saw the exploration of this concept as one of the key future tasks of MI(R). One idea was to use slots and flaps on aircraft wings to give a very low landing speed. The Westland Lysander army cooperation aircraft, which had gone into service in June 1938, already had this feature although overall the Lysander was considered unsatisfactory in its designated role. Its STOL characteristics could only be fully exploited from August 1941 when the Lysander was used, as Holland had envisaged for such aircraft, to clandestinely land and recover SOE agents from occupied Europe and later to resupply the Chindits in Burma. Inspired by the Lysander, Holland was confident that further STOL aircraft could soon be developed, without diverting production from conventional aircraft. Out of this he predicted:

> Some new form of force, of which, so to speak, the advanced guard mounted troops are autogyros and helicopters, the main body being transported in aircraft of the kind foreshadowed above, with stores being dropped by bomber aircraft. The whole scheme might be described as analogous to the former diversionary role of cavalry.[57]

Holland was acutely aware of the likely resistance to such a novel idea and was concerned to retain this research within the War Office, where he could exercise control, as he did not believe that the Air Ministry regarded the concept of autogyros and helicopters with any great favour.[58] He was, nonetheless, also unsure how such ideas would be received within the army and therefore wanted to try out the tactics with the staff of the Lochailort Training School. In the closing days of MI(R), its War Diary for 23 September 1940 said that a machine was ready to be constructed and only waited on permission from the Army Council to build and try it out.[59] Holland's doubts were well-founded; it was a Sikorsky helicopter of the US Air Commando that was first used in combat, rescuing wounded Chindits from behind enemy lines in April 1944. Britain first used helicopters operationally from 1950, during the Malayan Emergency. The tactic most famously came into its own with US special forces and the air cavalry during the Vietnam War. They are now the standard means of deploying special forces across the world.

Military Intelligence Chemical Committee

In April 1940 Holland and Jefferis made contact with the Tizard and Rothschild Committees on Chemical Warfare and established the Military Intelligence Chemical Committee under Lord Rothschild and Macrae as part of MI(R)c, with the specific aim of developing a new contaminant that would immobilize fuel in cars and destroy bulk fuel stocks in depots. MI(R) had been considering plans for the demolition of fuel depots in Belgium and Holland, as well as the destruction of the Romanian oil wells, since the start of the war. The committee was based around a number of staff at Imperial College London, including Professor Vincent Briscoe (physical and industrial chemist), Professor Ian Heilbron (organic chemist and fuel expert), Professor Alfred Egerton (industrial chemist and fuel expert), and a representative of the Ministry of Supply, Dr F. Roffey. The Ministry of Supply, which had its own scientific section and advisers, resented this new intrusion into their work by MI(R) and cast an unenthusiastic air over the proceedings. The committee collapsed after six months, when the risk of invasion diminished and MI(R) was dispersed, but Macrae managed to use the committee to MI(R)'s advantage by using its authority to requisition a staff car, on the excuse of needing a vehicle for testing. The failure of the committee's concoctions can be judged by the fact that this car survived as a very reliable staff car throughout the testing process and beyond.[60] In the event, the Royal Engineer demolition teams employed to destroy the continental oil tanks used the cruder expedient of Boys anti-tank rifles, Very pistols and petrol bombs!

Chapter Four

Recruitment and Training

Intelligence work prior to the Second World War was largely a task for gifted amateurs and training was haphazard, with an emphasis on 'reliability' born of interlocking social connections. The acceptance of Scheme D in March 1939 which sought the recruitment of twenty-five army officers and the subsequent expansion of MI(R) focused attention on how such men should be recruited.

The first source remained the traditional 'old boys' network' and several recruits were from Holland's old school, Rugby. Many of them were university graduates from Oxford or Cambridge. There were also ties of blood, as John Brunyate and General Sir John Shea were Holland's brothers-in-law. Some had pre-war business connections, including several directors of Courtaulds. As part of its partnership with Section D, SIS appear to have recommended several of its officers or shadowy unpaid 'honourable correspondents' that would be asked to carry out pieces of work from time to time. One of these, Kavan Elliott, was not a typical recruit to British Intelligence. Born in London, the son of a humble grocer's assistant, he left school at 15 with, according to his sister, no special aptitude 'except perhaps a touch of the devious' and worked briefly as a clerk in a debt collection agency. But Elliott had a natural aptitude for languages and answered an anonymous advert in the *Star* newspaper seeking men with language skills. This was ostensibly to teach English and French to the children of Croat businessmen in Zagreb, but was a typical device of SIS to trawl for potential recruits. After a few months he told his family he had joined Unilever as a 'soap salesman' and eventually was known as the General Manager of the Unilever subsidiary *Astra* in Zagreb – although Unilever had no record of his employment. Elliott's real job was to collect economic intelligence for SIS. Elliott later joined the local Section D network but, after his cover was blown by the *Abwehr* in May 1940, he returned to Britain and transferred to MI(R).[1] F.T. Davies had joined Courtaulds Ltd in 1929 and became a director in 1937, with responsibility for factories in France and Germany. With such a useful background, he wrote to the Under-Secretary for War in September 1938 volunteering for intelligence work, and was asked to report on Germany's economic preparations for war on behalf of SIS; he joined MI(R) in August 1939. It seems likely that Peter Fleming (Plate 6), described by biographer Alan Ogden as a combination of 'avant-garde travel writer and diplomat manqué', was unofficially asked to collect intelligence for SIS whilst covering the Sino-Japanese war as a journalist.[2] Douglas Dodds-Parker may have similarly been collecting intelligence on the victorious Nationalists at the end of the Spanish Civil War. Douglas Roberts had been born in the Caucasus, the son of the British consul at Odessa and had served in the South Russia mission in 1919. He had gone on to work for famine relief in Russia and in the mining and timber industries in the Caucasus and Eastern Siberia from 1924 to 1930, all giving ample opportunity to collect local intelligence. Ronald Hazell, who was recruited to the Polish mission, had carried out work for SIS whilst a vice-consul in Poland. The counter-insurgency and security aspects of the MI(R) missions were also important and some men were chosen from having prior experience with MI5, including John Mahwood and Henry Brocklehurst.

The transfer of MI(R) to the Directorate of Military Intelligence in June 1939 provided a new opportunity in the selection of staff. After the 1938 Munich crisis, the then DDMI, Frederick Beaumont-Nesbitt, had ordered Gerald Templer, then a GSO2 in MI1(a) (administration), to review Intelligence planning for mobilization and update the index of potential recruits registered with the Regular Army Reserve of Officers (RARO) and the new Officers Emergency Reserve (OER). The aim was to seek out suitable officers from the 'professional and literary classes, also public schools, universities, banks and commercial houses … from the Home and Indian Civil Services, the Consular Services and Missionary Societies'.[3] Clearly they were looking for the traditional well-bred and educated officer class. MI(R) was given access to this resource, as Holland firmly believed that an essential prerequisite of MI(R) was that recruits needed to have military training and many were drawn from the Royal Engineers.[4] This was a cornerstone of his view of guerrilla warfare carried out by 'officers and gentlemen' as opposed to the civilian agents of SIS. Nonetheless, the War Office was reluctant for MI(R) to risk its reputation by employing regular officers in anything with a disreputable air. Instead, the suggestion was to recruit officers from the Reserve or Territorial Army who could more easily be provided with a cover story. They were ideally to be 'possessed of means' (therefore not requiring a salary) and not tied to civilian jobs; men who were keen to see some temporary active service and who already possessed some useful experience.[5] Eventually a card index of around a thousand names was compiled. Potential candidates from the Military Intelligence list were sent a questionnaire and then called for interview. Until September 1939 (when he joined the BEF), the preliminary interviews were conducted by Templer with Joan Bright taking notes.[6] Brunyate later took over interviewing duties. Out of these was compiled a shortlist of potential MI(R) officers.[7] Geoffrey Household remembered being called to the War Office for an interview, his interest raised by the letter not bearing the usual OHMS franking but a discreet stamp. He was shown to a room which seemed 'excessively large' with at the far end a colonel (Templer) and 'an exceptionally lovely girl' (Joan Bright). The presence of a woman at such War Office interviews in 1939 was a novelty and Household believed she was there for the value of her snap judgement. It is equally possible that in a more chauvinistic age her presence was designed to throw interviewees off-guard (as was the technique of making them walk the length of a long room and then seating them next to a hot radiator). Templer was looking for the 'mass production of certain types' who would form the core of Field Security and the future Intelligence Corps, passing on the more individualistic linguists, writers, explorers and executives with an adventurous personality to MI(R). Some would have particular local knowledge, especially true of missions in Scandinavia and in East and West Africa, with the latter relying heavily on colonial service officers, big game hunters and others used to living in the bush.

Initially, MI(R) was only permitted to take men aged 31 and over from the Officers Emergency Reserve, leaving the younger, more active, men for the DMI (although the net was eventually widened).[8] Those not required for an immediate project were returned to their former duties or occupations but contact was maintained. Most of the civilian candidates were university graduates who had passed their 'Certificate A' at school or university OTC and therefore had some preparation for a commission. Holland insisted that they were then sent to an Officer Cadet Training Unit (OCTU) for an abbreviated regular military training. There were exceptions: Gordon Waterfield, a journalist, was recruited to MI(R) on the basis of his fluent Italian and Arabic, then immediately given an emergency commission in the new Intelligence Corps. His only apparent military experience was what he learned at the Lochailort Training School, where he was chosen for Mission 106 and, somewhat bizarrely, was sent in advance to the Middle East as an acting captain to sabotage the Djibuti–Addis Ababa railway (*see below*, p. 169). It remains a possibility that he was actually a former SIS officer. MI(R) was not a unit as such and existing officers attached to it wore their former regimental cap badges, while new recruits were commissioned onto the General List, wearing the anonymous-looking badge of the royal coat of arms (derided as the 'Post Office Rifles') or from July 1940 were badged to the new Intelligence Corps (Plate 34).

Autobiographical accounts of their recruitment and deployment often have a cultivated whimsical tone because it seemed un-British to appear to be too professional in what was viewed as the sometimes grubby world of Intelligence. The charming Malcolm Munthe claimed to have been recruited because of a note on his service record that he was 'very keen and a good linguist', and a mistaken belief that he was an expert on demolitions.[9] He was summoned to the MI(R) office from the Weedon OCTU, where he was in the process of being commissioned into the Gordon Highlanders, and was immediately sent with Andrew Croft to instruct Swedish Legion volunteers in Stockholm and then on to Bergen to organize the shipment of supplies to Finland. Following contact with Peter Fleming, Douglas Dodds-Parker was recruited in September 1939 from the Grenadier Guards Training Battalion and in March 1940, after completing the Cambridge 'Gauleiters' course, he was due to be sent to the new MI(R) Middle East/G(R). He arrived early at the office and Peter Wilkinson, after asking whether he knew anything about Poland, assumed Dodds-Parker was the officer detailed to take over his responsibilities with the Polish mission in London. They went off to discuss this at Dodds-Parker's club and in the meantime the officer actually intended for the Polish mission arrived but was sent to the Middle East instead![10]

Peter Kemp, aged just 25, was recruited while working for the Press Section of Postal Censorship, a medical board in September 1939 having declared him unfit for military service due to his still-healing wounds from the Spanish Civil War. During a casual meeting with Dodds-Parker after the latter's recruitment to MI(R) (the two men having met in Spain in June 1939), Dodds-Parker simply asked 'Would you like me to give your name to my people at the War Office?'[11] An interview with Brunyate followed and in late December 1939 Kemp was informed that he would be commissioned onto the General List and then undergo three months' training at No. 110 Cavalry OCTU at Weedon before joining MI(R).

Geoffrey Household had been a banker in Romania and had joined the TARO at the time of the Munich Crisis. He was next summoned for a test on his language skills in Spanish, French and German; having spent four years in Romania, it was assumed (incorrectly) that he could speak Romanian. After his interview with Templer, there followed two Intelligence courses in the summer of 1939, probably comprising the MI(R) Caxton Hall course (*see below*) and a ten-day long Military Intelligence course at the Royal United Services Institute. His training covered the use and organization of 'Commandos', the new opportunities provided by parachute troops, the 'rallying of large local forces by small parties of British' and the art of guerrilla warfare. Household had assumed he would be sent to Spain but on 20 August he received a terse telegram from the War Office ordering him to report within 24 hours. His destination was to be Romania, where in a very British way he had not bothered to learn the language: 'I could not speak a word nor even read a newspaper.'[12] He was to leave in four days and so went out to buy a uniform. He described his fellow MI(R) officers of the Polish and Romanian missions as 'nearly all amateur soldiers, picked for our languages or special knowledge, and put in the picture – trained is too strong a word – by the same courses'.[13]

One professional army officer was Peter Wilkinson from the Royal Fusiliers, who had been attached to MI3(a) in 1938 as a language officer and, with Alan Brown of the Royal Tank Corps (another future MI(R) Officer), had been in Prague at the time of the German invasion as part of a language course. After a casual conversation with Gubbins at the Army and Navy Club in May 1939, Wilkinson and Brown were invited to lunch with other prospective recruits and over brandy and coffee they were told that Gubbins was looking for suitable officers to train in guerrilla warfare, in the expectation that large areas of eastern Europe would soon be overrun by the Germans. Having expressed interest, Wilkinson then returned to regimental duties but in July 1939 he received a letter from Gubbins asking him to attend one of the courses at Caxton Hall. Returning to his regiment once more, on 22 August he received orders to report to the War Office on the following day and on 25 August was on his way to Poland with the MI(R) mission. On the basis of his weekend Caxton Hall course, he was optimistically expected to advise the far more experienced Polish Army on how to organize guerrilla units. He presumably spent the journey desperately reading the new MI(R) pamphlets for ideas on how this might be arranged.[14]

The first task given to MI(R) after the agreement on Scheme D was to produce a guerrilla field service manual (*see above*, p. 13) and this was the main reason for the recruitment of then Major Colin Gubbins (Plate 2) from the War Office training section, MT1. Gubbins had served for six months in North Russia in 1919 as aide-de-camp to Brigadier General Edmund Ironside and later reflected that 'to anyone who had studied the Russian revolution ... the crippling effect of subversive and para-military warfare on regular forces was obvious'.[15] He was posted to Ireland in late 1919 with the Royal Artillery, eventually becoming a temporary brigade major. Gubbins later complained that he was 'shot at from behind hedges by men in trilbys and mackintoshes and not allowed to shoot back!' but this was a general rather than a personal statement.[16] In October 1920 the 5th Division had organized a three-day Guerrilla Warfare Class for officers and NCOs at the Curragh, as an attempt to disseminate the lessons of the 'peculiar type of guerrilla warfare in which they were becoming more and more engaged.' This included 'practical tactical exercises carried out by the class itself in ambushes on lorry parties and cyclist patrols'.[17] Gubbins probably attended the course and he would certainly have seen the lecture notes which were printed and distributed to all units in the 5th Division and beyond as *Notes on Guerrilla Warfare in Ireland* (1921).[18]

Holland's ambitious intention was to provide a manual that explained and codified the general principles of guerrilla warfare, and how these could be applied to specific countries. This plan was abandoned in the urgency of the moment in favour of producing a basic guide. The resultant three pamphlets were produced in a matter of weeks and became the bedrock of the training programme of MI(R), offered up to foreign allies as a measure of MI(R)'s credentials and used throughout the war by SOE. The strategy of guerrilla warfare was outlined in *The Art of Guerrilla Warfare* (*see* Appendix 2) by Gubbins with input from Holland and was based on the latter's desktop study of historic conflicts involving guerrillas, with elements extracted in particular from *Notes on Guerrilla Warfare in Ireland* (1921), revised as *Notes on Imperial Policing and Irregular Warfare* (1933 and 1934). The original 1921 version of *Notes* was a practical set of instructions to avoid ambush and Gubbins turned this on its head to create a guide for offensive action, adopting the key principles of mobility, careful planning and stealth, and the use of the local population as a source of Intelligence:

> It is in mobility, in information and in morale that guerrillas can secure the advantage, and those factors are the means by which the enemy's superior armament and numbers can best be combated. The superior mobility, however, is not absolute, but relative – i.e. to the type of country in which the activities are staged, to the detailed knowledge of that country by the guerrillas, etc. In absolute mobility, the enemy must always have the advantage – i.e. the use of railway systems, the possession of large numbers of motors, lorries, armoured cars, tanks, etc. ... By the judicious selection of ground, however, and by moves in darkness to secure surprise, the guerrillas can enjoy relatively superior mobility for the period necessary for each operation. The enemy will usually be in a country where the population is largely hostile, so that the people will actively co-operate in providing information for the guerrillas and withholding it from the enemy. The proper encouragement of this natural situation ... will ensure that the guerrillas are kept *au fait* with the enemy's movements and intentions, whereas their own are hidden from him.[19]

Gubbins could also draw directly from the captured IRA instructions of September 1920 which warned 'our troops must not be drawn into an operation or into a general engagement with large bodies of military'.[20] *The Art of Guerrilla Warfare* echoed this advice by instructing partisans to 'avoid prolonged engagements' and instead to 'break off the action when it becomes too risky to continue'. The principle of superior mobility to the enemy was derived principally from T.E. Lawrence but the 'supernatural rapidity' of guerrillas was also stressed by Mao Tse-Tung in 1937.[21] Everything was underlain by Holland's fundamental principle that guerrilla action had to complement regular offensives by diminishing the ability of the enemy to concentrate its forces against a conventional assault:

> This object is achieved by compelling the enemy to disperse his forces in order to guard his flank, his communications, his detachments, supply depots, etc., against the attacks of guerrillas, and thus so to weaken his main armies that the conduct of a campaign becomes impossible.[22]

The ideal size of a guerrilla band was to be between eight and twenty-five – small enough to be mobile and find easy concealment but strong enough to attack a large target. They would live off the land and be able to move across country, as opposed to conventional troops who were focused on roads and railways and relied on good communications to keep them well-supplied. The 'Nine Points of the Guerrilla's Creed' summarized the basic principles in practical form and combined both audacious action and necessary caution:

1. surprise;
2. ensure operations were sure of success – breaking off action when it becomes too risky;
3. ensure a line of retreat;
4. choose areas where you have superior mobility;
5. confine most operations to night-time;
6. do not engage in pitched battles;
7. avoid being pinned down;
8. retain the initiative when the enemy launches counter-measures; and
9. act with 'boldness and audacity'.

'Tommy guns' were prioritized in the list of suggested weapons but when the Czechs consequently requested such weapons Gubbins faced the embarrassment of having to admit that the British did not actually have any submachine guns. The importance of leadership was stressed:

> In guerrilla warfare it is the personality of the leader that counts: he it is who has to make decisions on his own responsibility and lead his men in each enterprise. He must therefore be decisive and resourceful, bold in action and cool in council, of great mental and physical endurance, and of strong personality.

Such a leader might have titular authority but it was expected that they would rely on the advice of a serving military officer for the most effective direction and coordination of operations. The presence of a military mission 'from a third party' (i.e. Britain) able to provide advice, liaison and the supply of weapons and funding, as well as officers in the field, was also naturally recommended. The officers of these missions were to identify with the people with whom they were to serve 'at the risk of future regrets and disillusion', which implied allying with local political interests – something that Holland rejected but may have been a result of the influence of Laurence Grand.

With memories of the British Army's experience in Ireland, the importance of using a friendly population to gather intelligence was stressed. The 1921 *Notes on Guerrilla Warfare in Ireland* had observed that 'the leakage of information in Ireland is very great, and it may be generally accepted that no inhabitant or civilian employee is to be trusted'.[23] The *Partisan Leader's Handbook* therefore stressed that partisans should work hard not to aggravate the people, but instead foster their hatred of the enemy and their sense of resistance. This might be either by providing information to the guerrillas or at least by withholding it from the enemy. But, from experience in Ireland, Gubbins also warned that informers posed the gravest risk to the guerrillas: 'The most stringent and ruthless measures must at all times be used against informers; immediately on proof of guilt they must be killed, and, if possible, a note pinned on the body stating that the man was an informer.' The style was borrowed from Scheme D of March 1939 which included advice on the assassination of members of the Gestapo 'in order to produce in the minds of the local inhabitants that the guerrillas were more to be feared than the occupying secret police. In this way, (a technique which was learnt from the Irish in 1920) the business of collection of intelligence would become more and more difficult for the enemy.'[24] Based on British policy in Ireland and Palestine, Gubbins warned of a likely campaign of 'Searches, raids ... curfew, passport and other regulations' against the partisans, which would eventually force them to 'go on the run', surviving 'as a band in some suitable areas where the nature of the country enables them to be relatively secure'.[25] A deliberate omission was the effects on a partisan movement of reprisals against the civilian population. According to Gubbins, this was considered 'as a point best passed by in silence'.[26]

While *The Art of Guerrilla Warfare* provided an introduction to the topic at a strategic level, the *Partisan Leader's Handbook* and *How to Use High Explosives* provided practical guides for the fighting partisans, including how to mount road and rail ambushes, destroy an enemy post, concealment, care of arms and explosives, and how to counter the enemy's intelligence system.[27] *How to Use High Explosives* focused on the types of explosives and devices that were likely to be supplied by MI(R) and advice on the sabotage of industrial machinery (Plate 17). Given all the available sources, the main principles of guerrilla warfare were well understood by 1939 and Gubbins' contribution was not in innovation but rather in rapidly synthesizing them into a concise and easily accessible form.

Training courses for the MI(R) recruits were next required. Taking inspiration from Templer's ten-day Introduction to Military Intelligence course held in Whitehall (which some MI(R) recruits may have attended), some successful candidates to MI(R) during May and June 1939 attended a short course at Caxton Hall in conjunction with Section D and organized by Lesley Wauchope and Joan Bright of MI(R), comprising lectures on the methodology of irregular warfare and talks on the organization of the foreign armies with whom they were expected to work. Caxton Hall was a public building used for conferences, weddings and council meetings where the instructors and thirty students, all in civilian clothes, could slip in and out unnoticed. The syllabus was prepared by Gubbins but Wilkinson was not impressed and said the attendees would have better spent their time reading *The Seven Pillars of Wisdom* by T.E. Lawrence. Gubbins gave a 'good but somewhat superficial' lecture on the principles of guerrilla warfare and there were lectures on elementary demolition and radio communication. Two lectures were given by Brigadier Gambier-Parry, the head of the Signals section of SIS.[28] Significantly, Holland stressed that the course was not intended to produce fighting guerrilla leaders (which should come from nationals of the country concerned), but rather British officers able to organize supply and training as 'advisers' in the military missions. In the typically chauvinistic attitude of the time, it was phrased: 'What is likely to be lacking in the national characteristics of our Allies is the ability to organize thoroughly.'[29]

In November 1939, to extend the concept of the Caxton Hall courses, Gubbins, Crockatt and Brunyate went to Cambridge to discuss the possibilities of the university cooperating in establishing a politico-military course. The first of the eight-week courses was held from 15 January 1940 at Brunyate's former college, Trinity, and was intended to run three times a year under Professor Ernest Barker (Professor of Political Science) with some outside lecturers. It became known as the 'Gauleiters' course (after the title of the regional heads of the Nazi party).[30] After the first course, administration was passed to the MT7 branch of the War Office. Each course took forty army officers with special knowledge of particular areas of Europe, providing introductory lectures common to all and then dividing into Europe and Middle East sections. Going back to the original concept behind GS(R), the belief was that political chaos might well emerge abroad during (and after) the war and that specialist officers with language qualification and knowledge of current political problems would be better able to advise military missions and even direct troops and local organizations. As with the Caxton Hall courses, the students were not being trained as guerrilla leaders but rather as officers to protect British interests in the empire and help oppose enemy 'fifth column' activities. Besides instruction in physical and economic sabotage (or more precisely counter-sabotage), the course covered different systems of government (including fascist, communist and federalist), mob psychology, political history, historical geography, and economic and ethnographic history.[31] Students were graded and those earmarked for MI(R) could be detached from their regiments for suitable employment at a later date. In the event, the third course was delayed until January 1941 (after the demise of MI(R)), to allow time for Professor Barker to devise a new syllabus. Both the Caxton Hall and Cambridge courses were essentially theoretical, reflecting the somewhat academic outlook of MI(R) but in an effort to improve more practical-based training, in October 1939 John D. Kennedy had flown to Scotland to try to persuade the Lovat Scouts to create a specialized Training Wing. Nothing came of this initiative and it was not until the creation of the Lochailort Training School in June 1940 that this crucial gap was filled.[32]

Although practical instruction in guerrilla warfare was lacking, Holland was determined that all recruits should have some form of conventional military training. Arrangements were made with the Directorate of Military Training (DMT) for recruits, where necessary, to undergo an abbreviated training at an OCTU, the first course being held on 11 October 1939.[33] From the start of the war to the end of August 1940, some 200 MI(R) nominees were trained through OCTUs and either employed by MI(R) or given a posting in another branch of Military Intelligence.[34] Courses were arranged at 168 OCTU (Infantry) at Aldershot, 169 OCTU (Field Security Wing, Corps of Military Police) at Minley, 110 OCTU (Cavalry) at Weedon and a Royal Engineers OCTU.[35] These were standard courses rather than tailored to the specific needs of MI(R) and Harold Perkins' commission from Weedon was delayed because he had not yet managed to get round the cavalry jumps without falling off.[36] Lord Lovat described the course at Weedon as 'antiquated to the point of being antediluvian'.[37] The overall intention was to train seventy-five officers for MI(R) every three months in a package of training comprising,

(a) OCTU course (between eight and sixteen weeks depending on previous experience)
(b) possible additional training in explosives
(c) possible additional training in horsemanship
(d) course in guerrilla warfare
(e) Cambridge politico-military course

This level of training was never achieved, with the explosives training being particularly haphazard and the failings in training were made obvious with the deployment of the Independent Companies to Norway (*see below*, p. 107).

Lochailort Training School

Inspired by the planning for the Cambridge 'Gauleiters' course, in December 1939 MI(R) was asked to evolve a project for the reorganization of wider Military Intelligence training as a whole. Gubbins obtained details of French Intelligence training and a project was then put to the DMI.[38] Nothing resulted, but Holland continued to ponder the matter and funding was at least identified for any future initiative, which became increasingly urgent as MI(R) was drawn into field operations. In May 1940 Lieutenant Colonel Bryan Mayfield and Captains William Stirling, Jim Gavin, Ralph Farrant and David Stacey, all from the short-lived 5th Scots Guards ski battalion, went to Stirling's nearby estate at Keir following the return of the abortive *Knife* mission (see below, p. 105), whilst they awaited further instructions (fellow *Knife* team member Peter Kemp having returned to London to report to MI(R)). Here they came up with the basic idea of a more practical training school for guerrilla warfare. Stirling's estate had already been requisitioned and the area was too populated for what they had in mind, but the men realised that the wild and isolated north-west Highlands, within the vast 'Protected Area' where access was controlled to protect the coastline and existing military bases, offered the perfect territory to train troops to become self-reliant, experts in concealment and capable of survival in the harshest environments. Stirling and Mayfield went down to London to put the suggestion to Holland, who leapt at the idea as by now it was obvious that the Independent Companies, intended as guerrilla troops in Norway, were being dispatched with no specialist skills (see below, p. 107). On the evening of 9 May Holland successfully presented a proposal to a meeting of the DMT for the establishment of a guerrilla warfare training school for up to 500 all-services personnel.[39] Meanwhile, at White's Club in London (the unofficial wartime hub of British Intelligence) Mayfield and Stirling met the latter's cousin, Simon ('Shimi'), the Lord Lovat, and were reunited with Peter Kemp. Lovat was disenchanted with his existing role as a captain in the Lovat Scouts and Kemp was frustrated by a lack of action. Lovat and Kemp returned to Keir to join the rest of the *Knife* party, who would now form the nucleus of the instructors at the new school. They next had to find a location and accounts vary as to whether it was Stirling, Mayfield or Lord Lovat who eventually suggested the Victorian-Gothic Inverailort Castle (Plate 19) as the HQ of the new training centre. The castle was the centre of a shooting estate at the point where the River Ailort entered Loch Ailort (Plate 18), and 40km west of Fort William. It was a rugged area, on the foothills of Seann Cruach and An Stac, a landscape of mountain, moor and bog. The castle was isolated but had good rail links via the West Highland railway to central Scotland and London, and the local railway line also provided the opportunity to practise dummy attacks on railways. Kemp described Lochailort as 'a wild bleak beauty of scoured rocks and cold blue water, of light green bracken and shadowed pine, that is strangely moving in its stark simplicity and grandeur'.[40] Inverailort Castle, Glenshian Lodge and part of the Inverailort Estate were immediately requisitioned by Scottish Command but the owner, 81-year-old Mrs Pauline Cameron-Head, was in London when she received notice of this and quickly returned to find herself barred from the house and obliged to take temporary shelter in the local inn. By then she noticed that seventy to eighty tents had already been erected in the grounds. The centre was opened on 3 June 1940, at first with twenty-five 'keen but puzzled' subalterns and a similar number of NCOs from Nos 6 and 7 Independent Companies, followed rapidly by 400 hurriedly drafted student volunteers including the men from No. 10 Independent Company.[41] The aim was to train specific units for irregular operations and a wider pool of men as a reservoir for future projects.[42]

The training school was managed by the Directorate of Military Training, with MI(R), having recruited most of the initial staff, advising on course content. Jim Gavin remembered that not even the instructors were quite clear as to who controlled the establishment.[43] Mayfield was appointed Commandant, with Farrant as his deputy, and Stirling as Chief Instructor. The original War Establishment allowed for 13 officers, 16 NCOs and 109 other ranks as permanent staff, catering for up to 600 students at any one time.[44] Gavin had been on the Himalayan expedition of 1936 and the early instructors also included polar explorers Surgeon-Commander George Murray Levick (now in his early 60s, he had been on Scott's ill-fated polar expedition of 1910– 1913), Freddy Spencer-Chapman (from the Watkins Greenland expedition and 5th Scots Guards) with Andrew Croft and Martin Lindsay (formerly assistant adjutant, 5th Scots Guards) from MI(R). The Chief Fieldcraft Instructor was Lord Lovat, first assisted by Peter Kemp and Spencer-Chapman, ghillies from Lord Lovat's estate and three NCOs from the Lovat Scouts. On 9 June Second Lieutenant David Stirling, another veteran of the 5th Scots Guards, younger brother of William and another keen mountaineer, the future founder of the SAS, replaced Peter Kemp briefly as assistant to Lord Lovat. Tommy Macpherson, a member of the new No. 11 (Scottish) Commando, attended one of the early courses in the summer of 1940 and recalled that 'the staff were an interesting collection'. They included a burglar on release from Peterhead prison – 'who I don't think was fully retired' – who taught how to pick locks and open safes.[45] Warrant Officer Percival 'Wally' Wallbridge from the Small Arms School Corps, formerly senior sniping instructor to the BEF, was one of the firearms instructors and aimed to get recruits up to a speed of 20–25 rounds per minute from an SMLE. Some of the instructors, such as Peter Fleming and Peter Kemp, were there only for a few weeks as Lochailort was used as a holding area for such men until a more suitable project was found.

The HQ, with lecture rooms and accommodation for the officer instructors, was the 'Big House' at Inverailort (Plate 20); Glenshian Lodge housed the NCOs and the medical unit; and the students were accommodated in more challenging tents and later corrugated-iron nissen huts in the surrounding area. A range of brick and asbestos-roofed buildings were also soon added with a NAAFI, catering accommodation, a recreation hall, generator house, cook-house and medical block, drying room, shower room, wash room, boiler house, latrine blocks, paint store, two ammunition sheds, cinema, pistol range and eventually over fifty nissen huts.[46] The shoreline of the Loch also provided ample opportunities to practise small-scale assault landings, initially using four dinghies requisitioned from Mrs Cameron-Head's boatshed.

Some lectures were held in huts on islets in the River Ailort and Lieutenant Ronald Hall of the GHQ Auxiliary Units remembered that the students were expected to wade the river, sometimes with the water up to chest height, to reach their classes, which they then had to attend in wet clothes. The flavour of the course was apparent from the start when upon arrival, the train would come to an abrupt halt and the students had to scramble to leave whilst under fire from hidden instructors. The course, loosely based on the MI(R) pamphlets but owing much to Mayfield, Lovat and Stirling and the 'lore of the Lovat Scouts', taught fieldcraft and survival skills, guerrilla techniques and demolition methods, with an intense weapons training. There were gruelling obstacle courses and one innovation (now a standard in special forces training) was the 'Mystery House' where students would have to make their way through a derelict cottage, distracted by firecrackers, and fire at pop-up metal targets representing the enemy, whilst avoiding shooting representations of innocent civilians.[47] It was devised by 'Wally' Wallbridge and former Shanghai policeman William Fairbairn, to develop split-second decision-making and 'instinctive shooting' that delivered two rounds fired in quick succession into the chest of the opponent. With his former police colleague Eric ('Bill') Sykes, Fairbairn also brought new techniques of unarmed combat, based on Far Eastern martial arts, and knife fighting. It was at Lochailort that Fairbairn and Sykes conceived their famous fighting knife, the first pattern going into production by the end of November and becoming the enduring symbol of the Commandos. The finale of the course was a three-day exercise, including spending two nights in the open, known as the 'Captain Blood Attack'.

The signals wing at Lochailort was briefly under Peter Fleming (Plate 6), who brought back some of the signals equipment that had been so disappointing at Namsos (*see below*, p. 102). He established a wireless station on the hill above the hall to experiment further with ship-to-shore communications, the section eventually providing valuable technical information for planning future Commando operations. Fleming was not a signals specialist and moved to briefly assist Lord Lovat in the fieldwork wing before finally leaving to join XII Corps Observation Unit. Jim Gavin was the demolitions officer, assisted for six weeks by Mike Calvert, a pre-war Territorial Royal Engineers officer, who was another ex-5th Scots Guards and who served with the Royal Engineers during the Norwegian campaign. Both were particularly enthusiastic and inventive. Gavin had a habit of setting detonators under the seats of students in the lecture rooms in order to keep them alert. Calvert left in late July to join Fleming in XII Corps Observation Unit, and Spencer-Chapman left in August to prepare No. 104 Mission which would establish a similar school to train Independent Companies and 'stay-behind' parties in Australia. In the Military Intelligence training wing, Major Munn of the Royal Artillery, who had served on the North West Frontier of India, instructed on map-reading and aspects of Military Intelligence, and on 31 July was joined by John Wilson to teach on counter-intelligence and 'fifth column' activities from a police perspective.[48] Crucially, experienced polar explorer George Murray Levick applied medical and scientific principles to teach the students how to maintain peak fitness and endurance in survival conditions. Lochailort eventually became the hub of a network of Commando training centres in the area, but in 1942 it was taken over by the Admiralty as a Naval Training Establishment and designated HMS *Lochailort*.

Chapter Five

Escape, Evasion and Deception

Two of the less obvious contributions of MI(R) were in the creation of the escape and evasion organization (MI9) and in deception planning. Although its direct participation was short-lived, it is important to recognize MI(R)'s role in the genesis of these important fields of Intelligence.

Escape and Evasion

Valuable intelligence had been gained in the First World War from German POWs and from British servicemen who had escaped captivity; from the start of the Second World War there was a concern to put this potential resource on a more organized footing. In September 1939 Gerald Templer transferred to become a senior Intelligence officer with the BEF in France and on 28 September 1939 he wrote to the DMI, Major General Beaumont-Nesbitt, outlining an idea to communicate with future POWs in their camps by coded messages. Beaumont-Nesbitt passed this idea on to Holland, who endorsed the proposal and in a substantial report of 13 October 1939 (submitted to Beaumont-Nesbitt on the following day) suggested 'a very thorough organization'.[1] The matter was then referred to the Joint Intelligence Committee (JIC) and was progressed at remarkable speed with cross-service discussions in which Holland installed as War Office representative a recent recruit to MI(R), 45-year-old Major Norman Crockatt. The latter was an old school friend from Rugby and a veteran of the First World War (in which he had won the DSO and MC). He had later become head of the London Stock Exchange. Recommissioned only as 'fit for home duty', Crockatt was now collating information on Europe and supervising the MI(R) training programme. To prepare him, Holland provided a pile of books about escaping prisoners of war, borrowed from friends and libraries. At a conference on 24 November 1939 it was agreed by the RAF and War Office that the DMI would take the lead and select an officer to run a new service, to be designated MI9. Holland objected to the suggestion that this should be led by a former First World War escapee on the grounds that their personal experience might colour their views. Instead he suggested Crockatt, who had a reputation as a good coordinator, quick-witted and not a man to be bound by War Office bureaucracy. It was an inspired choice. Crockatt transferred to the new

MI9 on 4 December 1939 and its Charter was issued on 23 December, with five main tasks:

- to help British POWs in their escapes, so they could return to combat and use up enemy resources in guarding them;
- to help the escapees to avoid capture while in enemy territory;
- to collect and distribute information;
- to help deny the enemy information; and
- to maintain the morale of British POWs in enemy camps.

In April 1940 MI9 also absorbed the section of MI1 responsible for extracting information from captured POWs and in late 1941 Crockatt was promoted colonel and designated Deputy Director of Military Intelligence (Prisoners of War).

The key to assisting escaped Allied servicemen was meticulous preparation before they ever went into action. During the course of the war lectures on escape and evasion techniques were given to more than 600,000 British and Commonwealth service personnel. They were given training in how to deal with imprisonment, escape methods and how to blend in with the surrounding population when on the run. Ingenious practical equipment was invented to assist them. There were items that could be hidden in clothing and other objects to avoid detection, including razors that were magnetized to provide improvised compasses, miniature compasses that could be hidden as collar studs, fly buttons or contained in false boot heels, and fine wire saws hidden in boot laces. Maps were printed on silk or mulberry tissue paper and could be hidden in uniform linings or as handkerchiefs (Plates 21 and 22). After they reached the camps, escape tools were sent in aid packages, secretly marked so that the prisoners would know which ones to try to prevent the guards from searching. Red Cross parcels were sacrosanct but other parcels were sent from fictitious aid organizations such as the 'Prisoners Leisure Hours Fund', the 'Welsh Provident Society', 'Licensed Victuallers' Sports Association' and the 'Ladies Knitting Circle'.

Contact was maintained with prisoners within the camps by hidden radio receiver sets, either built by captives or smuggled in by MI9. The simplest were crystal sets that were built around a razor blade, pencil lead and a bent safety pin, and did not require an electrical power source. An improvised earpiece could be built into an empty food tin. Such sets allowed MI9 to send coded messages to the prisoners in BBC radio broadcasts, including the popular weekly *The Radio Padre*. Thus, when the Revd Ronnie Wright began his broadcast with the words 'Good evening, forces', the prisoners knew that the talk would contain a coded message. In addition, POWs were able to send information out of the camps using a system of codes contained in their letters to home. By the end of the war miniature transceivers built into two thin

cigarette case-sized boxes were smuggled into the camp (their genesis probably being the 'Gambier Parry belt sets' envisaged for MI(R) missions in
1940: *see below*, p. 94). MI9 also coordinated with SIS and SOE over contacts
with the resistance organizations that provided escape lines out of enemy
territory.

The search for Allied escapees tied up enemy resources but Crockatt
opposed mass escapes on the basis that the risk of reprisals was too great, a fear
that was most infamously proved correct in the 'Great Escape' from Stalag
Luft III in March 1944 when fifty recaptured Allied POWs were executed. It
also led to one of the most controversial episodes in the history of MI9. After
Italy surrendered in 1943, MI9 ordered the 80,000 POWs in Italy to remain
in their camps, assuming that they would soon be liberated by advancing
Allied troops. The instruction continued to be transmitted even after it was
clear that the Allied advance had been delayed and that the Germans were
about to take over the camps. In all, 50,000 POWs in Italy were seized by the
Germans and many faced a gruelling journey to camps in Germany and
Poland.

Deception

In February 1940 MI(R) was asked by the Joint Intelligence Committee to
set up the small Inter-Services Security Board (ISSB), with representatives
from the War Office, Air Ministry and Admiralty, with liaison officers from
MI5 and the Ministry of Supply (and later SIS), to coordinate and control all
security measures surrounding future strategic projects. Its first task was to
establish the extent of knowledge of existing plans and to introduce security
measures to better restrict access and prevent leakage of information. It would
also implement deception plans to conceal the location and nature of future
operations. Holland chaired the early meetings and MI(R) also provided
the Secretariat, with the *bon viveur* and former banker, 49-year-old Major
Edmund Combe as Secretary, assisted by the meticulous John Brunyate and
the seemingly ever-present Peter Fleming. Such was the importance of the
work, the committee met every day at 3.00pm. The first test of the Committee concerned the deception schemes surrounding the proposed Finnish
and Norwegian campaigns. A simple system of name substitution (Fig. 4) was
introduced for use in all correspondence, with the Finland/Norway campaign
to be known as the 'Middle East Reinforcement Plan'.[2]

As an example, the minutes of the ISSB Meeting on 9 March 1940 recorded
a need to 'request the Foreign Office to advise HM Minister, Odessa, by telegram of the impending arrival of certain British representatives in connection with transit of stores to Iraq', which was actually a coded warning order
for the Minister in Oslo to expect the arrival of the expeditionary force for
Finland. The ISSB issued and coordinated all British code names and numbers

Figure 4. Extract from substitution codes in connection with the projected
Norwegian campaign, February 1940. *(TNA WO 283/1)*

Name	Cover name	Name	Cover name
Scandinavia	Asia Minor	Namsos	Nicosia
Norway	Turkey	Narvik	Nikolaev
Sweden	Syria	Oslo	Odessa
Finland	Iraq	Stavanger	Smyrna
Russia	Persia	Stockholm	Sinope
Denmark	Cyprus	Trondheim	Trebizond
Bergen	Batum		

used by the War Office, Admiralty and Air Ministry and the secret telegraphic
addresses.[3] These followed common themes, selected to give no clue as to the
location or nature of the operation and were also to avoid trivialization by
the temptation to use humorous names. Censorship was manipulated, with the
connivance of newspaper editors, to distribute false information. A 'D' Notice
prohibited any mention of possible Allied intervention in Scandinavia and any
accidental leak of genuine information in the press was hinted to be a bluff. At
the same time, to divert attention away from Scandinavia, false stories regarding imminent operations in the Middle East were deliberately circulated in
the press, and then incompletely suppressed in what would appear to be a
'censorship muddle'. Former *Times* journalist Peter Fleming was responsible
for press liaison over the deception plans and also for monitoring German
reaction. The deception also included army commands drawing up lists of
requirements for desert issue uniforms and additional maps of the Middle
East being ordered from the suppliers, MI5 then ensuring the information was discreetly leaked to their web of turned agents or known Nazi-
sympathizing diplomats in Britain.[4]

An elaborate plan was produced in February 1940 for Advance Security
Officers (in civilian clothes, with fishing rods as cover) to be infiltrated into
the ports earmarked for the planned British landings in Norway on their way
to Finland (*see below*, p. 97). Originally this was to be a Section D operation,
MI(R) only being responsible for delivering the sealed orders to the local
military attaché. The Advance Security Officers were to organize the reception of the Allied forces and also to prevent 'by any way possible' efforts of
German agents to report news of the landings to Berlin.[5] Section D was to
provide six men for the operation under James Chaworth-Musters (head of
its Bergen network) but the plan was quickly amended and put completely
into the hands of MI(R) as the mission was to support a British military
operation.[6] Holland arranged for officers to be sent to the landing ports of
Narvik, Trondheim, Bergen and Stavanger as 'political officers' to arrange

the reception of British landings and to ensure good relations with the local population.[7] They flew out on 13 March but the Finns had concluded their armistice with the Soviet Union on the previous day and the planned landings were abandoned. The officers were soon to return to Norway as on 2 April MI(R) sent Advance Security Officers to the four Norwegian ports where it was proposed to disembark a British Expeditionary Force to bolster the Norwegian defences against the anticipated German invasion (*see below*, p. 99).[8] Holland's last meeting as chairman of the ISSB was on 16 April and responsibility for the ISSB secretariat then passed to MI1 (including the transfer of some MI(R) officers) but the foundations for the elaborate deception schemes that were later to prove vital in the plans for Operation Overlord in 1944 had been laid.

Chapter Six

Central and Eastern Europe

Poland was the anticipated flashpoint of war with Germany, and much of MI(R)'s work in eastern Europe and the Balkans was subsequently directed towards supporting its resistance. MI(R) involvement was led by Colin Gubbins (Plate 2), who had worked with the Polish Army during his time in Russia during 1919 and then served in the Polish section of the DMI in 1932, when he earned the nickname 'Gubbski'. Peter Wilkinson later recalled that the Poles 'had cast their spell over Gubbins, appealing particularly to the romantic side of his nature' and his loyalty to the Poles continued throughout the war.[1] Gubbins had joined MI(R) only after the demarcation of responsibilities with Section D was agreed and he was desperate for a more direct role in guerrilla warfare, frustrated by MI(R)'s reliance on Section D. To that end, he saw his work with the Polish and Czech forces in exile as the foundation of a new power base and took a proprietorial attitude towards their resistance organizations. The resultant discord had a significant impact in the argument to create the new SOE. The Czech and Polish resistance were already well organized but they gritted their teeth over offers of advice and direction from Gubbins because what they did need was material assistance from Britain in the form of weapons, explosives and especially money, as well as freedom to develop their own communications networks.

Poland

In May 1939, just one month after joining MI(R), Gubbins followed up earlier approaches by Holland and made flying visits to Poland, the three Baltic republics and Romania, meeting with the British military attachés but being discreet as to his particular interest. Guerrilla warfare seemed to offer particular potential in Poland, through 'the natural aptitude of the Polish people, both men and women, for guerrilla activities of all kinds, fostered by the national spirit during a century of oppression by Russia and Germany'.[2] The Poles were already making plans and Gubbins hoped that they would welcome British assistance, with the British ambassador in Warsaw informing him that the Poles 'could be trusted to the hilt' and urging that MI(R) give them concrete support.[3] Gubbins made two later trips to Poland, contacting the Polish General Staff and its Intelligence service and claimed much later that these trips 'were so secret that even the DMI was not informed and was very angry when he discovered'.[4] Why this should be is not clear as Gubbins had been meeting the military attachés and was the Chief of Staff-designate for the projected British mission to Poland. His frequent trips to Poland gave rise to the myth, created by the notoriously unreliable William Stevenson, that Gubbins had been involved in the smuggling of one of the Polish replica Enigma machines to Britain.[5]

In June 1939, following Gubbins' exploratory visits, the then DDMI (Beaumont-Nesbitt) told the Polish General Staff that the British were pre-pared to assist in the organization of guerrilla warfare and particularly in the demolition of the railway system – highlighting the railway line along the southern border of Poland that could be used for the transport of oil from Romania.[6] Following this, on 24 July 1939 Major Charaskiewicz, the head of the Polish guerrilla organization formed in May 1939 (on the basis of their experience of guerrilla warfare in late 1938 on the Ukrainian border), met MI(R) and Section D in London. This briefing would have a great impact on the thinking of Section D and MI(R), including the formation of the GHQ Auxiliary Units in coastal Britain. Charaskiewicz had formed small patrols of three to seven men along the Polish–German border, organized in groups of between seven and twenty-five patrols; they would allow their location to be overrun and would then carry out their pre-designated sabotage. Weapons and explosives had already been cached for their use. There was a parallel organization of larger partisan bands of up to fifteen men, who would carry out raids across the Polish–Slovakian frontiers and behind German lines. So far, 800 men had been put through a week-long training course. Like MI(R) and Section D, the Poles also had a technical section producing a variety of sabotage devices, but one omission was any thought of the use of wireless. Gubbins highlighted this problem with some irony, given the failure of wire-less communication in his later Independent Companies and the GHQ Auxiliary Units. At their meeting, information was exchanged on devices and MI(R) demonstrated to the Poles the latest clandestine wireless sets (supplied by SIS). The Polish delegation took back with them supplies of explosives and delay devices from Section D, as well as a copy of Gubbins' *Partisan Leader's Handbook*. The report of the meeting concluded with a need 'to consider the assistance that can be rendered by British officers, trained in guerrilla warfare, attached to a British mission in Poland for that purpose'.[7] This was straight out of *The Art of Guerrilla Warfare* but, at the time, there were no British officers trained in guerrilla warfare and the statement reflected the superiority complex of the War Office. While the War Office pondered how then to proceed, Section D began quietly organizing the movement of propaganda and sabotage materials into Poland from Scandinavia, using its contacts within the network of socialist parties allied to the German SPD.[8]

Gubbins returned briefly to Warsaw on 14–16 August and met Colonel Josef Smolenski, head of the Military Intelligence Bureau of the Polish General Staff. He was shown Polish wireless equipment and delay devices, some of which had been produced from the prototypes earlier supplied by Section D. Now the Poles wished to buy the new MI(R) mines and camouflet sets as well as explosives. They also wished to purchase sub-machine guns as championed by Gubbins in *The Art of Guerrilla Warfare* and it must have been galling to have to admit that the British Army did not yet possess such weapons.[9] Despite these contacts, the MI(R) August progress report had to admit there were still no real plans for British collaboration. Reference was made to technical collaboration over the development of clandestine wireless sets but in truth MI(R) could contribute nothing in this respect, it being an SIS responsibility. The Poles were polite about British recommendations in order to secure supplies of arms, and according to the MI(R) progress report 'the Polish officers appeared to be glad to discuss our views', however, the Poles would have realised that the British priority was not the defence of Poland *per se* but rather to encourage the Poles to extend their plans for guerrilla warfare by making preparations for demolition of the strategically important railway line along the southern border, carrying oil from Romania to Germany.[10]

The August progress report also announced that Gubbins and twelve MI(R) officers would be joining the official military mission to Poland, with a view to providing rear support for any guerrilla organization, although it was hoped 'One or two might prove in action to be real guerrilla leaders.'[11] In July the DMI had begun to prepare the sending of an official mission under General Carton de Wiart. General de Wiart had seen remarkable service in the First World War but had since retired to eastern Poland, living on the estate of Prince Karol Radziwiłł. Gubbins had briefly served with de Wiart in 1917 as a Royal Artillery liaison officer whilst de Wiart commanded the 4th Division, and was formally appointed Chief of Staff to the Polish mission (although he was not de Wiart's first choice).[12] Gubbins' real role was to head the small MI(R) component, funded by SIS, 'to stimulate and assist the Poles and Czechs in guerrilla warfare', through discussion with the Polish and Czech Military Intelligence officers already organizing that task.[13] Gubbins later justified his proprietorial view towards the Polish resistance on the grounds that prior to German occupation it had been the responsibility of MI(R) to liaise with the Polish General Staff over such matters but this exaggerated their actual contribution. It also ignored the fact that once Poland was occupied, the country might (under the terms of the DMI policy statement of September 1939) be considered to fall within the purview of SIS and Section D. There was a further complication in that SIS also saw Section D operations in

Poland as a convenient means of maintaining discreet contacts with the resistance, independent of the Polish General Staff.

The MI(R) mission eventually included fourteen officers as well as Gubbins (Fig. 5). They were drawn from the index of potential Intelligence officers, including Language Officers already in Poland and some men on the officer reserve lists who were resident in Poland. Several later became key figures in SOE's Polish organization and were among Gubbins' closest allies. Ronald Hazell was a vice-consul in Poland who had occasionally worked for SIS.[14] He later became head of the SOE EU/P section for Polish minorities. After the war he became vice-consul in Gdynia as a cover for a resumption of his SIS activities. Harold Perkins, who owned an engineering factory in south Poland, became overall director for SOE in Poland. While in Poland MI(R) recruited the well-travelled Michael Pickles, then working as manager of a Lodz sewing thread mill for J & P Coats; he had an earlier background in the oil industry. On his eventual return to England, Pickles was given an emergency commission and attended the Weedon OCTU before first studying Arabic in the School of Oriental and African Studies and then attending the new Intelligence Corps School at Matlock. He joined SOE in December and became head of SOE Polish Country Section.[15]

Figure 5. Members of the Polish mission, August–October 1939. (*TNA HS 4/224*)

Lieutenant Colonel Colin Gubbins	MI(R)	
Captain A.W. Brown	Royal Tank Regiment	
Lieutenant P.A. Wilkinson	Royal Fusiliers	
Captain J.S. Douglas	Royal Scots	Language officer already in Poland
Captain R.J.M. Wright	Royal Tank Regiment	Language officer already in Poland
Acting Captain W. Harris-Burland	OER	Paymaster
Captain Herbert J. Lloyd-Johnes	TARO	In charge of wireless equipment
Acting Captain F.T. Davies	OER (Grenadier Guards)	
Major J.C. Johnstone	OER	
Lieutenant Ronald Hazell	OER	Already in Poland as a vice-consul
Captain Harold Perkins	OER	Owner of a light engineering factory in south Poland
Lieutenant M.B. Rowton	OER	Already in Poland
Lieutenant M. Scott	OER	Already in Poland
Captain H.M. Curteis	Highland Light Infantry	

Those MI(R) officers on the mission who were in London assembled on 22–23 August. Wilkinson's orders were vague; he was told only on 22 August to report to the War Office on the following day, with the necessary kit for active service but also 'mufti suits and blue patrols'.[16] Like the others, he had only the Caxton Hall course as training for the evangelical mission to the Poles. They left Victoria station on 25 August together with the Romanian mission (*see below*, p. 87), under cover as a variety of commercial travellers, insurance agents and agricultural experts. Nonetheless, in the first of repeated errors in MI(R) missions, the officers had all been issued consecutively numbered passports; less suspicious ones had to be issued in Alexandria. Wilkinson recalled how F.T. 'Tommy' Davies, recently commissioned into the 1st Battalion Grenadier Guards, 'in a Brigade of Guards' tie, stood disapproving and aloof' amid the hearty mêlée of British Army officers in a variety of thin disguises. Herbert Lloyd-Johnes was described by Wilkinson as looking like an 'absconding financier' in a grey pin-stripe suit and a 'seedy bowler hat'. Without private means, NCOs from the Royal Signals attached to the mission were issued with matching sports jackets, grey flannel trousers and trilby hats.[17] In order to avoid travelling through Germany and neutral Sweden they took a tortuous route first by train across France and then by HMS *Shropshire* to Alexandria, docking on 31 August. On the voyage the two military missions, 'claiming to be so secret that they were not allowed to mix with their fellows, captured and held one of the ship's boats; and there, beneath the davits, some twenty of us lived and slept during the passage to Alexandria'.[18] Such ostentatiously mysterious behaviour was worthy of Section D and no doubt attracted much speculation! On 1 September they left in three flying boats for Athens but on landing at Piraeus they learned of the German invasion of Poland and then travelled on by Polish aircraft to Bucharest. They finally crossed the border into Poland in a fleet of taxis but the normal passenger train to Livow had already left and so an antiquated first-class carriage was added to the next goods train. From Livow they travelled to Lublin in a motor bus and on arrival there on 3 September learned that Britain had declared war on Germany, and so changed into uniform. Regular army officer Hugh Curteis, in the tartan trews of the Highland Light Infantry, especially delighted the local population. Gubbins described the scene at Lublin:

> While having our meal we heard on the radio that Britain had declared war on Germany. I immediately ordered my officers and men to put on their uniforms and we went out into the town square to rejoin our buses. The square was completely filled by a huge crowd, cheering and shouting 'England is beside us. Long live England.' We were each of us lifted bodily into the air and carried into our buses already loaded with flowers. My heart was filled with sadness and foreboding.[19]

They finally arrived in Warsaw later in the evening of 3 September and reported to de Wiart. One immediate complication was that the reserve officers recruited to MI(R) who were already working in the country had to be quickly recommissioned and their uniforms were made up from local cloth in Poland to look as much like British uniforms as possible![20] The MI(R) staff remained with the Polish GHQ until the Polish defeat, having had to purchase American motor cars and a 5-ton truck with which to follow the HQ as it was repeatedly forced to relocate. Caught off-balance by the rapid *blitzkrieg*, on 5 September Gubbins wrote a scribbled letter for Davies to take back to London for Holland. With his writing interrupted by air raids, Gubbins noted 'German operations are developing rather too quickly for our liking.'[21]

As later in Norway, the MI(R) mission found themselves in the role of interlopers. The speed of the German advance meant there was little they could do in practical terms other than give a wireless set to the hard-pressed Polish Army. Davies was sent back to England in a hair-raising flight in a civil aircraft via Riga and Stockholm, fired on by both Germans and Poles. He carried a desperate appeal from de Wiart to supply the Poles with fighter aircraft, light machine guns and ammunition before the borders were sealed.[22] Davies only reached England on 8 September and by then Poland was facing imminent defeat but Holland was focused on the wider strategic picture: on 10 September he sent a secret telegram to Gubbins to query what demolition the Polish Army were planning on the Cracow–Lemberg railway and the Galician oilfields.[23] The death knell for the Polish Army came with the Russian invasion on 17 September and Peter Wilkinson recalled that when Gubbins heard the news, he

> made a moving little speech in French in which he expressed his sympathy for the Polish predicament and his admiration for the courage with which the army had fought against overwhelming odds. He promised that Britain would fight on until Poland was once more free and its territory restored. After this we shook hands and took our leave.[24]

In actuality, Poland was abandoned to the Soviet Union by the western Allies. The mission evacuated Poland on 17/18 September and all but Curteis and Pickles reached Bucharest (Romania) over the next two days. Curteis had been separated from the rest of the party whilst liaising with General Dembinski's HQ and crossed from Poland into Hungary on 18 September, then returned to England via Athens (and rejoined his regiment in France). Pickles, not part of the original mission party, made his own way back to England through Silesia and the Baltic states. While in Romania, de Wiart and Gubbins wrote up the official report of the mission but its lessons regarding the *blitzkrieg* went unheeded. Gubbins also spent his time there trying to develop a plan for the demolition of the oilfields with the MI(R) Romania mission and returned to London on 28 September, still preoccupied with the fate of the Poles.

On 10 October 1939 Gubbins made a preliminary visit to Paris to discuss reconstituting the No. 4 Polish Mission, to work with the exiled Polish and Czech forces and also 'in conjunction with the Secret Service [i.e. Section D], maintaining close contact over matters concerning the possibilities of future rebellion in Poland'.[25] On 27 November Gubbins became Chief of the new Polish mission in Paris, with its HQ at 88 Rue de Varennes, assisted by Herbert Lloyd-Johnes in Paris and Peter Wilkinson as a rear link with MI(R) at the War Office. Beyond their general liaison duties, there was a more secret function, known simply as the 'Gubbins Mission', defined as:

(a) Provision of arms, wireless, special stores to the Poles and Czechs, for use in Poland and Czechoslovakia.
(b) Preparation of plans for guerrilla activities in Poland.
(c) Initiation and reception of plans for sabotage by Czechs and Poles.[26]

The Gubbins Mission was nominally independent but was 'in very close touch with MI(R), and takes its direction from the DMI'.[27] Gubbins now had freedom to satisfy his ambitions beyond the advisory role envisaged by Holland but this brought him into conflict with Section D. He could extend his sphere of influence across the Balkans, which provided the main supply lines into Poland, and also monitored Polish Intelligence links to the Finns and the Baltic States, where around 20,000 Poles had been interned, in case the Poles tried to engineer a revolt against Russian occupation. In such an event, MI(R) could then 'direct activities in that region as may be necessary'.[28]

Eager to secure practical support, at their preliminary meetings in October 1939 both the exiled Polish and Czech General Staffs agreed to allow MI(R), effectively Gubbins, to 'control the whole project' of guerrilla warfare.[29] The basis of operations was to be a Polish Bureau in London 'to take complete control under MI(R)'.[30] The French conceded that MI(R) 'should control subversive activities and movements in Poland' but Gubbins remained worried that they would try to usurp his deal. French Intelligence continued to resist British control in what they saw as French spheres of influence in the Middle East and controlled Polish Intelligence activities in Afghanistan and Iran.[31] MI(R) reported on relations with French Intelligence in April 1940: 'This fight continues.'[32] In wooing his Polish and Czech allies, Gubbins had not been entirely honest as to the resources he could offer with his small staff of four. Although the MI(R) report of April 1940 proudly states they were sending explosives into Poland via resistance contacts in Bucharest and Budapest, it makes no mention of the fact that they relied on Section D for much of the supplies and for their supply lines.[33] This was intensely irritating to Gubbins, who in October 1939, when discussing how to support the Polish resistance operating from Hungary, had acknowledged 'our first job must be materials and hardware. Therefore D must immediately work out lines on which to transport material to Hungary; this is to be delivered to D's agents.'[34] Grand had been typically exuberant in offering assistance: 'We can send in wagon-fuls, my dear Colin, wagonfuls.' He did, however, reasonably demand details of what the Poles actually needed and Gubbins was unable to provide this information until January.[35] Gubbins also resented that he was obliged to pass on any suggestions from the Polish and Czech intelligence services for sabotage in neutral countries to Section D for execution, at the latter's discretion. Adding to the frustration, Section D was also not necessarily prepared to share its own plans with MI(R), for fear that operations might by compromised by MI(R)'s official dealings with neutral General Staffs. Gubbins had to admit that 'Other activities are unknown to the War Office, except for plans in general terms for sabotage on Danube and on Austrian and Romanian railways.'[36] The situation was yet further complicated by other sections of SIS having active intelligence networks in Poland and Czechoslovakia and being responsible for all secret wireless traffic. This all left Gubbins feeling hamstrung but in one positive effort to reduce tension between Section D and the Gubbins Mission, Peter Wilkinson was attached to the Balkans section of Section D (responsible for most of the trafficking of supplies into Poland) under George Taylor (*see above*, p. 12).

In January 1940 Gubbins sought the assistance of the British Intelligence cover enterprize, the Goeland Transport and Trading Company, in shipping supplies to Poland along the River Danube, repeating his usual attacks against Section D in saying the routes promised by Grand were 'not in my opinion, too healthy or certain, and in any case demand a long interval for development'.[37] Gubbins ignored the fact that the purchase of the Goeland tug fleet had originated with Section D and was jointly managed by them with MI(R); William Harris-Burland of MI(R) (formerly Paymaster to the Polish Mission) was managing director of the company and Section D agent Charles Blackley was the 'Inspector-General' of the fleet. The fleet of tugs and barges had been purchased to deny their commercial use to the Germans and, if necessary, to scuttle them and block the Danube, but it was periodically used for gun-running by Section D and MI(R).[38] Some material was packed in wine or food crates addressed to the military attaché in Bucharest as diplomatic baggage but Harris-Burland warned that there should be no more than three or four such crates a month, so as not to arouse suspicion. Greater quantities of stores were shipped along the Danube disguised as crates of furniture addressed to the flat of a Section D agent in Budapest. The crates would be classed as goods in transit and, although sealed by customs in Romania, would not be opened there. The stores were secretly extracted whilst journeying up-river and the crates resealed with a fake customs seal – or the customs official would be bribed. Harris-Burland warned that the crates should not be packed or dispatched by a service department 'as they always give the show away'. He cited the last shipment where two crates were perfectly disguised but the accompanying shipping note carefully described the contents as fifty revolvers.[39] It took time for the British to properly appreciate the detail of requirements of resistance forces. The Poles had asked for pistols and MI(R) consequently acquired 200 .455 Webley revolvers, each with fifty rounds.[40] Peter Wilkinson in February 1940 delivered a consignment of arms, including a dozen of the large Webleys, to Polish contacts in Hungary on behalf of Section D, under cover as a diplomatic courier. Although concealed within bags of diplomatic mail, the box for the revolvers had been coated in creosote for water-proofing and Wilkinson commented that his sleeping car on the luxury Orient Express began to smell like a rabbit hutch.[41] When he finally reached Budapest the Polish contact complained that the revolvers were too heavy and that .455 ammunition was unobtainable in Poland. To the chagrin of Wilkinson, the contact therefore proposed to dump them in the River Danube.[42] What the Poles wanted were light, short-barrelled .32 or .38 automatic pistols that could be unobtrusively slipped into a pocket but these were difficult to acquire and the .455 Webley continued to be supplied (*see* Plate 18).[43] From December 1939 to the end of March 1940 the Poles were supplied with

- 4 wireless sets
- 130 revolvers
- 6,500 rounds .455 ammunition
- 1,000lb high explosive (plastic or blasting gelatine) with detonators, fuze, etc
- 200 pressure switches
- 600 delay action fuzes
- 500 incendiary bombs[44]

Gubbins was explicit in his proprietorial attitude when he complained in January 1940 that Grand was 'playing about with our Poles'.[45] Section D had begun shipping supplies to Poland via Scandinavia and Gubbins had initially been cooperative, writing to the Polish legation in London on 1 January asking a contact to arrange an introduction for 'a friend of mine, Captain Fraser' to the Polish resistance HQ in Stockholm, as Ingram Fraser (head of Section D Scandinavian section) was engaged on work 'with which I am intimately concerned and of which you are aware'. Gubbins asked that the Polish military attaché might be 'prepared to work in complete frankness with him immediately he arrives'.[46] By 7 April 1940 Gubbins had become concerned over Section D's increasing influence and wrote a terse complaint to the British military attaché in Stockholm (who had been working with Fraser) about Section D impinging on MI(R) interests and shipping material into

Poland via the 'wild men' of the Social Democrat and Trade Union groups who did not necessarily acknowledge allegiance to the Polish General Staff. Gubbins explained:

I have a clear-cut agreement with the Polish General Staff, in accordance with the instructions of the DMI [Beaumont-Nesbitt], that all preparations for activities within Poland must have the agreement of the Polish General Staff and ourselves, and that all planning, demands for stores etc. should be worked out in collaboration … If we allow wild men to act independently they will get out of hand, and either amuse themselves with private feuds or provoke incidents before the proper time … the official ruling in the W.O. [War Office] that as far as the Poles are concerned, we <u>control</u> and F[raser]. and his master [Grand] and colleagues <u>act as our agents</u>. Would you, therefore, very kindly in future send demands for materials direct to me; these I will check with the Polish G.S. [General Staff], and will then arrange delivery through F[raser] … You had better destroy this, but it would be as well to tell Fraser that in future your demands will come direct to us, giving him the reasons.[47] [original emphasis]

Whilst working in the Section D office in January, Wilkinson was not above doing some 'snooping' on Gubbins' behalf. To discover the activities of the French 5ième Bureau as regards the Czechs and Poles and their relationship to Section D, he proposed 'ingratiating' himself with Leslie Humphreys of Section D in Paris and getting the latter to allow his assistant Frederick Elles, who was Section D liaison to the 5ième Bureau, to give MI(R) some introductions to the French. At the same time Wilkinson reported back to Gubbins on the potential differences in policy with Section D after sneaking a look at some correspondence:

Whereas this department [Gubbins Mission] and apparently the Poles are agreed that the next year or so must be one of preparation rather than operation, this does not suit D's book. He sees in the Polish activities an opportunity for immediate dividend … I saw an instruction from him to his agents in Budapest to say that, although the Poles had evidently received orders from their Headquarters to go slow, his agents were to do all they could to make them re-consider this decision.[48]

This may not have been as damning as Wilkinson wished to suggest, merely commensurate with the rest of Section D's encouragement of small-scale sabotage on German transport links across the Balkans, which was in itself in line with the policy of the Polish General Staff. While the primary focus of the Polish General Staff and MI(R) was indeed to avoid serious confrontation and to build up the strength of the resistance for the future, 'At the same time they [Polish resistance] intend to undertake small acts of sabotage, which will not risk disclosing their major preparations, and which will be directed against German lines of communication and other objectives which are of specific advantage to the Allies.'[49] By April, General Sikorski was concerned that spontaneous acts of resistance might not be able to be prevented, due to the desperate state to which the population had already been reduced by the German and Russian occupiers. He therefore asked that the shipping of supplies to Poland be expedited. Gubbins, although no longer officially involved with the Polish Mission, joined in requesting that the provision of supplies to Poland be accelerated.[50] This was the context for the Blake-Tyler fiasco in Budapest (*see below*, p. 84).

After Wilkinson's mission to Budapest in February 1940 he and Gubbins came to the conclusion that MI(R) needed to either take control of the Section D supply organization or establish a rival network in order to increase the influence of the Gubbins Mission.[51] They were, however, constrained by limited resources (the Gubbins Mission consisting of only Gubbins, Herbert Lloyd-Johnes and Major Richard Truszkowski in Paris and Wilkinson in London) and the restrictions of the MI(R) charter. Gubbins therefore tried to take advantage of plans to install MI(R) officers as assistant military attachés in the Balkans legations as a new power base. In Bucharest Commander Dymock Watson already successfully liaised between MI(R), Gubbins Mission and Section D and managed a joint explosives dump in the legation. Watson (Plate 24) was described by Joan Bright as a 'green-grass-and-white-flannels type of man, with brilliant blue eyes and a wide smile. His gentle ways belied an iron determination and a specialised knowledge of the flow of the River Danube and its importance to the oil wells of Romania.'[52] In Belgrade Alexander Glen, the assistant naval attaché (ANA), acted jointly for the Naval Intelligence Directorate (NID) and Section D. Gubbins gave credit to the organization of Naval Intelligence in the region which, he pointedly claimed, 'contrast strikingly with the other department's organisations, which lack any definite arrangements for coordination and control'.[53] Gubbins really meant that he was not party to Section D's arrangements, complaining that whilst MI(R) and the Gubbins Mission knew of each other's plans for Romania (a disingenuous argument given that they were effectively one and the same!), 'neither knows precisely the extent of D's intentions in Romania, or what use is intended to make of Commander Watson to further these'.[54] He tried to raise further conflict by asking if NID were aware that their ANA in Belgrade was also acting on behalf of Section D. In fact, this was an official arrangement made between the two organizations.

Grudgingly, Gubbins had to eventually admit that 'in actual practice these rather rough and ready arrangements have worked fairly successfully' and that there had been no clashes between the organizations. Nevertheless, Gubbins wanted a stronger coordinating authority, based around an expansion of the assistant military attachés in the legations and giving a controlling role to MI(R) and himself. He particularly complained that the funds for MI(R) and the Gubbins Mission were reliant on a grant from SIS and he wanted a place on a new joint committee that would allocate such funds. Gubbins also wanted a sub-committee to coordinate demands on the supply lines to Poland and thereby exercise control over what was the whip-hand of Section D.[55] The formation of the ISPB in April as a coordinating committee (*see below*, p. 182) that included representatives of MI(R) and Section D (and was chaired by Holland) was one attempt to address these concerns, but it was purely advisory. Meanwhile, chafing for a more active role, on 5 February 1940 Gubbins suggested allying MI(R) with a proposal by Polish Intelligence for sabotage on the Romanian railways and on the Danube, using Polish refugees experienced in insurrection in Upper Silesia. He believed that such 'poaching' on Section D spheres of operation could be excused if presented as a Polish scheme:

> Attached is a scheme for sabotage in Romania, handed to me by the Polish General Staff, in case it be of interest to us. It is, of course, actually a D project rather than one of mine, as it deals with Neutral Countries, but as all the action would be carried out by the Poles, and the British part would only be of materials and not even supply of money, the distinction is hardly of importance.[56]

This came amid the renewed discussions between Lord Hankey and the DMI over the relative responsibilities of Section D and MI(R) and also cut across plans by Naval Intelligence to use the Goeland fleet on the Danube. Gubbins' proposal was an unwelcome complication and nothing more was heard of it. Such ruffling of feathers, including his intrigue with Czech Intelligence (*see below*, p. 82), may explain Gubbins' sudden recall to London on 23 March, with Wilkinson taking over in Paris and Dodds-Parker as his liaison officer in London.

The reputation of the Gubbins Mission for intrigue continued under Wilkinson and when Polish Intelligence asked for help in setting up a wireless network to work into Britain if France should fall, the French 2ième Bureau believed that the Mission was trying to cause trouble between them and the Poles. The French even tried to get the Mission expelled but it hung on until after the German invasion.[57] When Wilkinson left for the GHQ Auxiliary Units in mid-June his place was first taken by Harold Perkins, who had been on the original Polish Mission, and then was taken out of MI(R) hands by Brigadier Charles Bridge.

The conflict between the Gubbins Mission and Section D over Poland reverberated into SOE. In early December 1939 Section D recruited, on a six-month trial, the refugee Polish socialite and journalist Krystyna Gizcyka, born Krystyna Skarbek but better known by her later alias and naturalized British name of Christine Granville. Sent to Budapest, her task was to establish links with Polish resistance groups and set up separate communication lines for inserting Allied propaganda and funds into Poland, and for bringing out intelligence on the state of the country. There were immediate demarcation problems with Polish Intelligence objecting in principle to a Pole being employed by a foreign Intelligence service and Peter Wilkinson tried to warn off Section D from sending their own mission into Poland. A grudging agreement was finally reached with Polish Intelligence but it refused to give Granville any contacts in Poland and warned her that 'because she was in the pay of the English' she was no longer a trustworthy Pole. She was also warned that 'any movement in Poland which is not our movement is an enemy one'.[58] In 1940 the Polish resistance was not united and it therefore suited SIS to maintain alternative channels of communication but Granville's mission report in March was a mix of misinformation and exaggeration, and seemed to validate the concerns of Polish Intelligence.[59] She had contacted a rival group to the official ZWZ resistance called 'The Musketeers', founded by Stefan Witkowski in October 1939 and which had a range of German contacts, even infiltrating the *Abwehr*; some of their members were sent as agents to Soviet Russia.[60] This was a potentially important asset operating across Poland, Germany and Russia and Granville became a reception point in Budapest for couriers of both the 'Musketeers' and the Polish Socialist Party. Section D was, however, worried about her reliability and there were even suggestions of her being recalled to London. Granville made two further attempts to enter Poland in June but both failed and her position as a Section D agent had become ambiguous, her trial contract having expired. Her contacts with unofficial Polish resistance groups continued in Budapest through the autumn and winter of 1940 but Granville and her lover Andrjez Kowerski (Andrew Kennedy) were forced to flee Hungary in January 1941, taking with them a microfilm that showed the build-up of German armour along the Russian border – crucial evidence of the impending German invasion. Granville and Kowerski eventually made their way to Cairo but found an air of suspicion surrounding them in SOE, with a difference in opinion between those former officers of Section D and the Gubbins Mission over the policy to be taken towards the Polish resistance. Former Section D officer George Taylor, now Chief of Staff in SOE, was trying to reactivate contact with the 'Musketeers', to the horror of Gubbins and Wilkinson when they joined SOE. In May 1941 a conference with General Sikorski in London finally agreed that only those Polish resistance groups owing allegiance to the government-in-exile would be supported by SOE. Having been served a catalogue of complaints by

Polish Intelligence, Wilkinson recommended that Granville and Kowerski be suspended.[61] It was not until 1944 that Granville was eventually dropped into occupied France, where her exploits finally made her one of SOE's most famous agents. At the end of 1941 the 'Musketeers' did join the official Polish ZWZ resistance organization (Home Army), but Witkowski was charged with treason and was executed by a squad of the Home Army. His killers were subsequently shot by another dissident Polish group.

Czechoslovakia

Before the war Britain maintained links with the Czech Intelligence Service through its commander, Colonel František Moravec, who had escaped to England in March 1939. He became head of the Military Section of Dr Benes' Czech National Committee in exile and worked closely with SIS in developing an Intelligence network within occupied Czechoslovakia. In a parallel development, the Czech General Staff had in 1938 begun to establish a resistance organization, based on three-man cells who were well-equipped and focused on organizing escape routes for former soldiers.[62] The Czech General Staff in exile established a wireless link from Paris to their network, independent to that of Moravec, and sought support to extend it with a new secret wireless station in Belgrade. Gubbins saw this as another opportunity to establish a power base for MI(R) independent of SIS and as early as July 1939 he began to woo the Czech General Staff in Paris; as with the Poles, his key object was for the Czechs to act under MI(R) direction. The head of Czech forces, General Sergěj Inger, was not yet ready to sacrifice independence in return for outside aid – especially as, at that time, there seemed little that MI(R) could offer, but in late August 1939 new MI(R) officers Ralph Greg and John Walter met Colonel Kalla, the former military attaché in London responsible for Czech refugee camps, and established that the Czechs wanted financial aid and permission to form a Czech Legion.[63] MI(R) consequently proposed to create a camp for 2,000 Czech volunteers but this was rejected by the DMI. Taking advantage of Czech disappointment at the lack of SIS support in the 17 September rising, Gubbins held a rapid series of meetings with various Czech officers and on 11 October 1939 he met Kalla to again press the claims of MI(R). In line with the consistent MI(R) advice of damping down the aspirations of resistance before a major Allied offensive could be launched, Gubbins suggested a focus on passive resistance for at least the next six months. But he also sought to assume leadership of the resistance, with the Czechs 'working with, but under, MI(R)'. Gubbins was firm: 'The general policy regarding action to be taken at any time will be decided by MI(R)... We must stand firm on the fact that we are going to control.'[64] This is a very different tone to Holland's vision of an advisory MI(R) and stretched the brief of MI(R) to the limit, there being no immediate prospect of British military involvement in Czechoslovakia. Colonel Kalla 'appeared most willing to cooperate' but in return he wanted wireless equipment which Gubbins confidently declared 'This, of course, we can arrange', although this was beyond his domain. Two days later, on 13 October 1939, Lieutenant Colonels Fisera and Lukas agreed that all guerrilla warfare in Czechoslovakia would be put on a military basis, managed by a joint staff in London. The next day Gubbins met General Inger in Paris, and exuberantly reported that the latter was now 'willing to hand over the whole of the running of the organization to us' and would provide a staff officer to work with MI(R) in London.[65] The MI(R) War Diary consequently claims that the Czechs agreed that MI(R) would 'control the whole project' although, significantly, a more sober pencil amendment clarifies their role as being in an advisory capacity.[66]

Gubbins once again overreached himself when, on 18 November, he agreed to provide a wireless set for the Czechs to install in Belgrade and also to investigate means of shipping materials to Yugoslavia so that the Czechs could smuggle them into Czechoslovakia.[67] By 22 November there was suspicion over the respective claims of both sides in the negotiations. There was concern over the actual scale of the Czech resistance and the relationship of Inger's resistance network to Moravec's Intelligence organization. Gubbins also had to admit 'interdepartmental difficulties' in the supply of wireless sets – which was an SIS responsibility that they jealousy guarded.[68] Greg and Wilkinson met again with Fisera and explained there would be a delay in providing high-powered clandestine wireless sets but Fisera said that even a low-powered set would have to be a *sine qua non* before any shipment of supplies could be contemplated. There was further consternation when Fisera announced that the Czechs would send over an officer in a week's time to select suitable automatic pistols and sub-machine guns for shipping. MI(R) would then have to reveal they had no means of acquiring and supplying such weapons.[69] Holland was obliged to intervene in January 1940 and clarify the responsibilities of MI(R) and SIS to the Czechs, explaining that MI(R) would be responsible for the coordination (rather than control) of Czech activities with Allied strategy but admitting that the supply of wireless equipment and the delivery of supplies were in the hands of SIS.[70] Later that month an excited Gubbins confided to Wilkinson that the Czechs wanted support for a plan to attach mines to German barges on the Danube. He wanted Wilkinson to arrange for Section D to supply the necessary plastic explosives and delayed action fuses but he had to admit, 'Actually all the above business is really D's pigeon and not an MI(R) matter.'[71] Gubbins was clearly itching to take over the sabotage operations of Section D but he was eventually warned off pursuing the Czech scheme by the DMI, Major General Beaumont-Nesbitt, who was being asked awkward questions by the Foreign Office as to the nature of any British links to Czech Intelligence.[72] Beaumont-Nesbitt, following a disingenuous briefing note from Holland, falsely reassured the Foreign Office of the innocence of MI(R):

> One section alone (MI(R)) sees a member of the Czech intelligence organization from time to time, but only to be kept generally informed of what operations they propose to prepare against the Germans in their own territory, and what military material they require from us for those operations: at the same time we give as tactfully as possible our advice, purely from a military point of view, on the operations they are planning.[73]

Following this awkward scrutiny, on 29 February Wilkinson passed the Czech sabotage proposal on to Section D in Belgrade, where head agent Julius Hanau was already working closely with Czech émigré groups. It then became clear that the Czech Intelligence Service could offer little in any practical sense as their plan was predicated on using Yugoslav agents to conceal any Czech involvement which might excite reprisals, with Section D providing the explosives 'and perhaps money'.[74] Nothing came of the venture and it was independent Czech exile groups working with Section D who carried out a wide programme of sabotage across the Balkans, whilst the official Czech Intelligence Service focused on strengthening their organization within their occupied country.[75]

On 8 March Beaumont-Nesbitt wrote to Gubbins to try to control his ambitions, passing on a letter from the Foreign Office 'which will show you the line you must take with the Czechs'.[76] Gubbins was reluctant to face the Czechs directly and in response wrote, 'I think it would be better if you told the Czechs as regards my position in France vis-à-vis them … It will come better from you.'[77] Shortly afterwards, Gubbins was removed as head of the Polish/Czech Mission in Paris and it may have been with some relief in the DMI that he was posted to command the Independent Companies in Norway.

Hungary

MI(R)'s principal interest in Hungary was as a shipping point for supplies to Polish resistance contacts in Budapest, who would then smuggle the material over the border. There was considerable opposition to the work of SIS in the country from the British Minister (Owen O'Malley) and the military attaché, and this was encouraged by Gubbins and Wilkinson, leading to one of the most direct conflicts between Section D and MI(R). The scene was set in October 1939 when the military attaché, Lieutenant Colonel W.P. Barclay, wrote in conspiratorial tones to Gubbins about an emissary of a Polish resistance group who wished to be put in contact with SIS in Budapest. The reply from Gubbins included the following:

> Between you and me I mistrust PCS organization [SIS] entirely as they always try and pinch anybody who may be of use for their undertakings without any consideration whether he might not be more useful elsewhere.[78]

It is no surprise, therefore, that MI(R) wished to secure its own presence in Budapest. Consideration of sending an assistant military attaché (AMA) began in January 1940, officially to assist the passage of Czech and Polish refugees to France via Britain and, as Wilkinson noted, 'preventing the French from pinching all the best men, which is what is happening at present'.[79] Wilkinson also expected a future AMA to 'supervise without taking an active part' in the distribution of supplies to the Czechs and Poles through Section D's agents in Budapest. Wilkinson's interpretation of a discussion with George Taylor (Section D head of Balkan operations) over Section D's organization in Hungary was that 'Taylor tells me he would welcome anyone who could keep an eye on the two very irresponsible journalists there.' These were presumably Sydney Morrell and Hubert Harrison, who were running a very effective Section D propaganda campaign at the time, and Wilkinson's comment may again not have been entirely objective! With characteristic War Office self-belief, it was also vaguely hoped the AMA might be able to organize guerrilla activity in the country if the country was overrun, despite the minimal training considered necessary for the AMAs (*see above*, p. 18). A marginal note added 'This is very attractive.' It was estimated that an AMA might be able to carry on such work for about three weeks before being forced to flee.[80]

Harry Blake-Tyler, aged 39, was finally appointed as an AMA in the Budapest legation in April 1940. He had been commissioned into the Royal Berkshire Regiment as a second lieutenant in April 1939 and had a meteoric rise. By May 1940 he was a major.[81] His brief was to be 'chiefly concerned with the transit of stores and devices to Polish irregular organizations' and specifically 'for supervision of supplies from Gubbins mission to Poland'.[82] But, coloured by the views of Wilkinson, Blake-Tyler interpreted these orders as being to replace Section D operations rather than work in partnership. He falsely told Harrison that he came with orders from George Taylor to send him home. Blake-Tyler then 'attacked him [Harrison] on the question of getting his supplies [redacted] saying that he should have developed safer means, and that he, that is Blake-Tyler, was busy doing so'. With a modicum of sarcasm, Harrison 'wished him luck and said he would help him in any way he could'.[83] Relationships quickly soured further after Blake-Tyler met with Section D courier Andrew Duncan on 12 May. Blake-Tyler was first reported to be charming but then began a catalogue of complaints, urging Duncan to make a confidential, critical, report on the state of Section D in Hungary to the Minister, for forwarding anonymously to the Foreign Secretary. 'I began to suspect that Tyler's real aim was to get rid of the D organization in Hungary,' wrote Duncan.[84] Blake-Tyler then manipulated the somewhat naïve Duncan into asking about potential contacts with opposition 'Legitimists', which was a good enough excuse for the Minister, Owen O'Malley, to write to Sir Alexander Cadogan (Permanent Under-Secretary for Foreign Affairs) saying that he refused to have any further Section D activities in his legation. This included the storage of weapons and explosives awaiting shipment to Poland. Such action would clearly rebound upon MI(R)'s commitments to the Poles, and Douglas Dodds-Parker, liaison officer in London between MI(R) and what was still called the Gubbins Mission, needed to know if there was an alternative solution. He sent a message to Blake-Tyler on 21 May, trying to avoid direct censure by blaming O'Malley for the dispute:

> As existing method of delivery to Poles has broken down as result of YP's [O'Malley] attitude now most urgent to push on with your alternative method of shipment so as be able to resume deliveries as soon as Poles can receive.[85]

Despite his earlier bluster, Blake-Tyler had to admit that he had not actually devised any alternative ideas to those of Section D and he now realized there was a budgetary implication if he was to take over this work, naïvely enquiring if Section D would still pay the costs.[86] In desperation, Blake-Tyler submitted a plan on the next day which was essentially a reworking of the existing methodology of Harris-Burland and the Goeland tug fleet (*see above*, p. 75). He proposed shipping supplies disguised as 'machinery parts' from Alexandria to the Free Port in Budapest, which would be switched on the Danube for duplicate genuine crates, and the explosives offloaded onto lorries by Polish agents.[87] Wilkinson commented, with no sense of irony given that he bore a large share of the blame, that in late May 1940 he had to spend time dealing with 'one of those tiresome rows, typical of the intelligence community' with 'violent' telegrams being exchanged by Blake-Tyler and the Section D officers in Hungary.[88] It was left to George Taylor (Section D), Dodds-Parker (MI(R)) and Gladwyn Jebb (Foreign Office) in London to try to find a resolution. Taylor wanted MI(R) to call for O'Malley's request to ban Section D activities to be over-ruled 'for military reasons'. MI(R) could not support this, but at the same time realised it could not afford to antagonize Section D and 'did not wish to damage relations with D/H [Taylor] in view of our dependence on him in other areas'.[89] It was agreed that Blake-Tyler and the Minister be given a chance to try an alternative means of shipping materials into Poland – on the condition that if it did not work they would revert to the existing methodology. In recognition of the concern to appease Section D, it was Taylor who drafted the telegram for MI(R) to send to Blake-Tyler and the subsequent report by Dodds-Parker shows little sympathy for Blake-Tyler and O'Malley for having caused such problems: 'The Minister and B-T have their chance; it has not been necessary to coerce the Minister, though Jebb is willing. D/H is happy, having drafted the telegram.'[90]

Nothing came of the Blake-Tyler scheme and on 26 May Dodds-Parker was dispatched to Cairo to oversee MI(R)'s interests in the shipment of stores into Poland from the Middle East and the Balkans.[91] Conditions were worsening in Hungary and at the end of May there was a crackdown on the activities of Polish refugees and two Poles were arrested in possession of suit-cases of explosives.[92] Despite all of the recent angst, MI(R) had to abandon its plans for smuggling into Poland independently, and continued to rely on Section D couriers who smuggled explosives into the legation using diplo-matic bags, to the later dismay of O'Malley. The Polish military attaché (Colonel Jan Emisarski-Pindelli) later believed that better results would have been obtained by simply giving the Poles money to buy weapons at half the price of the cost of the courier service, saying it was actually funding rather than arms that they had needed. As it was, it proved impossible to transport most of the smuggled pistols from Budapest to Poland.[93] Blake-Tyler remained, and when Wilkinson met Emisarski-Pindelli in April 1941 the latter said he regarded Blake-Tyler as the only realistic British Intelli-gence officer he had come across in Budapest.[94] This may have been a diplo-matic comment and it is not clear what Blake-Tyler actually achieved while in Hungary. Laurence Grand complained that although he had turned over Section D's contacts within the Hungarian Army to MI(R), there had been no follow-up. MI(R) did contact Count Carl de Longay about a scheme for irregular activities against the Germans in Hungary but this was not pro-gressed in the face of the characteristic reluctance of O'Malley to support any clandestine operations that might upset the Hungarian regime. Despite Blake-Tyler's bluster, it was Ted Howe of Section D who quietly continued to make plans for organizing sabotage in the event of invasion, whilst Basil Davidson and the SIS head of station continued to discreetly fill the cellar of the legation with explosives.[95]

Chapter Seven

Romania and the Balkans

A key Allied objective in 1939–1940 was to deny Germany access to strategic economic resources. The Romanian oil wells and the transport network that brought the oil into Germany were a prime target and MI(R) focused its attention on the oil wells where British and French sabotage had put the oilfields out of action for five months in 1916. In 1939 Romanian foreign policy was driven by the overriding fear of Soviet expansion and uncertainty as to whether Germany or the Allies would provide better protection. Romania was heavily dependent on trade with Germany but Britain and France remained desperate to keep the oilfields, in which they had strong commercial interests, out of German hands and in April 1939 they offered an unrealistic guarantee of Romania's freedom from German aggression. King Carol tried to avoid being dragged into war and in September 1939 formally declared Romania's neutrality whilst threatening to destroy the oilfields if invaded, and using the risk of Allied sabotage to deter German aggression.

In April 1939 Holland wrote to the military attaché in Bucharest to establish if the Romanians had plans to destroy the oil wells in advance of German invasion.[1] Gubbins' brief follow-up visit in May was not hopeful, believing that 'the drive and initiative must come from, or be directly instigated by, trained personnel supplied by us, from outside'.[2] The complication was that in June an assessment for MI(R) in London by Lieutenant Commander Dymock Watson and Royal Engineers George Young and John Walter concluded that any successful destruction of the Romanian oilfields using British ground forces must have the cooperation of the Romanian General Staff. This would be a high stakes gambit but the report also concluded that a less dramatic sabotage of the transport links into Germany was also critical and could best be left to the covert operations of Section D whilst MI(R) continued to wrestle with the fate of the oilfields as a military operation. At first, the Chief of the Romanian General Staff and the Prime Minister, Armand Călinescu, seemed sympathetic and MI(R) began to negotiate the terms of cooperation and financial compensation. Support to the Romanians would be provided by a field company of Royal Engineers (8 officers and 204 other ranks), sent by sea from Egypt via Turkey and ferried from Constanza to the oilfields by troop-carrying aircraft.[3] Other sappers would be secretly infiltrated into the Ploesti oilfields as 'oilfield trainees' of the Astra Română company (an associate company of Shell). Adding to the complexity, the plan therefore also depended on the willingness of the Turkish government to turn a 'blind eye' to the passage of troops through their territory. On 24 August 1939 Dymock Watson headed for Romania to meet Herbert 'Tim' Watts, an ICI chemist already in the country, and prepare for the arrival of the main MI(R) mission, which left London on the next day (alongside the Polish mission) and travelled by rail and sea. The mission included Majors Stanley Green, J.V. Davidson-Houston and George Larden, and Captains Household, Ekserdjian and Stewart.[4] Stanley Green had once been secretary of Unirea but the choice of Davidson-Houston was less obvious. A Royal Engineer major, Davidson-Houston had been recruited to MI(R) in 1939 from the DMI and was an Intelligence officer specializing in Sino-Japanese affairs. In the casual spirit of the times, in July he was asked 'How would you like to go to Romania?'[5] Larden was another Rugby School 'old boy' and an expert in anti-aircraft defences in the London Territorial Royal Artillery. Holland had tried to persuade him to take two months' leave in May 1939 to allow him to make an unofficial tour of Romanian railways, but had failed to do so and had now been obliged to formally recruit him to MI(R) for the task. The MI(R) mission first undertook its standard surveys of the country. Larden and Davidson-Houston carried out a reconnaissance on the Romanian railways and roads with Major Rădulescu of the Romanian Army, while Commander Dillon (RNVR) and Stanley Green surveyed the River Danube. Their reports on the road and rail communications throughout Romania were compiled by October 1939, when a finished demolition scheme in the event of a German invasion was prepared and handed to the Romanian General Staff in the hope they would execute the plan if necessary.[6] Meanwhile George Young had flown out to Egypt to brief the Royal Engineers field company on their impending task.

After a hurried return to London to report on the current state of the country, Watson returned to Bucharest on 16 September to coordinate plans with the French 2ième Bureau and the British military attaché, and to elicit support from the considerable British expatriate oil community. The MI(R) mission was also briefly joined by Gubbins on his way back to England after the evacuation of the MI(R) Polish mission on 18 September. The optimistic intention was to destroy the oil wells, refineries and pumping stations in just 24 hours before they could be reached by an invading German Army.[7] Unfortunately it would take the Royal Engineers two to three days to arrive in Romania from Egypt and their equipment would have to be in place beforehand. Any inkling of such a move by German Intelligence was likely to trigger a pre-emptive invasion and there was doubt whether the Romanian authorities would ever actually agree to the deployment of British troops.[8] The demolition scheme was to be under the joint direction of the British military attaché (Lieutenant Colonel Geoffrey MacNab) and Colonel Leonida of the Romanian General Staff, but operational responsibility lay with Davidson-Houston of MI(R) and Major Rădulescu of the Romanian Army. Only the Chief of the Romanian General Staff and a few allies had been taken into the secret and, as a whole, the Romanian General Staff began to distance themselves from the Allies during the German ascendancy. A contingency plan therefore involved a more secret partial destruction by British and French oilfield engineers assisted by Royal Engineers covertly infiltrated into the country as 'oil trainees'. One dramatic idea, suggested by Leslie Forster (Chief Engineer of Astra Română), was to blow up the 'Christmas trees' at the wellheads of both the Tintea and Boldești high-pressure oilfields, causing fires that would burn for years and cut Romanian oil production by 50 per cent. Davidson-Houston, Watson, Green and Gubbins went to Ploesti to meet Forster, together with Edward Masterson and Gwynn Elias of Unirea and representatives of French Intelligence to work out the basis of this plan. Other oil engineers in the British oil companies were encouraged to enrol in the OER ready to carry out the demolition, if necessary. The British oil workers were said to be enthusiastic and only a few senior managers did not volunteer to take part. Some had good reason not to become involved: Reginald Young (Chief Chemist, Romano-Americana Oil company) and Charles Brazier (Technical Manager, Ploesti Oil refinery) were secretly working for Section D in planning sabotage on the rail transports into Germany.[9] The likelihood of Romanian cooperation diminished after the assassination of the Prime Minister, Armand Călinescu, on 21 September 1939 by the pro-Nazi Iron Guard, who perceptively accused him of conspiring to blow up the oilfields to prevent them falling into German hands. Justifying British and French suspicions, King Carol then admitted the British plans to the German air attaché – but claimed he had rejected them. Contradicting this denial, a few days later the German legation in Ploesti identified five 'oil trainees' as being obviously British officers in disguise.[10] These were members of the RE field company who had come to draw up a detailed reconnaissance. Embarrassingly, their names were circulated in the Romanian press with details of their military service taken from the *London Gazette*. In this confused political situation MI(R) still continued to try to make a deal with the Romanian General Staff, offering substantial financial compensation and the supply of explosives to the Romanian Army.

Gubbins left Romania on 26 September to return to England, leaving Watson in charge and on 30 September F.T. Davies arrived at Constanza in a flying boat with the more secret demolition material, including the new MI(R) limpet mines, pressure switches and camouflet sets.[11] These were stored in the British legation rather than being handed over immediately to the Romanian Army. Less sensitive supplies arrived shortly afterwards on the

SS *Fuadieh* at Galati, at the mouth of the Danube, on 2 October 1939.[12] The ship had been instructed to come up the river by night at high speed in the hope of avoiding attention but a combination of her lights and the wash that she created, which flooded riverside gardens, ensured her arrival was fully reported in the Romanian press. The ship carried 2 tons of explosives in 250 crates, two Morris trucks and other material for the Romanian Army, escorted by an officer and fifteen men of the RE field company. There was little doubt of the point of origin as the trucks were still covered in the sand of the Western Desert. The men were supposed to be disguised as deckhands, but their cotton dungarees and cloth caps were clearly more suited to the Middle East and warm clothes had to be bought for them in Galati. They had again all been issued with serially numbered passports. The unloading was supervised by Davidson-Houston and the material transferred to a mountain artillery barracks at Râșnov. It was clear that the crates had been packed in a rush. One crate contained slabs of gun cotton together with a half-empty bottle of methylated spirits. In with a Boys anti-tank rifle was a dartboard. One crate of .303 ammunition also included three hockey sticks and there was a consignment of Arab grammar books and a collection of pornographic photographs from Port Said. The explosives were used for training over the winter at the barracks by Romanian officers and selected oil company employees and in late October Davidson-Houston gave instruction to the Romanian Army on the new camouflet sets.[13]

Even as the MI(R) survey of demolition targets was delivered to the Romanian General Staff, in October 1939 the *Abwehr* concluded an agreement with the Romanian Secret Service whereby the Germans would protect the route of the oil transports into Germany. The Brandenburg Regiment arrived to covertly patrol the railways and ports, establishing their main base near the Iron Gates and placing sentries in civilian disguise on every train passing into Germany. In November the Romanian Secret Service agreed to tighten security on the oilfields and to report the movement of foreigners to the *Abwehr*, which also infiltrated its agents into the security section of the Romanian General Staff.[14] German Intelligence in Romania easily outmatched MI(R) and, incredibly, Dymock Watson's promotion to commander was published in *The Times* on 1 January 1940 – even reporting that he was serving in the Naval Intelligence Division! To protect the MI(R) team, Watson then had to be appointed assistant naval attaché while his assistants Green, Watts and Household were similarly taken onto the staff of the legation in Bucharest. It was evidently a pleasant assignment. Household recalled the MI(R) officers lived 'an unheroic life of luxury', eating in some of the finest restaurants in Europe and attending a cabaret every evening![15] Still trying to play both sides, the Romanian General Staff continued to make encouraging noises as a means of increasing their stock of explosives and asked for 300 of the MI(R) TV switches.[16] A further shipment of 100 tons of explosives was sent on 15 January 1940. Ominously, the Romanian government still refused to sign the formal agreement for cooperation until the demolition was regarded as imminent and, fearing the worst, on 9 February 1940 Gubbins suggested that 1,000 Polish refugees should be retained in Romania (rather than evacuating them) at a cost of £2,500 per month to provide manpower for the sabotage scheme if the Romanian authorities ultimately proved uncooperative.[17] In preparation, Household was sent to Egypt on a two-week demolitions course with the 54th Field Company of Royal Engineers. Once the plan was executed, one of Household's tasks would be to guide the Royal Engineers through Turkey to Ploesti. By April 1940 substantial quantities of British uniforms, arms, equipment and explosives were secreted in the legation ready for the sabotage.

Alongside the drama of planning major sabotage within Romania, there were on-going efforts to supply the Polish resistance across the border but on 5 April 1940 Watson reported that the Poles felt they had been losing too many agents smuggling the trickle of supplies from Romania and therefore would prefer to store bulk items such as explosives in a depot in Egypt or Turkey and only ship them at the time of a major revolt (a joint MI(R)/Section D depot was subsequently established at Alexandria). Watson did not want to close down the supply chain altogether and proposed to keep sending in as many delay-action sabotage devices and small arms as possible, shipped into Romania by the traditional means of diplomatic courier.[18]

The Romanian government finally agreed to accept a bond of $60 million from the British and French governments as compensation in case the sabotage proceeded and Ronald Hazell, previously of the Polish mission, was sent as AMA to Romania for 'observational duties' and to strengthen the MI(R) team.[19] The Romanians still wanted to organize the demolition themselves, whereas the suspicious British felt that, as they were paying for the work, MI(R) should participate to ensure it actually proceeded. The 54th Field Company, Royal Engineers, was finally made ready for embarkation, leaving Alexandria on 25 May 1940 on the SS *Deebank* bound for Chanak in Turkey. Here, the cargo carried as cover was unloaded and to preserve their disguise until ready for sailing for Constanza, the men worked as civilians repairing local roads and the harbour. Yet again they had been issued with suspicious consecutively numbered passports. Turkish authorities were nervous of their presence, especially after the entry of Italy into the war on 10 June, and their recall to Egypt was ordered on 22 June 1940 so as not to antagonize Turkish neutrality. The official demolition plan was finally dead and hope turned to the secret back-up plan using British oil workers. Watson made another attempt to smuggle 'oil technicians' into the Tintea high-pressure oilfield owned by Astra Românǎ to try, with the help of sympathetic employees, to blow up the wells. The plan was to use four or five small demolition parties, each with a local engineer whom the company guard would hopefully obey, running from well to well setting charges timed to explode simultaneously, the teams then escaping to Galatz and a waiting destroyer.[20] MI(R) was unaware that on 19 June, during their advance through France, the Germans captured documents from French Intelligence detailing the September 1939 sabotage scheme, drawn up by the French engineer who had been party to the planning meetings and naming the British Intelligence officers involved. Alerted to the plan, the *Abwehr* again easily saw through the disguise of the 'oil technicians', not least because the British officers were spending extravagantly in Bucharest, and planned their own counter-intelligence operation. Some 36 hours before the operation was due to be carried out, the Romanian Army took over responsibility from the oil companies for the guard on the oil wells; Romanian police then raided the final planning meeting of the conspirators and conveniently discovered damning evidence of British explosives on the oilfield, which had been placed there by *Abwehr* agents to add to the scandal. On 1 July the Romanian Prime Minister renounced the Anglo-French guarantee and membership of the League of Nations; on the same day the German legation demanded the expulsion of thirty British and French citizens implicated in the sabotage plans. They included not only the MI(R) mission but also Section D agents Reginald Young (the *de facto* Section D head agent) and Charles Blackley (who also worked with Naval Intelligence on the Danube), named in the captured French documents. A week later most of the men were expelled from Romania and travelled to Egypt, but Watson, Household, Green and Watts remained, protected by their diplomatic status. After King Carol abdicated on 6 September 1940 and Antonescu took power, Green and Household's final task was to take the considerable store of explosives in the legation out into the countryside and dump it in a lake.[21] In October they finally left Romania and reported to GHQ in Cairo but by then MI(R) had been disbanded and it was left to them to find new employment. Green found work in the control of refugees and Household joined the Field Security Section of the new Intelligence Corps.[22]

While MI(R) was locked in frustrating negotiations with the Romanian authorities, Section D had, from the start of the war, quietly got on with the task of sabotaging the oil transports into Germany. As far as possible, to improve security, it operated without contact with MI(R) but Watson was its quartermaster, supplying explosives from the joint store within the British legation. Thus, the Section D organization in Romania of British oil workers and 'crooks, down and outs, and people of doubtful character' was left largely intact when the MI(R) officers were expelled in July.[23] But in mid-September two German agents fire-bombed the house of the leader of a sabotage cell of oil workers, and the cell was arrested by the Iron Guard. Watson and fellow

MI(R) officer Herbert Watts in the legation were incriminated as supplying the cell but were protected by their diplomatic status. Fortunately, in October a combination of diplomatic efforts by the Minister and a bribe of £5,000 organized by the new SOE managed to secure the release of the Section D agents to Istanbul.[24]

Yugoslavia

Yugoslavia contained strategic zinc and lead mines, and the River Danube, bringing oil from Romania to Germany, passed through its territory. An unofficial and somewhat desperate MI(R) mission comprising General Sir John Shea and Michael Colefax was sent there from 2 November 1939 to 15 December 1939, tasked with investigating the efficiency and capability of the Yugoslav military organization and the transport network – identifying tunnels, bridges, etc., that should be destroyed in the event of German invasion. Shea was a brother-in-law of Holland's and, although aged 70, carried the gravitas of a retired Indian Army general (described by Elizabeth Holland as the 'personification of Empire'). who, although having no knowledge of the region and having retired from the army in 1932, could hopefully impress the Yugoslav General Staff.[25] It is entirely possible that he pushed Holland to recruit him as a 'last hurrah' for an old soldier who had first tasted action in 1895. Colefax was a merchant banker with an interest in the oil industry, but neither he nor Shea had any particular skills for the mission and MI(R) seemed unaware of the long-standing intelligence-gathering of SIS in the country. MI(R) also wanted to assess the Yugoslav armaments industry and its potential; in November 1939 F.T. Davies undertook a short course of instruction at Woolwich before making a whistle-stop tour of British armament factories in Birmingham, Glasgow and Chorley and then a French plant before joining Shea and Colefax in Belgrade during early December. He returned to London on 18 January and his report was incorporated into that of Sir John Shea. The mission had established a good relationship with the Chief of the Yugoslav General Staff thanks to Shea's reputation and the report was submitted to the Yugoslav authorities – but one might surmise that Yugoslav Intelligence was already aware of the key demolition targets and nothing came of the venture. Shea made a plea for at least a token measure of support to be provided to the Yugoslav Army (such as a battery of anti-aircraft guns with instructors) but was also realistic about raising too many expectations.[26]

With little to show from this effort and Davies still complaining of a lack of a clear policy towards Yugoslavia, in June 1940 MI(R) tried to send a 'shadow' mission into the country with the intention of creating a new military attaché post, supported by two AMAs with an SIS wireless set, who would try to learn of Yugoslav Army preparations for para-military warfare and advise on ways of countering German 'fifth column' activities. Following any German invasion, additional officers would be added to each Yugoslav Army corps with 'Gambier Parry belt sets'. As far as can be ascertained, such sets were a myth, possibly a result of SIS trying to impress MI(R) with whispers of its research which would eventually reach fruition as the MI9 'cigarette case' miniature transceivers. Yugoslavia was reported to have the cadre of a guerrilla organization and with the characteristic lack of War Office humility 'it is obvious we should be apprized of their organization and plans', with British officers attached to instruct them 'in methods of demolition and guerrilla warfare'. The need to recruit British expatriates onto the OER was also raised and it was hoped that instructors could be infiltrated into the country as 'clerks' in the legation.[27] Acting as a backdoor channel for Holland, Davies had earlier tried to raise support from the Foreign Office for the proposal by unofficially sending a briefing to his old contact R.A. Butler (Under-Secretary of State for Foreign Affairs), asking him to 'give it a violent push in the right quarter' in the Foreign Office as otherwise it might 'go the way of our previous efforts: the "filing cabinet"'.[28] The Foreign Office reluctantly gave provisional agreement for a mission to proceed into the country under cover, although already considering it 'too late'. On 4 June 1940 Captains Nicholas Hammond and Kavan Elliott (both formerly Section D), Hunt, John Pendlebury and Robert Cripps left for Cairo to await approval from HM Minister in Belgrade to proceed into the country, but they were left hanging around in great frustration until permission was finally refused in late August. (Elliott was then sent as AMA to Bulgaria, Cripps was diverted to Greece and then loaned to Section D, and Pendlebury established a joint Section D/MI(R) organization on Crete).

As seemed typical, while MI(R) was stymied by bureaucracy, Section D continued to successfully sabotage railway traffic in Yugoslavia and Austria, distribute propaganda and engage in a range of 'dirty tricks'.[29] The head Section D officer in Yugoslavia, long-time SIS agent Julius Hanau, had been successfully mounting operations from as early as March 1939 and had long-established contacts with the Yugoslav Army and the Intelligence Service. He and other Section D officers collaborated with sympathetic staff of the Yugoslav Army to prepare sabotage in the event of a German invasion and in August 1940 they met General Mikhailovich to discuss his plans for mounting guerrilla warfare. After the German invasion in 1941, former Section D agent Mate Bruslja helped the army carry out some of the planned sabotage on the Danube.[30]

Bulgaria

In late July 1940 Captain Kavan Elliott, former Section D agent in Zagreb and now stranded in Cairo with the rest of the MI(R) shadow mission to Yugoslavia, was appointed AMA in Sofia. After working for SIS before the war, collecting economic intelligence in Zagreb under the cover of General Manager of the Unilever subsidiary *Astra*, he had joined the local Section D network but in May 1940 his cover was penetrated by the *Abwehr*. Elliott returned to Britain and transferred to MI(R) before being sent to an abbreviated course at Mons OTC and commissioned onto the General List (later transferring to the Intelligence Corps). He was then given rushed training at Lochailort to become an explosives specialist before being sent to Cairo with the shadow mission. Elliott was finally sent to Sofia on 25 July 1940 as AMA. Here he worked closely with Aidan Crawley, the Assistant Air Attaché, with whom he carried out a survey of North Bulgaria and also worked under the direction of Norman Davis of Section D, helping to cultivate Georgi Dimitrov, leader of the left wing of the Bulgarian Agrarian Party. Elliott became the Party's explosives instructor and helped Davis organize Dimitrov's escape from Bulgaria in February 1941, before leaving with the legation staff in March. Elliott later joined SOE; he was captured after parachuting into Croatia in 1942 as part of *Operation Disclaim* and imprisoned in Colditz Castle. After the war he was part of an SIS Special Operations unit and then in 1946 travelled to Hungary as an SIS asset.[31] He was arrested by the Hungarian Intelligence Service in 1948 and was expelled from the country as being a British agent.

Albania

Holland claimed that MI(R)'s work in Albania occurred 'more or less fortuitously' and should have been the responsibility of Section D. In reality, activity was limited to a desk-top study and a 'watching brief' on developments provided by the AMA in Athens, Major L.G. Barbrook. In August 1939 Dr Malcolm Burr and Mr F.W.S. Pinder were sent to Yugoslavia and Greece to try to contact Albanian refugees. Dr Malcolm Burr, aged 62, was a noted etymologist, travel writer and Russian translator but his supposed expertise on Albania rested on his First World War experiences in nearby Macedonia and Montenegro. More information was gained from General Sir Jocelyn Percy who had previously been Inspector-General of the Albanian Gendarmerie. A report covering the potential of para-military activity in Albania was submitted in November 1939 to the DMI, suggesting the best success was likely to come from émigrés in Yugoslavia rather than in Greece but no action was permitted until Italy entered the war. Burr then joined the Foreign Office and Ministry of Information. It was left to Section D to undertake the practical work in trying to coordinate émigré activity but this was repeatedly constrained by the Foreign Office and C-in-C Middle East, fearful of antagonizing the Italians before they declared war or of over-extending the limited British military resources in the region.[32] In June 1940 Robert Cripps, aged 49, a retired lieutenant colonel and former Inspector of the Albanian

Gendarmerie School, presently stranded in Cairo with the rest of the projected Yugoslav mission, was sent to Greece as a cypher clerk for the anticipated MI(R) mission; when this failed to develop, he was loaned to Section D, first as a courier to Belgrade and then to establish new communication lines into Albania from Turkey and liaise with the disparate émigré communities. It was a thankless task which an over-enthusiastic and trusting Cripps did not handle well. He was accused of being 'a menace to our organization' and guilty of entertaining 'undesirable' Albanians known to be in the pay of the Italians.[33]

Chapter Eight

Scandinavia

With its plans in Romania stalled, it was in Scandinavia that MI(R) first had the chance to establish its credibility in action and much of MI(R)'s capacity until June 1940 was directed towards supporting the Finnish and Norwegian operations.[1] It was another frustrating experience but had significant consequences in leading to the formation of the Commandos.

Finland

Taking advantage of the West's preoccupation with Germany and emboldened by the lack of any effective opposition to their invasion of Poland, Russia invaded Finland in October 1939. Following the expulsion of Russia from the League of Nations in mid-December 1939, the British government decided to send weapons, supplies and airplanes to Finland's aid as a preliminary for an expeditionary force whose real objective was to secure the northern ore fields against future German occupation. MI(R) was initially only to send a few officers as advisers, and to provide training in some of Jefferis' sabotage devices, but it soon acquired a wider logistical role. Shiploads of arms were sent, including twenty-five fighter aircraft, 4.5-inch howitzers, machine guns and ammunition, and MI(R) was put in charge of supervising the delivery of these stores to the Finns. MI(R) was also asked by the DMI to investigate the possibility of creating a guerrilla organization in Sweden that could work with any British force sent there to operate against either the Russians or the Germans.[2]

The MI(R) teams were based around men with family or business connections to Scandinavia or experienced polar explorers who knew the conditions to be encountered in Finland's winters. Andrew Croft and Malcolm Munthe took over the first shipment on 19 December 1939, having been given just two hours' instruction in the use of his devices by Jefferis. Munthe had been brought up in Sweden, but had only recently been recruited to MI(R) and was pulled out of his training at the Weedon OCTU for the mission. Croft was an experienced polar explorer and a friend of existing MI(R) officer Martin Lindsay. First arriving in Stockholm, they introduced the MI(R)c devices to officers of the Swedish Legion volunteers and then proceeded to Bergen in Norway to supervise the unloading and shipment of the stores destined for Finland. One vital task was to measure the dimensions of the railway tunnels and some of the crates carrying aircraft had to be modified accordingly. They were followed on 21 December by Hjalmer Whittington-Moë, John Scott-Harston and Gordon O'Brien-Hitching, who went directly to Finland to give instruction on the use of the MI(R) devices. Born in 1912 in Hong Kong, lawyer Scott-Harston was an accomplished skier and linguist, although he may have originally been recruited to MI(R) because of his knowledge of China. Whittington-Moë was an engineer of Norwegian descent whose father lived in Finland.

O'Brien-Hitching, aged just 20, had been born and educated in Finland before leaving for Ireland in the 1930s. His father Jack had married a Finn in 1914 and after service on the Western Front and liaison duties in Finland at the end of the war had joined SIS in Stockholm. Jack became a journalist but maintained his Intelligence connections and rejoined SIS on the outbreak of the Winter War in November 1939. He helped organize the British volunteers to fight in Finland and became a company commander in the Finnish Foreign Legion. It seems likely that, on a briefing visit to London in November, he recommended his son Gordon for Intelligence work in Finland; Gordon was consequently recalled from enlisted service in the BEF in December 1939 and quickly commissioned. Better prepared than Croft and Munthe, the new recruits had been sent in December on a ten-day Royal Engineers demolitions course, although Scott-Harston and O'Brien-Hitching had only been commissioned onto the General List as second lieutenants three days before departure on 18 December 1939.[3] Recognizing the potential to gain intelligence on Russian organization and morale from prisoners taken in Finland (and even potentially to raise recruits for a Russian Legion to take part in future British operations against the Soviet Union), MI(R) sent Russian-speaking Major Gatehouse (Royal Warwickshire Regiment) and Captain Guy Tamplin (MI2b) to cultivate prisoners in POW camps. Tamplin had served in the First World War on the Lockhart mission to Russia and had lived for a considerable time in Riga. They set off on 16 January and returned on 14 February, then compiled a report on the organization, equipment, tactics and political views of the Russian soldier.[4] Tamplin remained with MI(R) and would soon find himself in the Middle East.

Croft, Munthe, Whittington-Moë, Scott-Harston and O'Brien-Hitching were back in England by the end of January. Munthe was sent back to Weedon OCTU to complete his course and undergo parachute training and Croft was put in charge of the development and preparation of Arctic clothing and supplies for the intended British expedition to Finland. But in February concern was raised in the War Cabinet over the congestion in Norwegian ports and on Swedish railways that was impeding the supply of materials to Finland. MI(R) was asked again to send out officers to investigate and on 20 February Croft and Munthe returned to Bergen with transport specialist

John Walter. Over the next three weeks the three men travelled 4,800km by rail and carried out a reconnaissance of Bergen and Trondheim ports. Walter returned to London on 8 March with a report but Croft and Munthe remained in Finland until its surrender on 12 March. In Finland the MI(R) officers saw at first-hand the simple but successful Finnish tactics against tanks, including using petrol bombs against their air intakes and ramming logs of wood into the tracks (techniques soon to be popularized against the threat of invasion in Britain).[5] Munthe became personally involved, including setting a camouflet mine on a railway line (*see above*, p. 36).

A British expeditionary force to North Norway and Finland was due to embark on 20 March, to secure the Lapland ore fields and defend Norwegian ports against any possible German counterattack. Holland was consequently instructed to send advance security officers to the ports of Narvik, Trondheim, Bergen and Stavanger to arrange the reception of British landings (the 'Avonmouth' and 'Stratford' expeditions) and to ensure good relations with the local population.[6] Major F.H. Palmer, Captains Currie and Torrance, and Lieutenants Hall, Metcalfe and May flew out on 13 March, followed by Captain F.T. Davies on the next day to give them final instructions. But even as they were arriving in Norway, they discovered the Finns had concluded an armistice with the Soviet Union and the planned landings were abandoned. The officers returned to England but MI(R) would soon be back in Norway. Gordon O'Brien-Hitching served as Reuters representative in Finland during March 1940, presumably acting for British Intelligence.[7] He was part of Fleming's No. 10 Mission to Norway in April but then rejoined the BEF and was wounded during the Dunkirk evacuation. Having first transferred to the Intelligence Corps and then to the 22nd Dragoons, he joined the Parachute Regiment and was killed in Normandy in July 1944. Scott-Harston was also part of the No. 10 Mission and later served with MI5.

Norway

Norway's control of the transport routes for the winter export of the northern Swedish iron ore, and its deep-water harbours opening onto the North Atlantic, made it strategically important. Unfortunately the whole Norwegian campaign in 1940 was dogged by poor planning and a British arrogance that gave little attention to local expertise. General Carton de Wiart ruefully reflected on his sudden summons to the War Office: 'It dawned on me the reason might be Norway, especially as I had never been there and knew nothing about it.'[8] The same might be said about most of the British commanders.

As it seemed ever more likely that the Germans would invade Scandinavia, on 2 April MI(R) again sent advance security officers (now under cover as 'assistant consuls') to the four Norwegian ports where it was proposed to disembark an Allied expeditionary force to bolster the Norwegian Army. Major F.H. Palmer went to Trondheim, James 'Hamish' Torrance to Narvik, Andrew Croft to Bergen and Malcolm Munthe to Stavanger (Fig. 6). No other provision had been made by the War Office to provide reconnaissance and their despatch was 'a small and somewhat pathetic attempt to fill that gap'.[9] The British plans were overtaken by the speed of the German invasion on 9 April. Palmer was immediately captured at Trondheim and spent the rest of the war as a POW. At Bergen, Croft woke at 3.30am to the sound of gunfire and went down to the quay to find the Norwegian garrison preparing for evacuation. At 4.30am the first German troops began to land and spread through the town. Croft and the consular staff swiftly burned all confidential documents and Croft raced to the top of the mountain railway to watch the German warships enter the harbour. He then calmly walked back through the now-occupied town to his hotel, already full of Germans, and managed to sneak into his room and collect his passport. Croft then went to the house of Ivar Borge in the suburbs where he found two other Englishmen, one of whom was the vice-consul and head of the Section D network in Bergen, James Chaworth-Musters. With a leg of mutton in one pocket of his overcoat and a loaf of bread in another, Croft and his two companions travelled cross-country south to Nesttun, where they separated. Croft went on to Hardanger Fjord, dodging German patrols, and at one point a sympathetic family hid him under their daughter's skirt in the back of a car. He crossed the mountain in waist-deep snow on skis and reached Bulken at 8.00pm on the evening of Saturday, 13 April, having travelled around 240km. He eventually reached Ålesund on the evening of Wednesday, 17 April, from where he was able to escape to Britain on HMS *Ashanti*.[10] He had only 24 hours rest in London before returning to Norway with Gubbins and the Independent Companies (*see below*, p. 107).

James 'Hamish' Torrance of the Highland Light Infantry, who had previously worked in the timber trade in Sweden and Finland, had been appointed Intelligence Officer to the 24th (Guards) Brigade on 25 February 1940 but was detached for 'special duty' on 6 March 1940 to join MI(R). Torrance, with the British consul and his assistant, managed to escape Narvik as the Germans entered the town and hid first in a mountain hut and then in the house of the town mayor until the Allied recapture of the town on 28 May. In Stavanger, the main port on the south-west tip of Norway, Malcolm Munthe hid in the Victoria Hotel with a wireless operator trying to contact the expected British landing party and helped burn confidential papers from the Consulate. He escaped the town with the consular staff and in a series of adventures, during which he was wounded in both legs and briefly captured, travelled to occupied Bergen where he imaginatively picked up some planks of wood and a bag of nails and then posed as a carpenter to enter the US

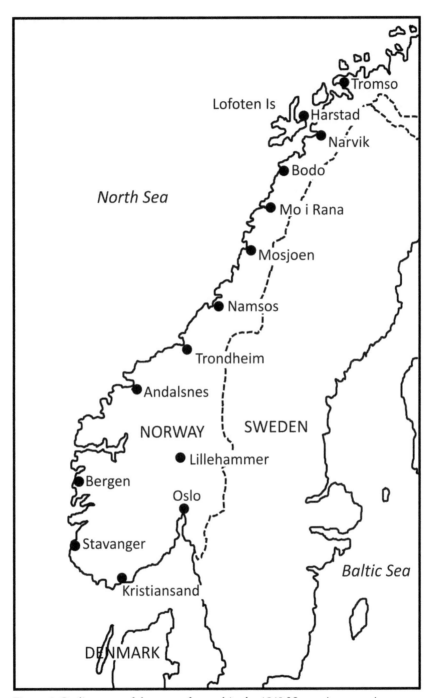

Figure 6. Outline map of the towns featured in the 1940 Norwegian campaign.

Consulate. From here he travelled with a forged Swedish passport by train to Oslo and then to Stockholm, playing *Deutschland über Alles* for travelling German troops on a concertina in which was hidden his British passport and other papers. He reached Stockholm in early June after his two-month-long trek and was appointed Assistant Military Attaché to avoid internment. This was soon after the arrest of the Section D network and so he was tasked with maintaining their existing contacts with the Norwegian resistance in Sweden and continuing the flow of Intelligence to SIS. He soon transferred to the new SOE, organizing training for prospective members of the Norwegian resistance currently refugees in Sweden and planning sabotage operations. Munthe was, however, later described in SOE as a difficult and demanding character and the Military Office at the Norwegian legation considered his lack of skill and 'gung-ho' attitude as more of a danger to his agents than to the Gestapo! The efficient Swedish Security Service, on alert after their penetration of the Section D cell, easily saw through Munthe's cover and had his 'Red Horse' network under surveillance. A number of arrests were made and Munthe was finally expelled in mid-July 1941, something of a relief to the Norwegian legation and the British Minister. He was lucky to reach Britain safely as a Swedish official had informed the German legation of his imminent departure and they were planning to shoot down the aircraft in which he was travelling.[11] Munthe was replaced as AMA by Andrew Croft, his former colleague in MI(R).

No. 10 Military Mission (Fleming Mission)
The day after the German invasion of Norway, General Hugh Massy, C-in-C North West Expeditionary Force (NWEF), requested MI(R) to plan for the landing of 'guerrilla bands' in Norway, to support future British operations. This was exactly the task that Holland had been awaiting. The task fell to F.T. Davies, Peter Fleming and Martin Lindsay, together with Lieutenant Carr RN from Section D. Carr had already led Section D's 'Cruising Club' operation in 1939 to survey potential landing sites in Norway and Section D had two embryonic sabotage networks in the country.[12] Events moved quickly and Peter Fleming was pulled out of a War Office meeting on 12 April between MI(R) and the Lovat Scouts (discussing the formation of what would emerge as the Independent Companies: *see below*, p. 107) and was ordered to immediately establish a wireless station at Namsos, north of Trondheim. This was needed to guide in a British landing (*Operation Henry*) by de Wiart as the north arm of a pincer movement against Trondheim (Fig. 6). Fleming's No. 10 Military Mission left the next day (Saturday, 13 April) and would be the first British landings of the Norway campaign. Fleming was clearly eager to see action but his deployment was a risk given his knowledge of the deception system surrounding Scandinavian operations.

Fleming's own account is one of studied casualness, claiming with journalistic licence that in April he had 'happened to hear' of the projected Namsos mission and 'had practically no difficulty at all' in getting himself appointed leader. He then claimed to have telephoned Martin Lindsay and said 'Come to Norway.'[13] Martin Lindsay had been on a Greenland expedition with Andrew Croft and had been first recruited to MI(R) by Fleming in September 1939 for the proposed Chinese mission. He had subsequently served in the 5th Scots Guards ski battalion and was now working with Fleming on plans for future guerrilla operations in Norway and so his deployment was not the whim that Fleming implies. Fleming ('Flea') and Lindsay ('Louse') were joined by the only recently returned Scott-Harston and O'Brien-Hitching as interpreters, and two Signals sergeants. They flew to Namsos on a Sunderland flying boat from the Shetlands, not knowing if the Germans had already landed. On the flight to Namsos Fleming's biography claims that he tried to persuade the pilot to divert and bomb Trondheim as an act of bravado typical of the adventurer, but was denied permission in the interests of secrecy. This may have been further artistic licence as the book also describes the bomb racks as being empty when it took off and it was clearly important to reach Namsos as soon as possible![14] They overflew Namsos and saw no sign of the enemy, but to be sure they first landed a few kilometres to the south in a creek. Reassured by local officials, they then flew into Namsos and established themselves at the Grand Hotel but when they tried out the wireless sets on the next day it was discovered that the Marconi H86 sets were too heavy and inadequate for the purpose. They were supposed to have an operating range of 30 miles [48km] but whilst they could receive messages from the fleet, they proved unable to transmit over the sea. Consequently, on the evening of 14 April the destroyers had to land the initial party of 340 marines blind, without the benefit of forward intelligence; it was the ignominious end of the planned MI(R) mission, but it was not to be a wasted effort.

General de Wiart flew in on 15 April and as his only staff officer was wounded during an air attack as the flying boat landed, Fleming and Lindsay agreed to serve temporarily as his staff officers. For de Wiart, Fleming was his 'general factotum number one', while Fleming described himself as not only chief of staff but also batman, driver and cook.[15] Fleming managed to get a signal back to the Admiralty early on 15 April, reporting on Norwegian strength and the situation with the naval landing party, as well as warning that the Germans were mounting daily reconnaissance flights. He also warned of the lack of local cover and the difficulty of moving a large number of troops through 1.2m-deep snow.[16] An immediate enemy reaction was delayed by Fleming, having quickly secured the local telephone exchange to prevent telephone and telegraph messages being passed to the enemy, and organizing roadblocks.[17] In reporting to Holland, Lieutenant Attwater RN believed

Fleming's presence 'had made it possible for him to cut communications with the rest of the country and had thus given the Navy three days' security for landing British and French troops with their stores before the Germans started bombing them'.[18]

The main landings began on 16 April with the troops remaining hidden during the day and moving quickly out of exposed Namsos towards Grong and Steinkjær at night. The evidence of their movements was camouflaged by the MI(R) officers buying up all the supplies of white linen sheets to lay across the disturbed snow. In their new role as staff officers, Lindsay accompanied the troops to Steinkjær while Fleming and his two Signals sergeants travelled to liaise with the Norwegian HQ at Kvam. There they discovered the only communication was by civilian telephone and there were no trained Norwegian Army signallers. They returned to Namsos and renewed efforts to make the wireless sets work, but still could not contact the Navy, reducing them to contacting the ships by signal lamps. Despite the British efforts to conceal evidence of the landings from aerial reconnaissance, the Germans were suspicious and confirmation came when French troops, who were being landed in twice the number of ships than expected, were unable to take cover before dawn. Caught in the open, they drew further attention to themselves by firing on a reconnaissance aircraft. All doubt was removed, and on Saturday, 20 April the Germans repeatedly bombed and strafed Namsos with more than sixty aircraft. In making out his list of equipment improvements for future operations, Fleming put 'more changes of under-clothing' as top of the list. More seriously, he also suggested better wireless sets, more despatch riders and a Royal Signals cable detachment with Fullerphones to avoid the use of civilian phone lines that proved too easy to intercept.[19] On 28 April Fleming was sent back to London to report on the situation on de Wiart's behalf and seek clarification of future orders. He returned to Namsos the next day and, according to de Wiart's memoirs, brought the depressing assessment 'you can really do what you like, for they don't know what they want done'. In fact, de Wiart had already received orders to evacuate. Fleming left with the rest of the British troops and was back in London on 6 May. Before departure, Fleming had the chance to try out his deception skills from ISSB in order to try to delay the enemy advance, and he faked some half-burned documents for the Germans to find, suggesting that the Namsen bridge had been wired with explosives and was protected by machine gun nests.[20] The bridge was finally blown up on 1 May by French sappers.[21]

Fleming and Lindsay were appalled by the lack of strategic direction for the campaign and the poor standard of equipment and training. On their return, both broke military protocol to make their feelings known. Fleming briefed the editor of *The Times* (his previous employer) on the failings of the Namsos expedition and on 7 May the newspaper, whilst taking care not to blame the troops or their commanders, directed criticism towards the government's leadership. Former Conservative parliamentary candidate Lindsay then presented a highly critical report on the organization of the Norway campaign to Attlee and the Labour opposition as the 'Lindsay Memorandum', which would play a major role in the downfall of the Chamberlain government.[22]

Knife Mission

Soon after Fleming's team flew to Namsos, an attempt was made to land an MI(R) party with a more active mission. On Monday, 15 April 1940 Holland learned that the Royal Navy intended to send a naval landing party to Sogne Fjord by submarine, in order to help extricate a Norwegian submarine, and asked the Director of Naval Intelligence for permission for it to be accompanied by a six-strong MI(R) party based on former members of the recently disbanded 5th Scots Guards. It was commanded by Lieutenant Colonel Bryan Mayfield (Scots Guards) with Major Ralph Farrant (Royal Artillery), Captains Stacey (Royal Artillery), Jim Gavin (Royal Engineers) and William Stirling (Scots Guards), together with Peter Kemp, an MI(R) recruit taken from the Weedon OCTU course. They were to take demolition stores, Bren guns, rifles and wireless sets with a mission to disrupt rail and road bridges linking Oslo to the north of Norway, hinder the German advance and supply contacts in the new Norwegian resistance. After having been briefed by F.T. Davies and John Kennedy in London on 23 April 1940, they sailed from Rosyth in the submarine HMS *Truant* on 24 April to land in Sogne Fjord; on the way the vessel was damaged by an enemy mine and had to return to Rosyth. The plan was to try again on the submarine HMS *Clyde* on 26 April and loading was in progress when news came that the operation had been cancelled by the Admiralty. The mission would be partially continued by Section D in May using Norwegian civilian volunteers and a pioneer of what became the 'Shetland bus'.[23] The main significance of the *Knife* mission turned out to be bringing together the future core instructors of the Lochailort Training School in a discussion on the need to improve practical MI(R) training.

No. 13 Military Mission (Brown Mission)

The main MI(R) mission to the Norwegian forces was the No. 13 Mission (Brown mission) which left for Norway on 17 April.[24] Its instructions were to 'act as DMI representative at Norwegian HQ ... to encourage every aspect of guerrilla warfare, if necessary by personal appearance with the Norwegian forces'.[25] But it was too late for the evangelical MI(R) to instil a great deal of interest in the Norwegian GHQ to divert (as they saw it) their retreating troops to guerrilla warfare. The mission was commanded by regular army Major Alan Brown (Royal Tank Regiment), who had been with Wilkinson in Prague in March 1939 as a language officer and, after attending a Caxton Hall course, had been recruited to the MI(R) Polish mission. With him was Captain

Robert Readhead (12th Lancers) and Sergeant Peter Dahl (a Norwegian hotelier working in London who had enlisted into the Royal Army Pay Corps) as interpreter. The mission would also try to make contact with the MI(R) advance security officers already in Norway and bring them under its control, although in the event these officers had been forced to flee upon the German invasion and were already trying to make their way back to England.

The mission travelled to Norway via Sweden, posing as civilians. After liaising with the military attaché in Stockholm they crossed the border on 19 April and, in British uniforms, travelled to the Norwegian GHQ at Oyer, where they briefed the Norwegians on their sketchy knowledge of the British plans. Any illusions as to their role and status were soon dashed as the Norwegian C-in-C made it clear that he preferred to work through the well-established British and French military attachés. In an effort to improve their credibility, Brown tried to expedite the shipment of Boys anti-tank rifles and ammunition to Norway but any credit they might have earned was destroyed when the War Office sent them on a slow passage by sea rather than by air, and the rifles and ammunition arrived in different locations. The Norwegian C-in-C was nervous about deploying guerrillas for fear of exciting reprisals but in a last effort to prove the methodology, Brown and Readhead were able to join Norwegian ski parties that moved east and west of Lake Mjosa on 22 April to try to cut German lines of communication. Brown's party was recalled before they could engage the enemy and he was evacuated on 30 April from Molde. He then went on to have a successful career with the Royal Armoured Corps. Readhead was a pre-war ski champion who had been commissioned into the army from university in 1936 and joined the 12th Royal Lancers but had been almost immediately attached to the Italian *Alpini* in 1937 and the Swiss Mountain Regiment in 1938. After commanding a troop of armoured cars in France, he briefly joined the No. 3 Military and Air Mission to Belgium in February 1940 (the 'Phantom' reconnaissance unit) before joining the 5th Scots Guards ski battalion in March, serving, like many other officers who had volunteered, as a sergeant. He was promoted captain in April 1940 when appointed to No. 13 Mission as one of the few British officers with training in mountain warfare. Unfortunately his Norwegian party had only limited military experience and had packed no demolition material; they were then diverted from their task by the need to assist British troops stranded in the mountains. In desperation, Readhead took command; whilst trekking northwards to try to reach British lines, he juggled the shepherding of the stranded troops with mounting small-scale ambushes from the wooded mountainsides on German troops passing on the road below. The Norwegian troops disbanded upon hearing of the Norwegian surrender of forces in Central Norway on 2 May and the now sixty-strong party of British stragglers split up into smaller parties and made their way to the Swedish border, covering 200km of German-held territory in ten days. Readhead worked under the military attaché in Stockholm until 8 July when he was finally repatriated to Britain under cover as a diplomatic courier.[26] He joined SOE and in 1945 was awarded the DSO after parachuting into Italy to take charge of partisan forces. One important contact that the mission made was Captain Martin Linge, who was attached to the mission from the Norwegian GHQ. He was evacuated with the rest of the NWEF and was attached to Section D before he and Sergeant Dahl joined the new Norwegian Independent Company which he came to command (which eventually became known simply as *Kompani Linge*).

Jefferis Mission
Millis Jefferis, head of MI(R)c, had previously served in a Royal Engineers field company and had more success at organizing demolitions in the wake of the Norwegian retreat. Jefferis, accompanied by Sergeant Tilsley, flew in a Sunderland flying boat from Scotland to Molde on 19 April, bringing with him 1,000lb of explosives, pressure switches and other demolition stores 'and his wicked face was lit with joy'.[27] They had raced to Hendon in Jefferis' car to catch their flight to Scotland and as a result he was fined £6 in his absence by the local magistrates for speeding![28] In Scotland they collected demolition supplies from HMS *Hood* and *Galatea*, before flying on to Norway. The mission from the War Office was to blow up railway lines in Central Norway but the Norwegians categorically refused to give permission. Jefferis joined up with Brigadier Morgan's 148 Brigade and provided a quick training for Norwegian engineers in the MI(R) pressure switches before skiing sabotage parties were dispatched south of Lillehammer. On 21 April Jefferis laid charges on the bridge at Ojer and blew it up after the last of the retreating British troops had passed over it and then helped organize the defence around Trettan, with 250–300 men and a single Boys anti-tank rifle. Cut off by the enemy, Jefferis, with Tilsley and two privates, sneaked through the German positions, blowing up two bridges on the way, and managed to rejoin the British forces on 26 April. He left Norway in a Sunderland flying boat on 28 April.[29] On his return Jefferis was asked to brief the Prime Minister, Neville Chamberlain, who used his report as part of a briefing to the War Cabinet.[30] For his remarkable service in Norway, Jefferis was awarded the Norwegian War Cross with Sword, and was Mentioned in Despatches – although this gets no mention in Macrae's egocentric account of MI(R)c!

Independent Companies
MI(R)'s focus had been on advising foreign governments on how to organize guerrilla warfare but the failure of the Brown mission in Norway and the frustrations in Romania had illustrated the difficulty of imposing their views onto foreign General Staffs without having a practical credibility. Ironically,

MI(R) had paid no attention to improving the capability of the British Army in guerrilla warfare and this lacuna was thrown into sharp focus when it failed in applying its methodology to the British forces in Norway. Brigadier Wyndham's review of MI(R) in August 1940 excused this, unconvincingly, by claiming the German invasion was 'unexpected' and took solace in the 'inevitable British improvisation'.[31] The intention was to insert self-sufficient guerrilla units along the coast of North Norway in order to disrupt German movements between the main British landings. The long coastline with plenty of potential isolated landing points and the ever-lengthening lines of communication of the German Army seemed to offer an ideal test-bed for Holland's concept of guerrilla warfare supporting conventional operations. Unfortunately the Independent Companies, as they became, were rushed into action with inadequate training and equipment and bore little relationship to the ideal as represented by *Art of Guerrilla Warfare*.

The first thought of the working group of Fleming, Davies, Lindsay and Carr, hurriedly convened on Massy's orders to consider 'guerrilla bands' for Norway, had been to use the experienced ghillies and deer-stalkers of the Lovat Scouts, which at the time comprised two battalions of scouts mounted on hill ponies. Their CO, Leslie Melville, met Holland, Fleming and an unnamed staff officer at the War Office on 12 April 1940 to discuss the Lovat Scouts forming part of a composite battalion of up to 1,200 men with the 5th Battalion, Scots Guards, divided into ten or twelve mixed companies which would land at different points on the coast; their HQs were to be located on trawlers in the fjords or with the Norwegian Army HQ on the mainland. Melville was unenthusiastic over the idea of dispersing his regiment and no decision could be reached. It was decided to continue the conference the next day under the weightier chairmanship of the DMI, Major General Beaumont-Nesbitt, but overnight came the unexpected news that the 5th Scots Guards had already been disbanded. A new proposal was that the Lovat Scouts be deployed as an independent unit to land north of Trondheim, and then travel 240km inland through the mountains and deep snow to cut a railway line. Melville was more enthusiastic about this option but Holland still favoured the original concept and after the meeting he immediately produced a brief for what became the Independent Companies.[32]

At 6.00pm on 13 April Holland went to the CIGS with his outline plan for drawing volunteers from existing regiments into a number of individual, self-sufficient companies and sending them into Norway to carry out small harassing operations against the enemy. With an historical perspective drawn from his original desk-top study, Holland likened them to a revival of the light infantry companies of the Peninsular War era.[33] By 6.20pm the principle was approved. A new conference was held under Brigadier A.E. Nye, Deputy Director, Staff Duties, in the afternoon of 15 April at which the establishment of the Independent Companies was agreed. Able to retain their regimental integrity in this new scheme, Melville was now more enthusiastic and he declared that a company of Lovat Scouts was ready to deploy almost immediately. But on 17 April the Lovat Scouts received a warning order for a move overseas and they were soon on their way to the Faroe Islands.[34] With the hope of using existing specialist troops dashed, in desperation it was decided to raise the Independent Companies from the second-line Territorial Army divisions across Britain (Fig. 7). Each brigade in a division was to provide one platoon of volunteers, drawing on each battalion to provide a section. Not for the last time would the War Office be wary of stripping front-line troops for the purposes of novel irregular warfare and Gubbins would soon face the same problem in raising army scout patrols to assist the GHQ Auxiliary Units in Britain. Details were circulated to Regional Commands on 20 April.

Once formed, the Inter-Services Planning Staff and the Director of Mobilization took over management of the Independent Companies and upon deployment they served under the expeditionary force commander.[35] But reaching agreement on their format and the subsequent organization of their supplies proved a huge burden on MI(R)'s limited resources and remained a source of bitterness to Holland. He later explained: 'Independent Companies were formed, and employed in Norway, under the aegis of MI(R), though such proceedings are matters neither of research nor military intelligence.'[36] MO9 was eventually created to manage the Independent Companies and the later Commandos. Colin Gubbins, unemployed following his removal from the Polish mission (and with Lionel Kenyon acting as Holland's assistant in MI(R)), was Holland's obvious suggestion to command the force and was appointed on 20 April. Already Gubbins had adopted the persona of an expert in the subject, based largely on his pamphlets on guerrilla warfare, and he cultivated an air of piratical mystery: 'It was said that he was a linguist who had fought with the White Russians after the end of the First World War or in some clandestine Balkan operation. Small irregular operations were said to be his *métier*.'[37] In truth, he had no practical experience of guerrilla warfare.

Ten companies were to be raised, each of twenty-one officers and 268 other ranks, self-sufficient in light weapons, explosives and supplies for 72 hours and furnished with £4,000-worth of gold sovereigns to buy additional supplies and transport. As with the rest of the expeditionary force, they lacked clothing suitable for Norway and what was provided was too heavy and bulky for a mobile campaign: a stiff, kapok-lined, Tropal overcoat was worn over a wool-lined leather jerkin and then a woollen battledress and one or more woollen vests. The whole ensemble did not even keep out the cold! The high percentage of officers was in the expectation they would be fighting at platoon or section level; each section of twelve men was therefore led by a subaltern.[38]

Figure 7. Parent divisions and commanders of the Independent Companies.

Independent Company	Date of Formation (if known)	Parent Division	Commanding Officer	Mobilized
No.1	20 April	52nd (Lowland) Division	Major A.C.W. May (Highland Light Infantry)	Matlock, Somerset
No.2	25 April	53rd (Welsh) Division	Major H. Stockwell (Royal Welch Fusiliers) (then Tom Trevor)	Ballykinlar, N. Ireland
No.3	25 April	54th (East Anglian) Division	Major A. Charles Newman (Essex Regiment)	Tonteland, Northumberland
No.4	21 April	55th (West Lancs) Division	Major J.R. Paterson	Sizewell. Suffolk
No.5	21 April	56th (London) Division	Major James Peddie (London Scottish)	New Romney
No.6	25 April	9th (Scottish) Division	Major Ronnie Todd (Argyll and Sutherland Highlanders)	Carnoustie, Fife, Scotland
No.7	25 April	15th (Scottish) Division	Major J. Young (Highland Light Infantry)	Harwick, Scotland
No.8		18th (Eastern) Division	Major Rice (Suffolk Regiment)	Brandon, Norfolk
No.9		38th (Welsh) Division	Major J. Siddons (Royal Welch Fusiliers)	Ross-on-Wye, Herefordshire
No.10		66th (East Lancs) Division	Major L. de C. Robertson (TA General List)	Catterick, Yorkshire
No.11	14 June	From volunteers of Nos 1–10 Independent Companies	Major Ronnie Todd	Gournock, Scotland

The Company HQ would include a Royal Engineer complement to organize sabotage and demolition as well as signals, intelligence, medical and support sections.

Each company would hold thirty days' rations, a one-day emergency ration and five days' mountain haversack ration of pemmican per man.[39] Having dropped the idea of a 'ship-home', the troops were expected to be mobile in rough terrain and with no other provision for transport except what they could requisition locally. They were only lightly armed, the heaviest weapons being the Boys anti-tank rifles and mortars in the HQ support section. Repeated revisions to the scale of weapons were made, centred around negotiations by Gubbins to acquire two of the new Thompson sub-machine guns per section in return for a reduction in the number of Bren guns.[40] No. 2 Independent Company was eventually issued with a sniper rifle and two Thompson sub-machine guns per section, three Bren guns for the HQ support section, one for each section and the Company HQ, three Boys anti-tank guns for the support section, two per platoon and one for the Company HQ.[41] The support section also had 2-inch mortars. Each company also had a supplementary allowance of 6,000lb of gelignite, 6,000 Ammonal cartridges and 200 anti-tank mines.[42] In an effort to strengthen their capability in conventional warfare, a troop of three MkVIb light tanks of the 3rd King's Own Hussars, accompanied by two 30cwt lorries and two motorcycles were intended to be attached to No. 5 Independent Company in its initial deployment to Mosjöen, sailing from Scotland on 7 May, but Mosjöen was evacuated before they could arrive.[43] The tanks were then lost on 14 May while being sent to reinforce Bodø on the MV *Chobry*.[44] On Thursday, 25 April Holland sent a memo to Stuart Macrae saying that the first four Independent Companies expected to depart must be equipped and trained by the following Tuesday. Bidgood and Macrae rushed around the country providing a bare modicum of training in the MI(R) devices while Norwood and Tilsley arranged for the shipping of supplies.

To administer what was designated as *Scissorforce*, Gubbins was allocated a small Operational HQ of 8 officers and 15 other ranks, supported by a comprehensive Headquarters Administrative Group of 16 officers and 179 men under Lieutenant Colonel B.L. Evans, including docks and personnel sections, a detachment from an ordnance ammunition company and base ordnance depot and a field security police section.[45] The Brigade HQ established itself at Gournock on the River Clyde, expecting to be able to train the new Independent Companies that began to assemble from across the country but this was clearly not to be a lean guerrilla force, with five batmen being held on the Operational HQ staff.

The men were supposed to be volunteers, although this could be loosely interpreted.[46] They were told that they were needed for a special mission demanding unusual and adventurous training, but with no indication as to the destination. For Charles 'Sonny' Wright, they were expecting 'to forget to be human beings, live off the land, murder and be tough. You had to survive.'[47] The companies were raised between 21 and 25 April with ambitious plans of training them in

(a) harassing of communications by destruction, or interruption, of railways, roads, tracks, etc., and by derailing trains;
(b) stalking and mopping up of isolated posts or parties;
(c) ambushing of supply columns or small parties; and
(d) intercommunication with local centres of resistance or relief of such centres if attacked.[48]

In practice, because of their immediate deployment, the Independent Companies were only able to focus on fitness training based on long route marches. Officers were given a 'map pack' with illustrated holiday brochures and touring maps plus the three MI(R) pamphlets on guerrilla warfare to read – with dire warnings that they were MOST SECRET and had to be returned to the War Office before departure.[49] No. 2 Independent Company, which only set sail on 10 May, was better prepared than most, having had time to undergo rigorous physical training in the Mourne Mountains, as well as shooting and tactical exercises – but as a consequence fifty-three of the original applicants were considered unfit and were returned to their units.[50] Some of the training was individualistic, to say the least. The CO of No. 9 Independent Company was Major Siddons, who had been commissioned from the ranks and had been a 'Black and Tan' in Ireland. One of his section leaders described him as terrifying, eccentric – and usually drunk! He lectured his men on how to kill someone with a table fork and used to jump up in the rifle butts during training and dare his men to shoot him.[51] Ernest Chappell enjoyed the training, 'running through the countryside in scruffy clothes and a bandoleer around my neck' and the greater sense of responsibility than was usual in normal regimental training.[52] There was no time to develop any *esprit de corps* and one of its officers, platoon commander Captain J.H. Prendergast from the Indian Army, complained they were 'drawn from many units, possess no field craft, no stamina'.[53] He continued: 'The idea seemed to be that merely to throw together such a unit with a wave of a wand would make it into a tough specialized force.'[54] The men continued to wear their former cap badges, emphasizing their ad hoc nature, and only No. 4 Independent Company had its own distinctive badge (*see* Plate 25). Fortunately the platoons tended to be drawn from a single regiment, thereby providing an important measure of cohesion at the level of the basic fighting unit. As a last-minute addition, they were assisted by eight officers of the Indian Army as the nearest thing to mountain warfare experts that the British

(*above*) **Plate 1.** J.C.F. 'Jo' Holland (1897–1956) late 1938 as a lieutenant colonel, just after being appointed head of MI(R). (*Elizabeth Holland*)

(*above, left*) **Plate 2.** Sir Colin Gubbins (1896–1976). MI(R) and later head of SOE. Photograph of 1944 shows his rank of acting major general; unfortunately for his pension entitlement, this rank was never confirmed. (*Walter Stoneman, 1944 © National Portrait Gallery, London*)

(*right*) **Plate 3.** Millis Jefferis, head of the technical section, MI(R)c. This photograph was taken after his promotion to major general. (*Walter Stoneman, 1945 © National Portrait Gallery, London*)

Plate 4. Laurence Grand (1898–1975), head of Section D, SIS. Photograph taken when later serving as a brigadier in the Far East. (*Lady Bessborough*)

Plate 5. Daniel Sandford in a press photograph of January 1941. It described him as a British officer who was training 'native Patriot troops' in Ethiopia and explained that a small party of British officers had entered Ethiopia six months earlier and had 'started a revolt against the Italians'. This was a typically Anglo-centric view of world events. (© *Acme*)

Plate 6. Peter Fleming (1907–1971). Pre-war travel writer who served in MI(R) and led XII Corps Observation Unit. (*Howard Coster, 1935 © National Portrait Gallery, London*)

Plate 7. Alan Warren's 1940 Military Identity Card stamped MI(R), Directorate of Military Intelligence. (*The National Archives*)

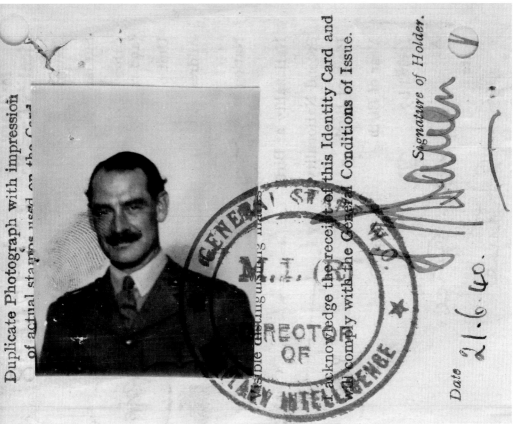

Plate 8. Limpet mine, showing how it was carried by a diver to the target. (*The National Archives*)

Plate 9. Grenade No. 74 ST, known as the Sticky Bomb. Removal of the metal casing revealed a gla sphere containing explosive, covered in a sticky stockinette. Developed over a long period during 1939 and 1940 as an anti-tank grenade using the 'poultice' effect to punch the force of an explosive charge that was stuck to the outside of a tank into the vehicle. Large-scale production did not beg until May 1941, by which time better alternatives were available. First used by the 8th Army and subsequently issued to the Home Guard. (*David Sampson*)

Plate 10. 29mm Spigot Mortar ('Blacker Bombard'). Developed by Stewart Blacker for MI(R) durin 1940 and first saw service with the 8th Army in 1941, although it has become particularly associate with later Home Guard use. Photographed at No. 3 Home Guard Training School, Onibury, Shropshire, May 1943. (© *IWM*)

(top) **Plate 11.** Switch No. 1 Pull. Designed in 1939 to set off trip wires, etc. (*Kate Atkin*)

(middle) **Plate 12.** Switch No. 2 Pressure. Designed in 1939 particularly to blow up railway trains as they passed over it. (*Kate Atkin*)

(bottom) **Plate 13.** Switch No. 3 Release. Designed in late 1939/early 1940 as a sabotage device to be hidden under a weighty object to trigger an explosive charge when that weight was removed. (*David Gordon*)

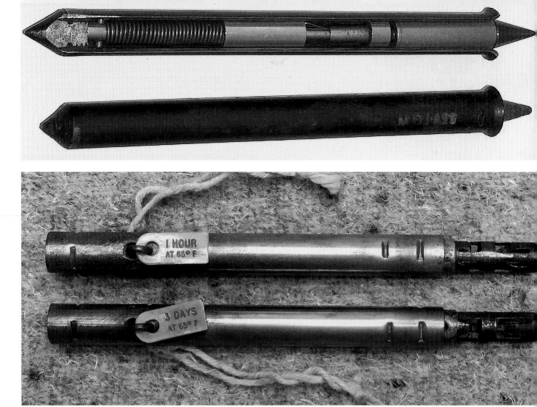

Plate 14. Switch No. 8 AP. Designed in the spring of 1940 as an anti-personnel device. Buried vertically in the ground, it would fire a .303-sized bullet when trodden upon and was consequently known as the 'de-bollocker'. (*David Sampson*)

Plate 15. Switch No. 9 L Delay. Developed in 1940 as an alternative to the Section D Time Pencil and used the principle that a lead alloy wire will stretch and break at a set rate. (*David Gordon*)

Plate 16. Avro Rota Autogyro under military evaluation in 1938. Senior Service cigarette card of 1938. (*Atkin collection*)

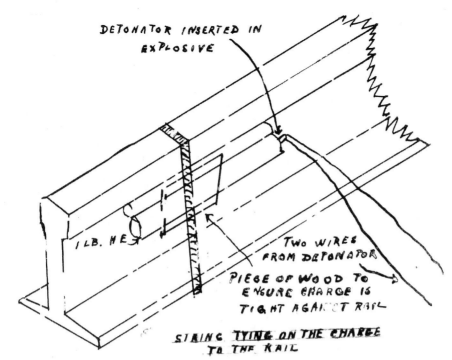

Plate 17. Illustration from *How to Use High Explosives* by Millis Jefferis (1939). This was one of the original MI(R) training manuals but it was only with the creation of the Lochailort training school in 1940 that a systematic programme of instruction in demolition could be established. (*Atkin collection*)

Plate 18. (Top) Webley Mk VI revolver, .455 calibre, of the type supplied to the Polish resistance by MI(R) in February 1940. The disappointed Poles said they wanted lighter .32 Automatics and some were dumped in the Danube. (Bottom) Colt 1903 .32 Automatic, which became the standard weapon of SOE. (*Kate Atkin*)

Plate 19. Aerial photograph of Lochailort, Scotland. Site of the MI(R) training school.
(© *Crown Copyright: HES*)

Plate 20. Inverailort Castle. HQ of the MI(R) Lochailort training school.
(*Photo: Keeshu, licensed under the Creative Commons Attribution-Share Alike 3.0*)

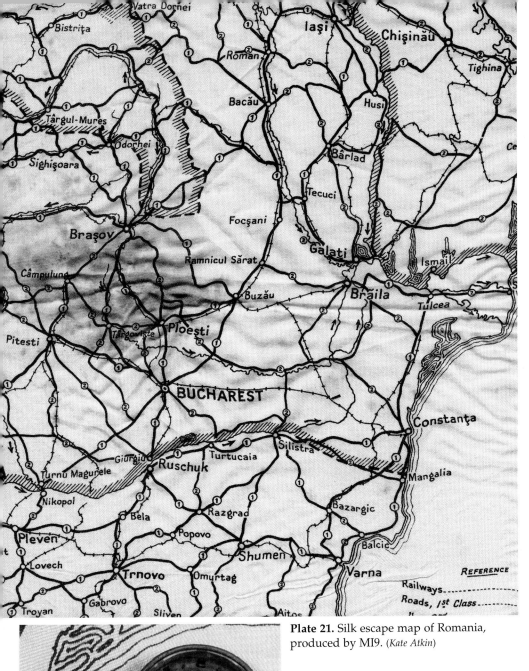

Plate 21. Silk escape map of Romania, produced by MI9. (*Kate Atkin*)

Plate 22. Early miniature compass produced by MI9. Alan Warren was offered an early version, disguised as a collar stud, for his mission to France in June 1940. (*Kate Atkin*)

Plate 23. MI(R) failed to destroy the Romanian oilfields in 1939–1940 and they remained a key strategic target. This photograph of Ploesti oilfield was taken during an air raid by the USAF in 1943. (*US Army CMH*)

Plate 24. Dymock Watson, assistant naval attaché and head of MI(R) operations in Romania. Photograph taken after his promotion to commodore. He later rose in rank to vice admiral. (*Hay Wrightson,* © *National Portrait Gallery, London*)

Plate 25. The shoulder flash of No. 4 Independent Company was one of the few distinctive badges ever worn by units of MI(R). It is based on the shoulder flash of the 55th West Lancashire Division. Modern reproduction. (*Atkin collection*)

Plate 26. Armed 'Puffer' of the type used by the 'Gubbins Flotilla' in Norway. (© IWM: N184)

Plate 27. Bridge destroyed at Mo i Rana, Norway, during the retreat of the Scots Guards and Independent Companies, shown under repair by the German army. (*Atkin collection*)

Plate 28. Bridge destroyed at Potthus, Norway, during the retreat of the Scots Guards and Independent Companies, shown under repair by the German army. (*Atkin collection*)

Plate 29. Ethiopian Patriots armed with captured Italian Carcano rifles being trained at El Wak on the Somalia/Kenya border in early 1941. (© *IWM*)

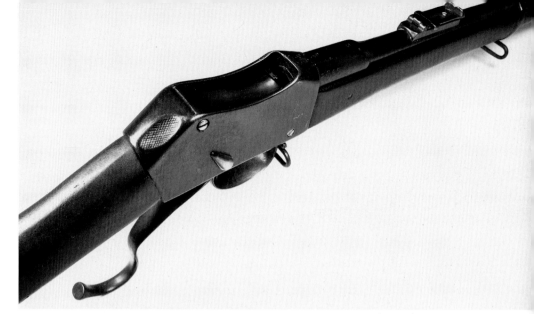

Plate 30. Martini-Enfield single shot .303 calibre rifle, probably made in Egypt, of the type supplied to the Ethiopian Patriots by MI(R). (*Kate Atkin*)

Plate 31. Shoulder flash of Middle East Command and cap badge of the Sudan Defence Force. (*Kate Atkin*)

Plate 32. Maria Theresa Thaler (London mint) of the type provided by Mission 101 to the Ethiopian Patriots. The originals were minted in 1780 and all later copies continued to carry this date. Those supplied to the Ethiopian Patriots by MI(R) were mainly minted in Bombay and London. (*Kate Atkin*)

Plate 33. Reconnaissance photograph taken of Leopoldville, capital of the Belgian Congo, in 1940 by Mission 19. Part of a large series of photographs taken in case the British felt obliged to invade the Belgian colony. (*The National Archives*)

Plate 34. MI(R) was not a unit as such and existing army officers continued to wear their regimental cap badges. Newly recruited officers were initially badged to the General Service Corps (left) before transferring to the Intelligence Corps (right) when it was formed in July 1940. (*Kate Atkin*)

Plate 35. J.C.F. 'Jo' Holland as a major general in 1947. He retired in 1951 but died shortly after in 1956. (*Elizabeth Holland*)

Army could find, although in truth their expertise was on dry foothills rather than snowy mountain valleys. They had only been ordered to proceed from India on 22 April and flew from there one week later. They reached Glasgow on 4 May, only meeting the Independent Companies just before sailing. One positive note was that the Companies each had interpreters, recruited from Norwegians in London and commissioned by the Norwegian Embassy.[55]

The hope for efficient, self-contained wireless communication proved illusory given the existing technology and the difficult conditions in Norway. The Independent Companies HQ at Bodø had a 250-watt transceiver that linked to Wick in Scotland and a No. 11 set that was supposed to link with base sets in the Company HQs in Mo and Mosjöen (Fig. 6).[56] Each Company had six 'Marconi sets' and also twelve dispatch riders.[57] Unfortunately the heavy Marconi sets proved too cumbersome and were deemed useless (*see below*, p. 118).[58] The Irish Guards War Diary records an opinion of the Independent Companies who worked with them in *Stockforce*: 'when supporting our flanks throughout the forthcoming operations, it was very difficult to contact them, and more than often impossible to know if they were even there. They lived up to their name as Independent Companies and retired and advanced at will.'[59] In practice, the whole force in Norway had to rely heavily on civilian telephones for communication. Although an important step towards the formation of the Commandos, the Independent Companies were a pale reflection of the ideal expressed in *Art of Guerrilla Warfare* and their employment in Norway must have been intensely frustrating for Holland and Gubbins. They were not tested as guerrillas and were used instead as conventional light infantry, but lacked the equipment for that role. It may have been this failure, together with MI(R)'s disasters in Romania, that contributed to Hugh Dalton's dismissal of the army's ability to organize guerrilla warfare when trying to take control of what became SOE (*see below*, Chapter Twelve). General Auchinleck, who took up his post as GOC Anglo-French forces in North Norway on 13 May, admitted that he had not expected much from the lightly armed Independent Companies: 'To be a successful guerrilla, you must, I think, be a guerrilla in your own country.'[60]

A key objective of the German invasion of Norway was the seizure of the northern iron ore port of Narvik (Fig. 6). German troops occupied the port on 9 April 1940 but they were cut off when their supply ships were destroyed by the Royal Navy. The recapture of Narvik was an Allied priority but to avoid the cost of a frontal assault, the plan was to encircle the port and it was crucial to prevent any German relief from the south. The Independent Companies were to disrupt any German advance up the road from Mosjöen or any sea or parachute landings along the route, harass enemy lines of communications and sabotage bridges, tunnels and railway lines, mop up isolated enemy posts and ambush supply columns. It was also hoped such activity would raise the morale of the local population and encourage the formation of local guerrilla bands. In line with the classic understanding of a guerrilla's role, Gubbins was ordered to refrain from attempting 'prolonged frontal resistance' to any enemy advance but rather to impede their advance by harrying action and demolitions on their flanks and lines of communication.[61] Yet even as the Independent Companies were being readied for deployment, the Allied plan was collapsing and their role changed to being part of a conventional fighting withdrawal against sustained assault – for which they were neither prepared nor equipped. The British forces which had landed at Åndalsnes and Namsos in Central Norway were forced to evacuate and by 5 May the Germans were free to advance and relieve Narvik. Their immediate target was Bodø, where the airfield could be used to resupply the besieged German forces.

No. 1 Independent Company, drawn from the 52nd (Lowland) Division, arrived at Rosyth from Matlock, Somerset, on 26 April and the next day sailed on HMS *Arethusa* with the Brigade HQ for Mo i Rana (229km south of Bodø and 98km north of Mosjöen: Fig. 6). They were briefed by Gubbins whilst at sea but the ship was ordered to return to Scapa Flow on 28 April and disembarked the Brigade HQ and Gubbins, who was ordered to report on 2 May to General Massy at the HQ of the North-West Expeditionary Force in London to clarify his orders. Without the brigade staff, No. 1 Independent Company finally sailed from Scapa Flow for Mo i Rana on 30 April in the *Royal Ulsterman*, with orders to 'get to know the country intimately. Make use of locals but do not trust too far. Use wits and low cunning.'[62] Mo controlled the most northerly road into Sweden and there was an airfield a few kilometres to the north which would bring German air power closer to Narvik. They landed in the early hours of 4 May and established an outpost to the south at Finneidfjord.[63] The men were advised to disperse and conceal themselves on arrival but to retain the ability to concentrate rapidly against any enemy sea or airborne landing parties, their mobility being dependent on commandeering local craft and transport.[64] They carried twenty-eight days' normal rations and thirty days' mountain rations.[65] They were clearly expecting to have to go to ground for a considerable period as guerrillas but this was soon to prove impossible when they came up against experienced German mountain troops at divisional strength. Communications were an immediate problem and Massy warned that communication with the *Scissorforce* HQ to be established at Bodø would have to be by 'civil telegraph'.[66]

Admiral Cork, commander of Allied forces at Narvik, had only been advised of the imminent departure of the Independent Companies for Norway on 29 April and was confused as to the implications for Allied strategy, signalling London on 4 May, 'Request I may be informed of the general policy regarding Bodø, Mo and Mosjöen ... These areas do not, I presume, come under

Narvik Command. Are there any other Allied forces to the south of me?'[67] Nos 3, 4 and 5 Independent Companies sailed on 5 May from Gourock, on the same day that the Germans began their advance north from Grong, and even as they were *en route* the Admiralty explained their rationale to Cork, saying that it was only possible to maintain small forces at Mo and Mosjöen, protecting the road leading to Bodø, and the role of the Independent Companies was 'to carry out extensive demolitions on road leading north from Namsos . . . and to delay advance of enemy for as long as possible and prevent landings from sea or by parachute'.[68] Two days later Cork was given formal control of the forces south of Narvik, until Auchinleck assumed command of all land forces on 13 May.[69] Massy, still in London, was keen to send the remaining Independent Companies in Britain as demolition parties to occupied Southern Norway but this was deemed impractical and the campaign came to a close before their deployment could be agreed.

No. 3 Independent Company under Major Newman (who would win a VC on the St Nazaire raid in 1942), with the HQ staff and signals section, sailed on the *Royal Scotsman* and landed at Bodø before setting up *Scissorforce* HQ at Hopen, 17km to the east. A company of 1st Scots Guards from 24th (Guards) Brigade had already established its HQ there and it was eventually established that *Scissorforce* would take command of the company, rather than replace it.[70] No. 3 Independent Company then established a guard at the ferry crossing at Rognan, at the head of the Saltfjord.[71]

Nos 4 and 5 Independent Companies on SS *Ulster Prince* and HMS *Arethusa* were to relieve a company of French *Chasseurs Alpin* at Mosjöen. Gubbins decided to travel with them and see them settled before joining his HQ.[72] Mosjöen lay 316km to the south of Bodø, but it was believed that, if necessary, the troops could fall back on No. 1 Company at Mo and thence back to Bodø (Fig. 6). Unfortunately the Allies were outmatched by the experienced German mountain troops who advanced over 240km of difficult terrain in a single week, hindering any effort to mount an effective rearguard or to organize a guerrilla campaign by men who had little military training, no experience of the local landscape and lacked skis. By the time the Independent Companies landed at Mosjöen (a small collection of wooden houses around the fishing port) on 9 May the enemy were within 40km of their position. The French Alpine troops were already on the quayside and they left on the return sailing of the *Ulster Prince*. Fortunately the Germans had been temporarily halted at the crossing of the Vefsna river at Fellingfors by a small force of 400 determined, but exhausted, Norwegian troops. As he landed, Gubbins received confirmation of his earlier orders from Massy:

> Your first task is to prevent the Germans occupying Bodø, Mo and Mosjöen . . . You will take all possible steps by demolition and harrying

tactics to impede German advance along this route. Your companies operating in this area should not attempt prolonged frontal resistance but should endeavour to maintain themselves on German flanks and continue harrying tactics against their lines of communication.[73]

This was to prove a hopeless dream. No. 4 Independent Company established a defensive perimeter around Mosjöen to protect against an attack from the sea while No. 5 Independent Company was sent to reinforce the Norwegians at a point just 16km south of Mosjöen, where the exposed road was constricted between the Bjørnaa river and steep hillsides. Here, a platoon under the experienced Captain Prendergast of the Indian Army crossed a spur in waist-deep snow and, maintaining their ambush position in freezing conditions overnight, on the morning of 10 May ambushed a patrol of German cyclists leading the advance, killing or wounding around fifty of the enemy, cutting them down in seconds and before they could fire more than two shots. Prendergast commented 'I had learned my art in a far country and brought it to perfection here.'[74] This rare success gave a flavour of what the Independent Companies might have achieved if circumstances had allowed but, hampered by a lack of skis, No. 5 Independent Company began to be outflanked and the men were obliged to retreat. Gubbins' first plan was to withdraw north towards Mo, covered by No. 1 Independent Company, but the route was passable only on skis and during the afternoon of 10 May came news that the Germans had landed at Hemnesberget, on the Ranfjorden west of Mo, and that No. 1 Independent Company and Norwegian forces were hotly engaged. Gubbins therefore decided to bypass Mo i Rana and escape by sea to Bodø while the better-equipped Norwegians continued to slow the German advance towards Mo i Rana as best they could. By early morning on the 11th, Mosjöen was in German hands but the two Independent Companies and a light anti-aircraft unit were able to escape by sea that evening from Sandnessjøen on the north shore of the Vefsed Fjord, on a Norwegian coastal vessel chartered by Gubbins for 5,000kr and escorted by HMS *Jackal*. Although the Bofors guns of the anti-aircraft unit were destroyed before evacuation, the force left their valuable food stores intact. The Independent Companies transferred to HMS *Cossack* at the mouth of the fjord and then sailed north to Bodø, arriving there on the morning of 12 May. Commander Napier of HMS *Jackal* later wrote of the action at Mosjöen:

I was deeply impressed with the personality and leadership of the Commanding Officer, and the quality of his officers and men. They had lost all their gear, were short of food and sleep, and had been hard at it fighting a delaying action against superior forces, unsupported in a strange country, and subjected to the complete German air superiority. They were of a very fine type, and their cheerfulness and enthusiasm beyond praise.[75]

When they arrived at Bodø, the troops of No. 4 Independent Company established themselves at Straumen Island (opposite Bodø) whilst No. 5 Independent Company moved to Fauske to protect the northern end of the ferry crossing. They were joined in the early hours of 14 May by No. 2 Independent Company under Major Hugh Stockwell and the HQ Administrative Group. The lack of coastal support was a major handicap but plans had been made to send a flotilla of trawlers and drifters from Scotland as the 'Gubbins flotilla', under New Zealand submariner Lieutenant Commander William R. Fell.[76] Fell brought his flotilla to Harstad but the trawlers were declared unsuitable and were replaced by four or five local fishing boats ('puffers'), armed with Lewis guns (Plate 26). They came down to Bodø on the evening of 13 May, slipping singly into the harbour to avoid attention from the air. The 'Gubbins flotilla' was then assisted by the *Scissorforce* Intelligence officers Andrew Croft and Quintin Riley as it protected the sea flank of Bodø and ferried supplies to the southern outposts, 'landing our stores in different fjords, all of which reached up into the mountains of the mainland like the fingers of a score of hands'.[77] It was on their second supply trip that Fell met Gubbins, having walked 6 or 8km across rough ground from the moored 'puffer'. Commander Fell described Gubbins as 'the most unconventional General I'd ever seen, dressed in a khaki shirt, with sleeves cut off at the shoulder, a pair of slacks and enormous army boots'.[78] As well as ferrying supplies, Fell, Riley and Croft organized two sabotage raids, although only one was successful and it is not clear what they were actually attacking. Fell described how Croft brought six 'thugs' on board, with haversacks full of demolition charges. He took them through a maze of small islands and then up another fjord to the chosen landing site. They arrived around midnight and then Croft and his men jumped out and headed up a ravine.

> Quintin and I took part in various small raids of a somewhat hair-raising description. With Bill at the helm we would travel about 50 miles [80km] south to land in the small hours behind enemy lines, creep up on a sentry guarding a bridge, dig, position and tamp our explosives, and creep back to watch the resulting explosion from a safe distance, hoping to God that Bill would reappear and take us off.[79]

Croft told Fell 'that was the best fun I've ever had'. His team had found the gully crossed by the bridge that had been repaired after being blown up the week before. They set a half hour fuze and 'it went up beautifully, the timbers flying up in sparks and flame then down our valley nearly to where we were lying!'[80] Fell picked him up the next night. The next raid was 16km further south and took place a week later but they were spotted and forced to retreat. After that they reverted to transporting stores.

With the original plan of acting as guerrillas in tatters, *Scissorforce* was now placed under the command of 24th (Guards) Brigade and Brigadier William Fraser, as part of a conventional strategy to hold off the enemy long enough for the airfield at Bodø to be completed. As reinforcements, on 15 May NWEF sent an urgent request to the War Office that the remaining Independent Companies should be sent immediately to Norway, even if they had to complete their training at Harstad.[81] The German invasion of the Low Countries dramatically changed the landscape of the war and No. 9 Independent Company was already sailing down the Clyde when the deployment was cancelled.[82] Gubbins was well aware of how poorly they were equipped for their new defensive role as light infantry:

> Independent Companies are not equipped for defensive role. They have nothing but rifles and brens and cannot really hold a position against better equipped troops. They are meant for offensive guerrilla action only, i.e. cut and run. I would welcome a chance to use them for this ... Independent Companies have no D5 telephones on cable, and the Marconi W/T sets are useless – this is the experience of every Company. In this defensive role telephones are essential.[83]

The Independent Companies became involved in a series of fighting withdrawals from Mo i Rana to Bodø (Fig. 8), rather than the short sharp raids that Massy and Gubbins had envisaged and the campaign would simultaneously make and blight Gubbins' reputation. Mo i Rana controlled the 229km-long mountain road running along the narrow Saltdal mountain valley up to Bodø and also the most northerly road into Sweden. No. 1 Independent Company had arrived at Mo i Rana on 4 May as its lonely defender but on 9 May General Mackesy (then commanding land forces at Narvik) ordered Fraser to strengthen its defences with the HQ and two battalions of 24th (Guards) Brigade.[84] The plans for reinforcement were disrupted on 10 May by a daring German attack on Hemnesberget, a ferry crossing 25km south-west of Mo on the Ranfjord. Leapfrogging their main advance, the Germans commandeered a Norwegian coaster, *Nord-Norge*, at Trondheimsfjord, and embarked 300 infantry and two mountain guns. Still flying the Norwegian flag, they sailed up the Ranfjord. The Royal Navy had been tracking the *Nord-Norge* but with the inadequate communications which characterized the campaign, were unable to contact the forces at Mo to warn them of its approach. Shortly before 7.00pm, *Nord-Norge* approached the wooden pier at Hemnesberget, defended only by a platoon from No. 1 Independent Company and about 120 Norwegians. The Allies opened fire as the steamer approached but their small arms could not compete against the 20mm cannon

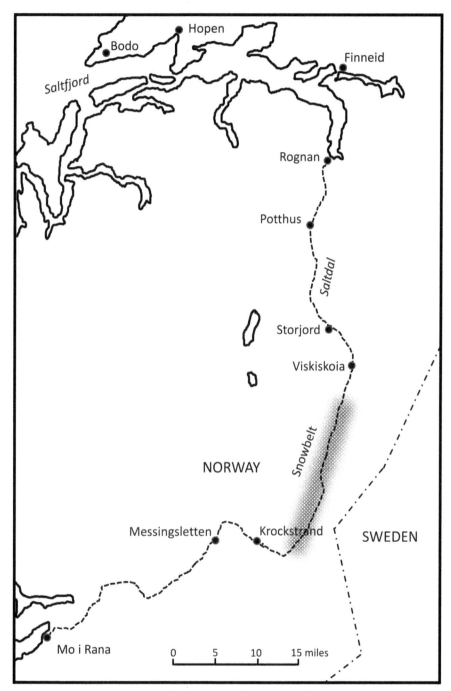

Figure 8. Map showing the line of retreat from Mo i Rana to Bodo, Norway, in May 1940.

and machine guns on board the steamer and they were beaten back from the wharf. The Germans established a bridgehead, whereupon HE59 seaplanes were able to reinforce the landing with more troops, mortars and machine guns. At 10.30pm HMS *Calcutta* and *Zulu* managed to sink the *Nord-Norge* at the wharfside but counter-attacks the next day by the rest of No. 1 Independent Company and Norwegian troops in fierce street fighting failed to dislodge the enemy. This base could now serve as a jumping-off point for any flanking attack on Mo i Rana, supporting a main assault from the south, and risked making Mo untenable.[85] The Germans began to expand across the peninsula and in response, on the night of 11 May, Fraser dispatched three companies of the 1st Battalion, Scots Guards under their CO, Lieutenant Colonel Thomas Trappes-Lomax, supported by a troop of four 25-pounder field guns and a troop of four Bofors anti-aircraft guns as the intended advance party of the whole of 24th (Guards) Brigade. No. 1 Independent Company became a supernumerary company of the Scots Guards. Mackesy signalled the War Office in an air of confidence:

> Time has come cease constant withdrawals and check enemy advance northwards. Essential prevent enemy using aerodrome vicinity Mo and to block road from Mo to Sweden. Am therefore taking all necessary steps achieve this object. Force sent tonight [11 May] will be followed by HQ 24 Guards Brigade, 1st Battalion Irish Guards and such other troops as I may consider necessary.[86]

The Scots Guards arrived at 4.00am on 12 May after having suffered repeated bombing along the route. But the strategy of making this the brigade HQ broke down almost immediately. Major May, CO of No. 1 Independent Company, sent a message to Gubbins at 12 noon advising that no further reinforcements should be sent because of the risk of loss through bombing and reported that unopposed German reconnaissance aircraft were now flying along the Saltdal Valley towards Bodø.[87] Despite having only arrived at Bodø that morning, Gubbins immediately drove south to Mo i Rana to see the situation for himself but a major change was occurring in the higher command.[88] On 13 May Auchinleck relieved Mackesy as the new GOC Anglo-French Forces in North Norway but he had no experience of Norway or of mountain warfare and, from his HQ at Harstad, was obliged to rely on second-hand situation reports. He accepted that Mo, lacking any air cover, was too exposed to resupply by sea and, although Fraser had warned that Mo could not be held by its current garrison, ordered that the Irish Guards and 24th (Guards) Brigade HQ should now be sent to Bodø which, protecting the southern approaches to Narvik, was to be held 'permanently' while Mo was to be held for only 'as long as he [Trappes-Lomax] could'.[89] Auchinleck had persistent difficulty in accepting the precarious nature of the Mo garrison and, unable to shake his belief in the inherent superiority of the British Army, pinned his hopes on 'when they [the Germans] come up against really determined opposition they will sit back and think on it'.[90] He had not seen the well-equipped German 2nd Mountain Division in action. Fraser, who had only just returned to duty from wounds received at Narvik, sailed on 14 May to give the bad news to Trappes-Lomax that he should not expect further reinforcements and while there reported by telephone to Auchinleck on the parlous state of the defences. The plans were pushed further into disarray later that day when MV *Chobry*, carrying the 1st Battalion Irish Guards, the three tanks of the 3rd Kings Own Hussars, 24th (Guards) Brigade HQ and other units to Bodø, was attacked just before midnight by a Heinkel III, 48km from Bodø. The CO of the Irish Guards, Lieutenant Colonel Walter Faulkner, his second in command and all the company commanders were killed or wounded, along with 100 of their men. The 700 survivors of the battalion had to return to Harstad to re-equip but the tanks were lost. A few hours later, while travelling back to Bodø from Mo i Rana, Fraser's ship (HMS *Somali*) was so badly damaged in an air attack by Stukas that it had to immediately return to Scapa Flow for emergency repairs, taking Fraser with it. The 24th (Guards) Brigade had lost its CO (at least temporarily) and one-third of its strength in the space of 24 hours.

As the senior surviving battalion commander, Trappes-Lomax might have expected to take temporary command of the Brigade until Fraser's return (having done so earlier when Fraser was wounded at Narvik), but he was isolated from the rest of the command. Trappes-Lomax was also outranked by Gubbins, who was an acting colonel, and on 15 May Auchinleck reported to Dill that 'I have put Gubbins in command at Bodø.' Taking advantage of Gubbins' eagerness to impress in his first field command, on the following day Auchinleck ignored the earlier first-hand opinion of Fraser and May and ordered Gubbins: 'I wish the detachment at Mo to hold on to its position, and not withdraw.'[91] Despite the disaster on the MV *Chobry*, Auchinleck was still expecting the imminent move of the 2nd Battalion, South Wales Borderers and the HQ staff of 24th (Guards) Brigade to reinforce Bodø and promised to do whatever he could to provide further men. Yet the fate of Gubbins' new command was going from bad to worse.

On 14 May No. 1 Independent Company and a Norwegian force had been obliged, under fierce attack, to abandon the outer defence of Mo at Finneid and had fallen back 16km to the main outer defence line of the Scots Guards at Stein, 4.8km west of Mo i Rana. In the afternoon of 17 May five battalions of German mountain troops with three troops of artillery and supported by Stuka dive-bombers began their attack on the heavily outnumbered Allied force. The Germans moved up the coastal road and spread out onto the hills to the east, taking full advantage of their mountain warfare experience and ski troops, and the crucial absence of Allied air cover. Although forcing heavy losses on the Germans, the defenders were repeatedly outflanked on the hill-sides and were forced to retreat, the 25-pounder guns losing their communi-cations equipment in the process (meaning they could only manage direct fire with open sights thereafter), while German ski troops attacked the Scots Guards' transport near Mo i Rana and threatened to cut off Trappes-Lomax's line of retreat. There were also rumours of German parachute landings further to the north, raising fears that they would blow up the bridges on the single road leading back to Bodø. More bad news came on the evening of 17 May when the cruiser HMS *Effingham* struck a rock about 20km from Bodø; it was carrying the second attempt to bring the Brigade HQ to Bodø along with the 2nd Battalion, the South Wales Borderers, French Chasseurs, ten Bren Carriers, two field ambulances and 130 tons of stores. The ship had to be scuttled but fortunately the troops were transferred to the destroyer escorts and returned to Harstad to be re-equipped. The only consolation was that No. 2 Independent Company managed to salvage four Bren Carriers from the wreck. The delays in making good these reinforcements further hampered the chances of holding on to Mo.[92]

During the night of 17/18 May Gubbins again made the long drive down to Trappes-Lomax's HQ in his temporary role of brigade commander, arriving at 5.30am with a repeat of the order from Auchinleck that Mo i Rana was to be firmly held to halt the German advance. It was a difficult meeting, with Trappes-Lomax no doubt smarting over being passed over and still expecting Fraser to return to duty, while Gubbins was keen to establish a good reputa-tion with Auchinleck. Trappes-Lomax maintained the earlier consensus that the position was untenable without further reinforcements and Gubbins was obliged to agree, but as there seemed to be no immediate threat of attack he at first suggested holding the town until an evacuation down the Ranenfjord and by sea could be arranged. Trappes-Lomax believed this was impractical in light of German air superiority and the expanding German base at Hemnes-berget, and signalled a poor military judgement by Gubbins.[93] In return, Gubbins believed the Scots Guards 'do not understand this type of fighting' – although in truth this was a failing shared by the entire British leadership.[94] Gubbins' suggestion would have left the road to Bodø open to the enemy but may have reflected a fear that the road was likely to be cut by parachute troops or by bombing the bridges, losing the whole force at Mo.[95] Trappes-Lomax's alternative was for a rapid but well organized withdrawal north along the Saltdal valley until it could reach a secure position to defend Bodø. Gubbins reluctantly agreed to Trappes-Lomax's strategy of a fighting retreat, inform-ing Auchinleck of this by telephone before returning to Bodø. The *Scissorforce* War Diary states: 'After reviewing the situation he [Gubbins] decided that Mo could not be held much longer without risk of disaster and gave the order to withdraw, obtaining authority by phone from GOC at Harstad.'[96] Auchinleck was clearly mystified by the inability of the British forces to hold their ground and, although he accepted Gubbins' assessment, he moaned 'Why our soldiers cannot be as mobile as the Germans I don't know, but they aren't apparently.'[97] He did not appreciate that the British were not only outnumbered but lacked the training, equipment (particularly skis) and experience of the German mountain troops and their officers. Although later stating that Trappes-Lomax withdrew 'precipitately', abandoning most of the stores and equipment, Gubbins was with Trappes-Lomax when the orders were issued and, according to the Brigade Chief of Staff, there had been general agreement over the plan.[98] Gubbins himself had been guilty of leaving his own stores intact at Mosjöen. Gubbins' energy was not in doubt and he returned almost immediately from Bodø during the night of 18 May, in time to see the start of the withdrawal. One problem was that the inadequate w/t communications meant that No. 1 Independent Company and a company of Scots Guards did not receive the order to withdraw and were lucky to be able to rejoin the main force.

The demolition of two bridges over the River Rana (Plate 27) bought time for Trappes-Lomax to rapidly move his force 51km to the north to a defensive position at Messingsletten Bridge, which had been secured by the arrival of the Scots Guards company by road from Hopen (Fig. 8). This, and his own repeated journeys back and forth between Mo and Bodø, made Gubbins doubt Trappes-Lomax's concern over the dangers of crossing the 'snow belt' but he failed to take into account the dangers of moving a whole battalion along a single track narrowed by snow drifts and then being left exposed on the plateau, whilst under enemy fire and with no air cover. The Scots Guards reinforcements were offset by the detaching of No. 1 Independent Company to secure the ferry crossing at Rognan, on the south side of Skjerstad Fjord (which would be crucial for enabling the final retreat to Bodø). Desperate to gain as much time as possible for Bodø to be put into a good state of defence, Auchinleck ordered Trappes-Lomax 'You have now reached a good position for defence. Essential to stand and fight.'[99] Indeed, Auchinleck quite unrealistically wanted the heavily outnumbered Trappes-Lomax to try to recapture Mo i Rana. Gubbins had told Auchinleck's Chief of Staff, Colonel Arthur Dowler, on 19 May in Bodø that he was happy with Trappes-Lomax's performance – but upon learning that Auchinleck had ordered Trappes-Lomax to make a stand, Gubbins backtracked and said 'he [Gubbins] did not altogether agree with his [Trappes-Lomax] plan'.[100] At midnight on 19 May Auchinleck authorized Gubbins to 'remove any commander of any rank whom you think is not resolute or willing to fight'.[101] It was only while Gubbins was still *en route*, at 6.00am on 20 May, that Trappes-Lomax received the signal from Auchinleck to make a stand and he immediately replied that the best way to protect the Scots Guards' ability to defend Bodø would be to get across the exposed 'snow belt' as soon as possible, onto ground where there was more cover and his force would be less easily outflanked. Gubbins was incensed that Trappes-Lomax had responded without consulting him first but after assessing the situation on the ground and another telephone conversation with Auchinleck, Gubbins issued orders that allowed Trappes-Lomax to act as he saw fit to ensure the survival of his battalion:

(a) You are to maintain contact with the enemy and impede his advance by every means in your power.

(b) You will only withdraw from any position you hold if in your opinion there is serious danger to the safety of your force. You must bear in mind that your object is to delay him all you can, and that can only be done by hitting him hard; this I wish you to do.[102]

No. 3 Independent Company had come up between Storjord and Rognan to guard against any German parachute landings on the British line of retreat but there remained a serious risk of the Germans bombing the bridges at Storjord and Potthus. By midnight on 20 May three defensive lines had been created to allow an ordered withdrawal through the snow belt. But on 21 May Gubbins issued fresh orders, stressing that there was to be no further retreat without authorization:

Just heard you are continuing retreat. If so this is against my orders as cannot believe you [are] seriously endangered already in view no contact with enemy yesterday you must hold enemy as far south as possible. This is my final order.[103]

Yet Gubbins admitted on the same day that the position of the Scots Guards was precarious, with the risk that parachute landings would cut off their line of retreat. Effectively, the Scots Guards were to be sacrificed in order to buy time to build a line of defence at Storjord, but even this strategy relied on the timely reinforcement of not only the two other battalions of 24th (Guards) Brigade but the unlikely provision of additional air and naval support.[104] Making the situation worse, Trappes-Lomax was ordered to return his motor buses to Bodø so they could bring up reinforcements to Storjord, slowing his retreat through the snow belt and increasing thereby the chances of a massacre. Based on his earlier order to preserve the battalion, Trappes-Lomax therefore took the instruction to hold the enemy 'as far south as possible' to be a matter of judgement. Histories have tended to take the side of Auchinleck and have glossed over the wavering of Gubbins, but the fighting retreat of Trappes-Lomax, from one prepared defensive position to another, timing his retreat across the snowfield by night in the pre-positioned lorries and motor buses (which he had failed to release to Gubbins) was a minor triumph of the Norwegian campaign. On the evening of 21 May the Germans first attacked Trappes-Lomax in earnest at Messingsletten, forcing a retreat to Krokstranda, where the second line of defence was centred on another demolished bridge across the river (Fig. 8). A combination of enfilading fire from the German mountain troops who dominated the higher ground and attacks from the air again forced a withdrawal, although it took the Germans a day to repair the bridge and follow the retreating British, who were covered by three of the Bren Carriers rescued from HMS *Effingham* and now manned by a detachment from No. 2 Independent Company sent down from Bodø. The delay in the German pursuit crucially allowed the British to cross the snow belt during the night of 22 May and the troops then headed for the third prepared line of defence at Viskiskoia, guarded by No. 3 Independent Company.

While the battle along the Saltdal valley was progressing, between 20 and 26 May the South Wales Borderers, Irish Guards and 24th (Guards) Brigade staff finally reached Bodø. There was not time to reinforce Trappes-Lomax directly, but their continued resistance would allow Gubbins to establish a new line of defence further to the north, through which the exhausted Scots Guards could then pass. Dowler sent back a glowing report on Gubbins to Auchinleck, saying the operations around Bodø could not be in better hands.[105] In turn, Gubbins told Dowler that he was satisfied with his officers and did not require any changes but his attitude soon changed under pressure from Auchinleck and Dowler, both unable to comprehend Trappes-Lomax's withdrawal. Dowler concluded on 22 May that the Scots Guards

> does not understand, nor is it trained, for fighting in the type of country in which it now finds itself. The impression I get is that it fails to secure its flanks by occupying the high ground on either side of the valley. As this is a matter of common sense, one is forced to the conclusion that leadership has as much to answer for as lack of training.[106]

This assessment again woefully failed to appreciate the total air superiority of the Germans and the lack of mountain warfare training or equipment of the British forces. Gubbins' reward was soon in coming. When Fraser returned to Harstad on 23 May he was declared unfit for service because of his earlier wound and at 1.00am on 23 May Gubbins was formally appointed CO of the newly designated *Bodøforce*, comprising 24th (Guards) Brigade, the Independent Companies and attendant support units.[107] On that afternoon, Gubbins drove south again to the Scots Guards and, following the clear wishes of Dowler and Auchinleck, relieved Trappes-Lomax of his command. Trappes-Lomax did not deny that he had acted contrary to that part of his orders instructing him not to withdraw but equally pointed to the instruction that allowed him to act in the interests of preserving his battalion.[108] Trappes-Lomax was poorly treated both by Auchinleck, who was ignorant of the local landscape, and by the ambitious Gubbins, who was too ready to win favour with his new superior officer against the opinion of his officers on the ground and his own observations.

With the utmost irony, after dismissing Trappes-Lomax to Harstad, Gubbins reconnoitred the situation for himself and, realizing how exhausted were the Scots Guards, accepted that his order to hold the defences at Viskiskoia until 27 May (giving time for the South Wales Borderers to complete the defences of Bodø) was impractical. Gubbins' first order to the new CO of the Scots Guards (Major Graham) was therefore to order a continuation of the withdrawal towards Storjord! The Germans attacked the crossing at Viskiskoia on the afternoon of 24 May, supported by Stuka dive-bombers. The Scots Guards occupied the centre of the position and the site of the demolished bridge, while No. 3 Independent Company and Norwegian ski troops occupied the high ground on the far side of the valley to prevent a flanking movement. By 4.00pm No. 3 Independent Company had been driven back and at 6.00pm Gubbins ordered Graham to further withdraw behind a new blocking position that had been established 22km to the north at the bridging point of Potthus (Fig. 8). Here *Stockforce* had been assembled from the reinforcements at Bodø, under the CO of No. 2 Independent Company, Major Hugh Stockwell.[109] Stockwell was later described as being excitable and by turns courteous and brutal, refined and coarse, headstrong in some circumstances, hesitant and indecisive in others, but 'One only of his qualities remains constant: his courage under fire.'[110] *Stockforce* comprised the 1st Battalion, Irish Guards, No.2 Independent Company, Norwegian troops including a heavy machine-gun company and two mortars, plus the troop of 25-pounder guns from Trappes-Lomax's *Park* force. No. 3 Independent Company also joined *Stockforce* after its withdrawal from Viskiskoia along with No. 4 Independent Company from Bodø. *Stockforce* had been brought down from Bodø by steamers on the Saltdalfjord to Rognan and then had to reach Potthus by route march and a fleet of lorries and buses. Potthus was just 16km south of Rognan and would have to be held until Gubbins could establish a new defence for Bodø at Finneid on the north side of Skjerstad Fjord. Here a chain of lakes and an arm of the Svartisen Glacier provided the last natural line of defence before Bodø, 68km to the west. No. 1 Independent Company guarded the ferry crossing at Rognan and held reserves of rations and ammunition.

The defences at Potthus were based around the girder bridge (Plate 28) that carried the road across the river, 100m wide at this point and swollen with glacial meltwater, and a smaller bridge over a tributary flowing into the Saltdal a few hundred metres downstream. Cover was provided by the wooded hill-sides. *Stockforce* began to occupy its positions in the evening of 23 May. The Irish Guards held the centre in front and behind the bridge where there was enough time overnight and during the next day to dig trenches and gun emplacements, and for No. 2 Independent Company and Norwegian troops holding the flanks to clear fields of fire through the woodland. No. 3 Independent Company formed part of the reserve, with the Bren Carriers acquired by No. 2 Independent Company. The exhausted Scots Guards passed through the line at 11.00pm on 24 May and the girder bridge was blown up behind them. The subsequent battle at Potthus lasted for 36 hours, often at close quarters on the flanks where wooded hillsides allowed the enemy to approach to within 50 metres before being spotted. For most of the men, including Stockwell, this was their first time in battle.[111] The Germans attacked on the morning of 25 May with 4,500 men of the 2nd Mountain and 181st Divisions and in the afternoon managed to break through to the bridge, forcing the Irish Guards on the east side to cross the river whilst under fire, using rifle slings as a makeshift rope, while the men of No. 2 Independent Company further on the flank had to make their way more than a kilometre down a tributary before they could cross safely to escape back to the Allied positions. Stockwell was obliged to commit his final reserves and the Germans were thrown back by a fierce counter-attack during the night and early morning but the danger of being outflanked remained.

Even as they fought this desperate battle, the overall strategic plan for Norway had changed. On 23 May the Cabinet ordered that North Norway be abandoned once Narvik was recaptured and its port facilities destroyed, the attack being planned for 27–28 May. The British consequently began to prepare for a general withdrawal and in the early hours of 26 May Gubbins was ordered to prepare an evacuation of his forces from Bodø. Later that morning, with a risk of *Stockforce* being cut off, he authorized a withdrawal to Rognan from where troops could be transported across the fjord to Finneid and then by road to Bodø. Heavy German fire and air attacks meant that Stockwell was not able to begin to extricate his men from their positions until 7.00pm. No. 2 Independent Company provided covering fire for the Irish Guards to withdraw from the bridge but it was only when two Gloster Gladiators arrived to give the Germans a rare taste of strafing in the campaign that the rearguard of the Irish Guards was able to break contact and withdraw without worse casualties. By the early hours of 27 May the Germans were advancing on both sides of the river but fortunately the Norwegians were able to cover the British retreat. There then followed a bitter fighting retreat for 16km along the west side of the Saltdal valley, the German mountain troops working their way around the flanks and ambushing the retreating troops wherever they could. From Rognan they were evacuated the 10km across the fjord to Finneid by a relay of a large car ferry and ten smaller armed 'puffers' of the expanded 'Gubbins flotilla'. The timed demolition charges on the jetty exploded when the last ferry was only 50 metres away, showering the troops with burning debris, whilst the first of the arriving German troops began to fire on the boats. A report by Lieutenant Commander Fell of the 'puffer' fleet gave a flavour of the action:

> By 02:00, most of the transport lorries had been destroyed, Bofors guns embarked in the puffers ... Only my puffer, a loaded ferry and a small demolition party remained. Sniping was beginning. At a given signal fuses of three large demolitions were fired and my puffer moved off. The ferry failed to start. A sapper managed to cut the fuse to the ferry landing stage, thus saving the crowded ferry. The other demolitions took place covering my puffer and the ferry with debris. The ferry caught fire but had by now drifted about 20 metres from its pier and grounded. With some difficulty we got alongside and started to tow [it] clear. Observed three men wading out from shore towards us. Midshipman Fletcher and a subaltern volunteered to man the dinghy and rescued all three. Proceeded to Finneid and disembarked all troops and vehicles.[112]

The intention had been to establish a defence at Finneid (Fig. 8), through which *Stockforce* could retreat, with the South Wales Borderers forming the last line of defence in Bodø itself. But, to the shock of the Norwegians, the British withdrew almost immediately from Finneid, before any immediate German threat to the position, and were successfully evacuated by destroyers on the nights of 29–31 May. Thankfully low cloud during the evacuation prevented reconnaissance by the Luftwaffe. Nos 2, 3 and 4 Independent Companies were evacuated on the first night on HMS *Vindictive* and were then transferred to the *Royal Scotsman* which immediately left for Scapa Flow. The last British soldiers to evacuate were Croft and Riley, whom Gubbins had sent on several missions to quietly drain civilian petrol filling stations in the surrounding countryside as the plans for the evacuation proceeded. They then sailed in Fell's puffer to open the valves on the main petrol and diesel depots on two islands on the northern outskirts of the town, draining the fuel into the sea, before escaping to Harstad.[113] Here, the exhausted Croft, Riley and Fell ferried troops from the puffers to the naval vessels for the final evacuation on 8 June.[114]

The Independent Companies returned to Scotland on 10 June, having suffered losses of around 400 men, killed, wounded or missing. Only now could they undertake the training that had originally been anticipated at the new training centre at Lochailort. Nos 1 and 4 Independent Companies were sent to help defend Scapa Flow while Nos 6, 7, 8 and 9 were sent under Stockwell to guard the Land's End zone, based in Carbiss Bay. From there,

Nos 6 and 9 were sent to the Scilly Isles to protect the forward radar stations. Stockwell organized training in demolition and sabotage and was reunited with William Fell and Quintin Riley, who were now in Combined Operations, running the small boat raiding training centres on the Scillies and at Newlyn. On 17 October Nos 1, 2, 3, 4, 5, 8 and 9 Independent Companies were combined to form No. 1 Special Service Battalion, later No. 1 Commando. Nos 6 and 7 Independent Companies combined with the new Nos 9 and 11 Commandos to form No. 2 Special Services Battalion. On 30 October Stockwell was posted to command the Lochailort Training School, now under the control of the Director of Combined Operations. He later commanded the 82nd (West African) Division and after the war became deputy Supreme Allied Commander of NATO.

Raiding Forces

Buoyed up by the optimism surrounding the imminent deployment of the Independent Companies, the first meeting of the Inter Services Project Board (ISPB) was held on 3 May, under the chairmanship of Jo Holland, to discuss the request of General Massy and the Chiefs of Staff Committee to consider the feasibility of coastal raids against German-occupied Norway.[115] The ISPB report recommended operations to disrupt communications and force the enemy to increase coastal patrols, which might then be attacked by the Royal Navy. The philosophy was clearly that of MI(R), with operations to be undertaken by uniformed troops landing from small motor boats released from destroyers lying offshore; it relied on a considerable level of inter-service planning which would eventually form the basis of commando operations.[116] At the same time Section D wasted no time in putting its own spin on the proposal and organized a raid on the Voss area, using civilian agents landed from a fishing boat, operating as civilian 'Norwegians freeing Norway' – the approach later developed by SOE. The practical results were limited, although a power station was damaged, arms caches were secreted and contact was made with resistance groups.[117]

MI(R)'s initiative in creating the Independent Companies was diminished by their premature deployment but they had set in motion a significant train of thought. Dudley Clark is said to have sketched out the idea for the commandos on 30 May before suggesting it to the CIGS on 5 June and his autobiography pays scant attention to the obvious precedent of the Independent Companies. Around the same time Churchill demanded raids of between 1,000 and 10,000 troops who could develop a 'reign of terror' in ceaseless 'butcher and bolt' raids against the German-held coastline. Holland was concerned over a lack of clear strategy in the new enthusiasm for raiding and the encouragement of subversion in enemy-held territory. Holland complained that the vision by the General Staff of coastal raiding parties risked making them as ineffective as the 'innumerable and somewhat futile' First World War trench raids, and a waste of the specialist troops involved. In a burst of his famous temper he commented 'Unless someone sees the much greater possibilities in this scheme, it is likely to be as pathetically ineffective as most of the ideas of the General Staff.'[118] Brigadier Wyndham incorporated Holland's view in the August 1940 review of MI(R), maintaining that such operations were of little use unless directed at 'worthy objectives and with a definite purpose of sufficient importance to justify the expenditure of blood and treasure involved. The policy of raiding for the sake of raiding left an evil memory from the last war.'[119] Holland feared that, whilst giving the politically useful appearance of taking action, raids would only cause petty inconvenience to the Germans whilst prematurely revealing the methodology before it was needed for strategic operations. This would form the basis of the long-running debate as to the strategic value of acts of resistance in occupied territories.

The Joint Chiefs of Staff discussed Dudley Clarke's proposal for the commandos on 6 June and, just three days later, volunteers were sought for a force of initially 40 officers and 1,000 men, building up to a force of around 5,000 men. They would be organized in a new section of the Directorate of Military Operations (MO9) which soon became Combined Operations. MI(R)'s role thereafter would be limited to suggesting targets.[120] At last, Holland's campaign to have irregular warfare organized as part of the mainstream of military operations rather than various ad hoc initiatives had been achieved. In October 1940 Joan Bright joined MO9 and commented: 'No longer Independent Companies under Intelligence, but Commandos under Military Operations, I said to myself and thought of Colonel Holland.'[121] In the Middle East Colonel Adrian Simpson was head of MI(R) Middle East aka G(R). His proposal to form a distinct Middle East Commando was approved on 29 June and it was formed under MI(R)'s Major George Young (*see below*, p. 154). As a sop to Churchill's impatience, a raid by the new Commandos was quickly undertaken and of necessity had to use the existing Independent Companies as their basis. Clarke went to the Independent Companies camp at Glasgow and asked for 100 volunteers who on 14 June became No. 11 Independent Company under Ronnie Todd. They moved to Hampshire and made ready for *Operation Collar*, a reconnaissance raid involving 115 men; they were landed by eight civilian motor boats on the coast south of Boulogne on 24 June but failed to gather any intelligence or capture prisoners. *Operation Collar* was followed by a disastrous raid on Guernsey on 15/16 July (*Operation Ambassador*). The results of the early Commandos were as limited as those of the Independent Companies until the same issues of recruitment, training and supply could be resolved.

The premature deployment of the Independent Companies contributed greatly to Holland's frustration over the organization of irregular warfare. Brigadier Wyndham noted that the calculated approach to irregular warfare that Holland had promoted in MI(R) led to 'a tendency (largely unjust in my view) to disparage our present efforts because they have not yet produced results'.[122] With MI(R) being criticized for being too careful in its planning and Section D facing equal criticism for being too rash, Wyndham in his review of MI(R) not surprisingly complained of a lack of clear policy from the War Office and government to reconcile itself to this form of warfare. As a consequence, 'the pursuit of para-military activities has, unfortunately, been launched prior to the adoption of a settled long-term policy'.[123] Written in August 1940, this was a dig at Churchill's exhortation to 'Set Europe Ablaze', the creation of SOE and the inflexibility of the War Office which failed to integrate the use of commando operations into its existing structures.[124]

Chapter Nine

Western Europe and the Americas

The remit of MI(R) precluded work in Germany but in January 1940 MI(R) was asked to investigate a suggestion from General Koeltz of the French General Staff to sabotage German rolling stock by whatever means. One suggestion was to pay agents to put delayed-action bombs on German rolling stock passing through Hungary and the Balkans. MI(R) responded in typical fashion by producing a desktop study of German rail and water transport on 26 February 1940 but the conclusion was that the plan was too dangerous.[1] Ironically, Section D's agents were already successfully sabotaging German railway stock passing through Austria, Yugoslavia and Romania.[2] Any work against Italy, its occupied territories or on the Iberian peninsula was blocked by diplomatic nervousness before Italy entered the war.

France and the Low Countries

In the complacent attitude of the time, little attention was given in 1939 to the possibility of the fall of Western Europe and there were minimal attempts to coordinate MI(R) with continental military intelligence services. France was Britain's major ally and GS(R) Report No. 8 and the MI(R) progress reports were passed to the French General Staff. The conclusion of the August 1939 progress report would have made uninspiring reading, admitting 'on the present scale, the work is little more than busy-bodying'. The French were particularly sensitive to any suggestion of the British attempting to tell them how to run their intelligence service and unfortunately much of the chauvinistic ethos of MI(R) in offering advice to foreign general staffs fitted into that mould. Section D had quietly established an office in Paris on the outbreak of war and began to work at a practical level in concert with their French equivalent, 5ième Bureau (on the condition that they did not carry out operations within France itself), but in January 1940 Wilkinson doubted that the 5ième Bureau even knew of MI(R)'s existence.[3]

MI(R) was more prepared to risk the wrath of the intelligence services of the Low Countries and as early as 29 September 1939 Jo Holland took a paper to the JIC to recommend a plan for the demolition of key assets in Belgium and Holland in the event of an invasion. This (as in Romania) would be undertaken by specially trained Royal Engineer units.[4] Originally, three Royal Engineer field companies were to carry out demolition in any retreat but this was later refined to focus on the oil stocks in Rotterdam, Amsterdam and Antwerp. MI(R)'s main role was to provide maps and initial targeting but what became *Operation XD* was undertaken by units of the Royal Engineers and naval demolition parties, under the overall command of the Royal Navy. The Kent Fortress Company, RE, sailed for France on 10 May. The main landing party set fire to the oil tanks at Rotterdam using Boys anti-tank rifles, while another detachment of three officers and thirty other ranks landed at Ijmuiden and travelled to Amsterdam by train, where the oil tanks were blown up even as the men were under fire. Oil tanks at Antwerp were destroyed and, in addition, the unit also rescued 36 tons of gold.[5] In France, after a delay in getting authorization from the authorities, Second Lieutenant Mayler, attached to MI(R) with half a dozen British soldiers, set fire to 200,000 tons of oil at Gonfreville near Harfleur on 7 June using a Very pistol and improvised petrol bombs.[6] In all, 2.2 million tons of oil were destroyed in *Operation XD*.

Operation XD was a military operation, albeit conceived by MI(R), but in what was probably a concerted enterprise, officers of Section D and MI(R) were sent to European banking centres to negotiate the extraction of gold, industrial diamonds and securities. Taking advantage of their pre-war business and diplomatic contacts, Section D successfully sent Louis Franck to Brussels and Monty Chidson to Amsterdam (fictionalized in the 1959 film *Operation Amsterdam*). For MI(R), F.T. 'Tommy' Davies, described as flamboyant, volatile, ruthless and a whirlwind of energy, crossed to Ijmuiden on the morning of 14 May on HMS *Havock* for a mission whose 'destination, mission and plans' were unknown to the British naval commander. Nonetheless, he was provided with an official Royal Navy car and drove to Amsterdam where he tried to negotiate the destruction of several million pounds' worth of US bearer bonds in the care of the Bank of the Netherlands. In his report, a frustrated Davies was more pessimistic about the mission results than the account in the MI(R) War Diary, pointing out that all he had been able to do was make suggestions to the bank authorities. Surrender was clearly imminent and the president of the bank was reluctant to take action, concerned for the interests of the bank shareholders (which extended to refusing to transfer the bank's gold reserves to the government). When Davies left Amsterdam the Dutch were wiring up the bank vaults for demolition, although there is no record of the securities being destroyed before the Netherlands surrendered later that day. A disappointed Davies returned to Ijmuiden, surviving two encounters with patrols of German paratroopers who were trying to cut the Amsterdam–Ijmuiden road, and escaped in an MTB to rendezvous with HMS *Havock*, waiting anxiously offshore.[7] More successfully, Davies went over to Calais shortly before the Germans arrived and, thanks to his pre-war links to the company, removed several hundred thousand pounds' worth of platinum from Courtauld's factory.

Belatedly, on 23 May 1940, with the German invasion well under way, Jo Holland produced a briefing paper for the forthcoming 27 May ISPB meeting titled 'Organization of Civil Resistance in Belgium and France'. He considered that the military authorities in France and Belgium were now too preoccupied with the fighting to organize civil resistance and sabotage and therefore it would be necessary for the British, in conjunction with the civil authorities, to organize a committee for civil resistance in specific areas to recruit, instruct and organize volunteers to carry on resistance after occupation, with stores of sabotage material cached in preparation. In a typically bureaucratic conclusion, the only action proposed was to raise this with the Allied coordinating committee and for a representative of MI(R) to go to France to advise the French authorities as to the most suitable type of organization required, and to organize the import of sabotage materials.[8] This was exactly the sort of 'busy-bodying' that Holland had warned against before the outbreak of war and it was unlikely to appeal to the French. Unknown to Jo Holland, SIS had already quietly reactivated its First World War intelligence network in Belgium as 'Network Clarence' and Section D now took its typically more direct approach; Laurence Grand wrote to the Paris Section D office suggesting they and 5ième Bureau work together to create arms dumps and organize stay-behind parties.[9] They did what they could but it was already far too late; as the Dunkirk evacuation got under way, the 5ième Bureau encountered problems in recruiting stay-behind parties and the speed of the German advance overtook their plans for demolition of transport links, while the French government was still reluctant to sanction a sabotage programme of its infrastructure. A number of arms dumps were, nevertheless, established behind the current enemy lines in Belgium and in France with the 5ième Bureau locating sites for explosives dumps and recruiting the 'guardians', and Section D supplying the necessary explosives and devices and transporting them to the dumps. Also included were translated copies of Section D's *Home Hints* and MI(R)'s *Art of Guerrilla Warfare* pamphlets. Section D also worked with 2ième Bureau to provide last-minute explosives training for saboteurs in France and Belgium.[10]

Having failed to contribute in a practical sense to the last minute plans for resistance, MI(R) did despatch one mission that would set a precedent for the future insertion of agents into occupied Europe. Alan 'Cocky' Warren (Plate 7), a major in the Royal Marines, had joined MI(R) in May 1940 to fill the vacancy for a GSO2 left by Douglas Roberts' transfer to the Middle East. In what was probably a spur of the moment effort, Warren was sent on 2 June to try to contact and rescue wounded British troops stranded on the French coast after Dunkirk. Before leaving, he described being offered one of the first of MI9's collar-stud compasses and a map of France printed on a silk handkerchief.[11] MI(R) also offered an SIS miniature wireless transceiver that would fit into his waistband – but he declined. Such sets might not have actually existed (*see above*, p. 94). Warren, with two recently commissioned second lieutenants (Hodges and Sinclair) from Camberley OCTU left for a stretch of coast between Boulogne and Étaples on the 32ft minesweeper MV *Halcyon* to land in a dinghy with the intention of then ferrying rescued troops back to the minesweeper lying offshore. The party rowed ashore but discovered German troops camped at intervals along the beach. They remained for three days, with Hodges and Sinclair unsuccessfully searching neighbouring villages for any British troops in hiding, but the signal torches were not strong enough to make contact with the ship for the return voyage and after another three days, with their original dinghy discovered by the enemy, they were obliged to buy a rowing boat and spent 13 hours at sea before being rescued by the Dungeness Lightship.[12] No troops had been rescued, although one captain of the BEF did manage to reach the waiting minesweeper independently. The embarrassment added to the list of failures of MI(R)'s attempts at practical action and Churchill called the operation a 'silly fiasco'.[13] The mission did at least establish the potential of being able to land on the enemy coast and was quickly followed by missions by Section D and SIS. It also brought Warren to the attention of Sir Roger Keyes, the new head of Combined Operations, and Warren left MI(R) on 20 June 1940 to become GSO2 (Intelligence) to Keyes. One of his first tasks was to collect intelligence for the early commando raid on Guernsey; he later joined SOE and organized stay-behind parties in Malaya.

Britain

The Secret Intelligence Service (SIS) had been preparing the contingency of a deep-cover British resistance (Section VII) from early 1940 but the Chiefs of Staff meeting on 7 May remained confident in the belief that the Low Countries and France provided a secure buffer to invasion across the narrow Straits of Dover.[14] Such confidence was shattered when, on 20 May, the first Panzer units reached the English Channel. A pessimistic report to the War Cabinet on 25 May concluded 'should the enemy succeed in establishing a force, with its vehicles, firmly ashore – the army in the United Kingdom, which is very short of equipment, has not got the offensive power to drive it out'.[15] On the same day Jo Holland had Peter Fleming (recently returned from Norway) attached to Home Forces, tasked with investigating the use of the new Local Defence Volunteers (LDV), whose intended role was still ill-defined, in fighting as guerrillas behind enemy lines if Britain was invaded. This would re-establish one role of the First World War Volunteer Training Corps and satisfy the aspiration of the founder of the LDV (General Kirke) for them to act in the spirit of the Boer Commando. This was, however, strenuously resisted by other sections of the War Office.[16] On 26 May the evacuation of the British Expeditionary Force began from Dunkirk but the War Office still considered any move to create a resistance which assumed an at least temporary occupation of parts of Britain to be defeatist. Instead its priority was to use irregular warfare to support an active military campaign, in line with the strategy long championed by Holland. The meeting of the new Inter-Services Project Board held on 27 May under Holland's chairmanship had been intended to focus on the need for irregular warfare in France and Belgium but was now obliged to consider contingency plans for Britain following any invasion, raising again the respective roles of Section D and MI(R). Consequently, John Dolphin, who had been developing the idea of the Section D Home Defence Scheme, and MI(R)'s Peter Fleming attended an expanded meeting.[17] An analysis of previous German offensives particularly identified the need to disrupt lines of supply and a settled consolidation of the enemy forces:

> When a part of the country had been overrun, and at a time when the strain on a loose line of communication must have been great, and the strain on operating personnel in advanced elements must have been greater, little was done either to deny the enemy essential supplies, or to ensure that the invader had no rest.[18]

Section D had pre-empted the debate and, alongside its efforts in France, the civilian sabotage and intelligence Home Defence Scheme (HDS) was said to be 'already partially organized' and contact made with regional army commanders and the civil regional commissioners.[19] Under Viscount Bearsted, the HDS would provide a short-term civilian guerrilla force in line with the layered approach to resistance advocated by SIS. An immediate guerrilla campaign would support regular forces but it was assumed that this would not long survive and it was critical that there be no contact with the true resistance organization, known only as Section VII, that would take no part in the immediate anti-invasion campaign in order to protect its long-term survival. Holland did, at least, manage to get the meeting to agree that, while Section D should organize a specialized sabotage programme, guerrilla activities in England acting in concert with regular forces should be controlled *on a military basis*:

> The regular defences require supplementing with guerrilla-type troops who will allow themselves to be overrun and who thereafter will be responsible for hitting the enemy in the comparatively soft spots behind zones of concentrated attack.[20]

It was assumed by Holland that these 'guerrilla-type' troops would be based on the new Independent Companies (even referred to in reports of the ISPB meeting as 'the MI(R)s'); five companies were still in Scotland after their deployment to Norway had been cancelled. Grand continued his plans undeterred, preparing for a situation that the War Office refused to contemplate, whereby SIS would take control in occupied areas where the army had ceased to operate. Meanwhile, within days of the ISPB meeting, Fleming had moved to Scotland as an instructor at Lochailort and MI(R) plans floundered. Instead, it was General Andrew Thorne, commanding XII Corps in Kent and Sussex, who independently established his 'Observation Unit' of army guerrilla patrols, basing his concept on a visit to a Prussian estate in 1934 where he had learned of the local tactic of 'stay-behind' units of peasants.[21] Fleming credited Thorne as being the first officer to see the potential if 'the enemy in his bridgeheads were harassed by light forces left behind for the purpose' and attacking lines of communications and concentration areas.[22] This is a surprising statement given the concept behind the Independent Companies but was true regarding anti-invasion planning in Britain.

The Germans entered Paris on 14 June and shortly afterwards the Chiefs of Staff formally warned the War Cabinet of a risk of imminent invasion.[23] There was disquiet among some in the War Office over Section D's intrusion into the invasion landscape and Holland was tasked with offering the outline of a military alternative. There is a suspicion from the Davies Plan (*see below*, p. 144) that Holland may still have been thinking along the lines of Scheme D and the inclusion of a civilian resistance, but realized that he would not be able to formally present such an option. Fleming had been interrupted in exploring the option of using the LDV but they and the Independent Companies were at the heart of Holland's thinking. Holland consequently briefed the Chief of the Imperial General Staff (General Sir John Dill) and C-in-C Home Forces (General Ironside) on the potential of LDV sections to support army commando units. Ironside took the idea to Churchill and the War Cabinet for approval on 17 June as the genesis of the GHQ Auxiliary Units:

> Steps were also being taken to organise sections of Storm Troopers on a full-time basis, as part of the LDVs. Tough and determined characters would be selected. Some of these would be armed with 'Tommy' guns.[24]

Gubbins later maintained that 'Auxiliary Units' as a name was conceived as giving no indication of their role and appeared uninteresting.[25] There were indeed many units with 'Auxiliary' in their title but it would not have escaped the War Office that 'Auxiliary Units' was the name given to the paramilitary unit of the Royal Irish Constabulary, formed in December 1920 from former British Army officers to carry out counter-insurgency operations against the IRA, and which became notorious for reprisals against civilians.

Despite reference to the proposed guerrilla troops as 'MI(R)s', Holland did not seek operational control of the Auxiliary Units but did suggest Gubbins as the commanding officer. Gubbins had returned from Norway on 13 June with 24th (Guards) Brigade but on 17 June Fraser resumed command of the latter, leaving Gubbins once again unemployed and looking for a post where he could retain his present rank of acting brigadier. Surprisingly, in view of his efforts in MI(R) and his subsequent career in SOE, Wilkinson later maintained that Gubbins 'had little confidence in sabotage and subversion as such; in fact [he had] a somewhat old-fashioned sense of propriety' but believed Gubbins accepted the post out of loyalty to Holland.[26] In turn, three of the fourteen Intelligence Officers appointed in 1940 came from MI(R). Andrew Croft became the Intelligence Officer in East Anglia, Hamish Torrance in Northumberland and Scotland, and Peter Fleming with XII Corps Observation Unit (which was absorbed into the Auxiliary Units). Peter Wilkinson, his colleague from the Polish mission, took charge of organization and plans, and compiled the first training manual (*Calendar 1937*).

As was the case with the recent formation of the LDV, the Cabinet had little idea how the Auxiliary Units would actually operate and Gubbins initially rejected both the model of the existing Polish resistance and a concept suggested by Holland in his visionary paper of 7 June. Holland had envisaged units operating from behind enemy lines in concealed hides, constructed and supplied before any withdrawal and ready to support any counter-attack. Such a force would rely on local guides and would have wireless communication. After the war Gubbins explained the pressure in that 'Time was the essence ... at the shortest we had six weeks before a full-scale invasion could be launched; if we were lucky we might have until October.'[27] Nonetheless, and despite Gubbins' burgeoning reputation as a guerrilla expert from his pamphlets, he struggled to settle on an effective methodology, the Auxiliary Units going through three iterations before mid-August, differing significantly from the ideal he had expressed in *Art of Guerrilla Warfare*. The MI(R) War Diary, compiled in November 1940 by Joan Bright, implied that the Auxiliary Units had from the start been created to use 'Much the same methods as Captain Fleming is using in Kent with his little headquarters', but this was only written using hindsight.[28]

First there was a confusion in basic principle. Wilkinson recalled the 'slight muddle' in thinking 'because nobody could quite make up their minds whether we were trying to set up something for immediate action against the Germans in the event of an invasion. Or, whether we were trying also to set up a nucleus of an English secret ... a British Secret Army.'[29] Wilkinson favoured the development of a civilian resistance organization to operate in the long term and it can be supposed that Holland championed a uniformed organization to support the regular forces. Wilkinson believed that Gubbins fell half-way between the two opposing views but it was beyond the remit of the War Office to prepare for resistance following an enemy occupation and so Gubbins followed their wish for a short-term, uniformed body, in continuance of the MI(R) strategy. From the outset, therefore, there was a clear rejection of the Auxiliary Units as a resistance organization.[30]

Influenced by the well-established focus of MI(R), Gubbins first envisaged the Auxiliary Units Intelligence Officers (eight were appointed by 13 July) acting only as advisers to local LDV commanders, who would form their own small covert units to extend its harrying function. Despite Wilkinson later claiming one of Gubbins' early tasks had been to take over the Section D Home Defence Scheme (HDS), claiming, unfairly, that it was 'hastily and unofficially set up earlier and proving a source of embarrassment to all concerned',[31] Gubbins and the Director of Military Intelligence (Beaumont-Nesbitt) initially believed the remit of the new Auxiliary Units was sufficiently distinct as a military force that it could still work alongside the hidden saboteurs of the civilian HDS. Facing the imminent threat of invasion, an acceptance of the existing saboteur organization may have been born of necessity.[32] This changed in late July when it was agreed that the Auxiliary Units should absorb the HDS because 'the risk of reprisals incurred by allowing civilians to engage in sabotage activities was too great'.[33] (This concern clearly did not apply to encouraging resistance forces abroad.) The Auxiliary Units Intelligence Officers began to recruit on behalf of the LDV and on 5 July Gubbins wrote to LDV Area Commanders to advise them of the intention for the new teams, which would 'take action against the flanks and rear of such forces as may obtain a temporary footing in this country ... The personnel will consist of existing LDV volunteers and others who will be enrolled therein for the purpose.'[34] The operational responsibility for these teams 'will be decided between the local military commander and the LDV commander'. Consequently, the Auxiliary Units Intelligence Officer would merely act as an adviser 'in the closest touch with the military commander and the LDV commander so as to assist in every possible way [with] the selection, training and organization of these sub-units, and the provision and storage of equipment'.[35] Gubbins' letter was subsequently used as licence by some Home Guard commanders to claim that the later Auxiliary Units Operational Patrols should come directly under their command.[36]

The purely advisory model lasted not much more than a week after Gubbins' letter to the LDV commanders. The next iteration was for the Auxiliary Units to become more directly involved and form their own 'village cells' from the LDV as an extension of the LDV's guiding role, to secretly lead army commandos through their territory and also undertake their own sabotage missions. Gubbins produced a briefing note for the Intelligence Officers on 17 July summarizing the new strategy which combined the methodology of the HDS with the concept of the Independent Companies.[37] The cells would operate while the invading forces were advancing through any bridgeheads, it being stressed that as many cells as possible needed to be formed in the shortest possible time. Some officers went on to form fifteen cells in a week.[38] The next priority of the Intelligence Officers was to lay down large weapons dumps ready for the putative army commando units to use behind enemy lines and to ensure coordination between them and the village cells. Unfortunately, it was quickly realized that there were not the resources to create such commando units for home defence and another rethink was necessary.

It was not until 15 August that Gubbins arrived at the final methodology for the Operational Branch of the Auxiliary Units, based on Fleming's innovations in the XII Corps Observation Unit, which, in turn, had taken inspiration from Holland's 7 June paper and the existing Polish model. General Thorne had originally created twenty army 'Battle Patrols' of twelve men in each battalion, ready to fight as small units of guerrillas behind the enemy lines and slow down the enemy advance, cutting off German supply lines to the sea. Their role was also considered offensive, able to disrupt any enemy retreat and so enable its complete annihilation. It was only when Peter Fleming was brought down from Lochailort to command the Unit and expand it with LDV patrols and the use of Holland's concealed hides that they became the model for the Auxiliary Units. Fleming was not hopeful about their survival:

> The whole scheme in its early stages was typical of the happy-go-lucky improvisation of those dangerous days, and though we gradually built it up into something fairly solid I doubt if we should have been more than a minor and probably short-lived nuisance to the invaders.[39]

Fleming warned that their life expectancy would then be just 48 hours.[40] He was joined by Mike Calvert in July, after the latter spent time seated in a corridor outside the cramped MI(R) office, writing a paper close to Holland's heart on 'The operations of small forces behind enemy lines, supplied and supported by air.'[41] Together, Fleming and Calvert demonstrated the potential of the guerrillas by infiltrating General Montgomery's 3rd Division HQ. Calvert mined bridges and railway lines, filled the basements of country houses liable to be used as German HQs with explosives ready to be detonated and over-enthusiastically booby-trapped Brighton Pier. Unfortunately, an inquisitive seagull set off one of the charges, producing a spectacular chain reaction which destroyed the pier.[42]

In the new model, patrols of six to eight men under a sergeant were formed from the Home Guard (rebranded from the LDV on 22 July). Their base of operations was a secret underground 'hide-out' (as Gubbins first called them), the men preferring the more-positive 'operational bases'. The patrols were managed and equipped from a new administrative HQ and training base at Coleshill House, Highworth, Wiltshire, and a training base was also established in Scotland at Melville House in Fife. Eventually army Scout Patrols (equivalent to the XII Corps Observation Unit Battle Patrols) were introduced in November, but in a reflection of earlier experience with the Independent Companies, only by taking soldiers from reserve units and depots.[43] The Scout Patrols did not have any specialist training in irregular warfare and their own training, therefore, was initially just one step ahead of the Home Guard Patrols that they were expected to train. Later, however, they would become a source of skilled recruits to the SAS.

The Auxiliary Units were not a national organization but were first established in the vulnerable coastal counties of the south-west, and along the south and east coasts of England and South Wales in the likely invasion areas, plus the two anomalous inland counties of Herefordshire and Worcestershire (to help protect the Midlands from attack up the Severn Valley or from Ireland). Never envisioned as the 'last-ditch' defence or 'resistance' of modern romanticized myth and very different in character from the already established resistance created by SIS Section VII, the Auxiliary Units were part of a multi-faceted strategy to delay the enemy advance and cut its supply lines ready for the field army to counter-attack.[44] As such, their role was a covert extension of the wider task of the Home Guard to hold nodal points, attacking predetermined targets on the flanks and rear of an advancing enemy and using their hidden operational bases to extend their lifespan beyond that expected for the rest of the Home Guard. This fulfilled Holland's vision of guerrilla units under military discipline supporting a conventional campaign but there was a structural failure in their inability to operate strategically after 'going to ground' as only the army Scout Patrols had wireless communication. The principal tool of the Auxiliary Units were packs of explosives, primed with the new plastic explosive and fitted with a variety of time delays produced by Section D and MI(R)c to allow time to escape, but the Training Officer, Nigel Oxenden, eventually complained that the increasing range of booby-trap devices only encumbered the patrols and produced a 'mental fog'.[45] Peter Fleming was scathing about what he saw as the romanticism of Gubbins and his staff 'for whom an enemy is hardly worth killing unless he can be killed with a tarantula fired from an airgun by a Bessarabian undertaker on Walpurgis night'.[46]

Despite Gubbins' post-war hyperbole of being given a 'blank cheque' to form the Auxiliary Units, the resources provided were initially limited – after all, the men were not expected to survive long enough to make extravagant expenditure worthwhile.[47] Thus he was not able to implement the recommendations for weapons as described in *Art of Guerrilla Warfare*:

> Undoubtedly, therefore, the most effective weapon for the guerrilla is the sub-machine gun which can be fired either from a rest or from the shoulder – i.e. a tommy-gun or gangster gun; in addition, this gun has

the qualities of being short and comparatively light. Special efforts must therefore be made to equip each band with a percentage of these guns. Carbines are suitable, being shorter and lighter than rifles, and the long range of the rifle is not necessary. After carbines come revolvers and pistols for night work and for very close-quarters, and then rifles.[48]

Initially the only automatic weapon issued to the Auxiliary Units was the cumbersome Browning Automatic Rifle; there were no carbines and instead each patrol had two of the standard Home Guard M1917 rifles. They were, however, all issued with revolvers or automatic pistols.

The ISPB meeting of 27 May had recognized the need for obtaining intelligence on enemy movements and stated that 'Some form of "watcher" organisation linked with a command centre on the lines of ADGB [Air Defence Great Britain] control is required.'[49] Grand created a primary intelligence-gathering wing to the HDS that Gubbins then struggled to incorporate into the structure of the Auxiliary Units.[50] The experience of MI(R) was in collating rather than collecting intelligence or running civilian agents, and in practice the Operational and Special Duties branches of the Auxiliary Units functioned uncomfortably as two independent organizations throughout their history. When Gubbins received authorization to create an HQ 'Special Duties' on 11 July 1940 it was a necessary means of formally absorbing the HDS with a cryptic comment that the organization had already commenced activities.[51] His staff would be responsible for managing the existing civilian agents but, unlike the SIS resistance, there was no wireless communication. The system relied on the unlikely success of relays of runners passing on messages through the battlefield, fast enough for GHQ to act upon the intelligence. Optimistically, a progress report to Churchill on 8 August 1940 identified a role of the Auxiliary Units to 'provide a system of intelligence, whereby the regular forces in the field can be kept informed of what is happening behind the enemy's lines'. Gubbins may have had more in mind the intended Scout Patrols, operating in similar fashion to the recently successful 'Phantom' units of No. 3 Military Mission in France as the report went on to explain how 'to supply Home Forces with information of troop movements, etc. from behind the enemy's lines, selected units are also being provided with wireless and field telephone apparatus'.[52] This was wishful thinking and for much of 1940 Viscount Bearsted of Section D continued to run his rudimentary HDS network *en bloc* under the name of 'Auxiliary Units (Special Duties)'.[53] Even when the TRD wireless set was introduced in 1941 for the Special Duties Branch, this short-range, high-maintenance set, with a reliance on fixed direction aerials, was a pale and impractical reflection of the wireless-linked intelligence network created by SIS. Fortunately by then GHQ had other, more efficient, options for collecting field intelligence. The network was maintained, thereafter, more for its potential to manage internal security (the use of telephony reducing the need for training of the volunteer operators), than for any serious anti-invasion purpose.[54] The incorporation of the Special Duties Branch did offer one possibility of personal interest to Gubbins. His original request was for the SDB to be commanded by a GSO1 (lieutenant colonel) but this was downgraded to a GSO2 (major). Had he been successful, Gubbins, as overall commander of the Special Duties and Operational Branches, could have retained his temporary rank of brigadier!

The MI(R) influence in the Auxiliary Units largely ended by the close of the invasion season in 1940, when the degree of immediate panic was reduced. The much-travelled Fleming left XII Corps Observation Unit in November for SOE, Calvert went to the Mission 104 Training School in Australia, and Andrew Croft joined Combined Operations in December. The last remaining member of MI(R) was 'Hamish' Torrance, who left the Auxiliary Units in April 1941 for SOE and commanded the Norwegian commando in the Lofoten raid of December 1941. Most significantly, Gubbins and Wilkinson left the Auxiliary Units for SOE in November 1940. By mid-August Wilkinson had already become disillusioned as to the direction of the Auxiliary Units, believing that as the organization expanded it became 'virtually a guerrilla branch of the Home Guard'.[55] By November the opinion was being expressed that the Auxiliary Units, conceived in the immediate invasion panic, had served their purpose now that regular forces had been strengthened but Gubbins is reputed to have ensured their survival by a timely lunch with War Office staff at the Cavalry Club.[56] The strongest argument was that the volunteers had been assured that they would not be returned to normal duty in the Home Guard and the War Office could not be certain that the threat of invasion would not return.

Both Wilkinson and Gubbins recognized the limitations of the Auxiliary Units in being designed to meet the specific crisis of 1940. For Gubbins: 'We were expendable. We were a bonus, that's all.'[57] He believed they would have justified their existence 'based heavily on the fact that they were costing the country nothing in either man-power or in weapons ... their usefulness would have been short-lived, at the longest until their stocks were exhausted, at the shortest when they were caught or wiped out'.[58] The report on the progress up to 1 September 1940 concluded that 'it was in fact doubtful whether many of them would have survived the first few days of invasion'.[59] In 1995 Wilkinson considered that they would have been, at best, a 'flea-bite' behind enemy lines, sowing a degree of confusion but not able to offer a decisive contribution. He even concluded, 'I think that in the cold light of reason, it is at least arguable, as many senior officers held, that they were not worth the effort put into them.'[60] They would, however, have provided a useful distraction away from the real British Resistance, which was ordered to remain 'quiescent' during the actual invasion in order to protect its long-term role.[61] Wilkinson wrote in 1997: 'any suggestion that Auxiliary Units could have provided a framework for long term underground resistance is, in my opinion, absurd'.[62]

Wilkinson admitted that he and Gubbins 'had to crank up the organization as enthusiastically as we could in order to "sell" it both to the rank-and-file, and to higher authority'.[63] This wartime marketing exercise has had long-lasting consequences and historian Arthur Ward later reported how Wilkinson was 'obviously irritated by the myth of a secret society of ninja-like assassins that was becoming an accepted part of Aux Unit folklore'.[64] Overall, the multi-layering of the official guerrillas of the Auxiliary Units with a variety of unofficial and only vaguely sanctioned guerrilla and resistance units would hopefully have confused the Gestapo as much as it has modern historians, and all served to obscure and protect the existence of the SIS British Resistance.

The Davies Plan – Scheme D reborn

There was great suspicion in the government regarding the moral and practical consequences of encouraging British civilians to become involved in any fighting after invasion, although as the agreement for Scheme D had demonstrated, there were fewer scruples in encouraging foreign civilians to become *francs-tireur*. The Home Office issued a press release on 11 May advising civilians to leave the fighting to the army and the ISPB meeting of 27 May 1940 stopped short of directly recommending the organization of civilian armed resistance, although it did propose 'The whole population, whether in formed or loose formations, or whether as individuals, must be instructed in the sort of contribution they can make to assist the services, and must be encouraged to make their contribution, should the need arise, with the same ruthlessness we may expect from the enemy, whether he is provoked or not.'[65]

The government policy against arming civilians was published in *Official Instructions to Civilians* on 18 June and was partially drafted by Holland's deputy, the quiet and reserved Lionel Kenyon. Rejecting such a policy, F.T. Davies submitted an unofficial plan for a civilian resistance which, although admitting that his idea was unorthodox and even unconstitutional, briefly excited some interest before being quashed by the C-in-C Home Forces and the War Cabinet. Jo Holland may have allowed Davies to circulate his plan, tolerating individual freedom in the same way as he allowed Fleming and Lindsay to circulate their report of the Norwegian campaign (*see above*, p. 105), but it is also tempting to see it as part of a machiavellian attempt by Holland to revive Scheme D for use in Britain but under military control. Davies had likewise been used as a back-door conduit to argue the case for 'shadow missions' with the Foreign Office (*see above*, p. 94). Now Davies raised his plan for a British resistance with Lieutenant Colonel Arthur Cornwall-Jones, Assistant Secretary to the War Cabinet, and on 17 June, having seen the papers relating to the formation of the Auxiliary Units that were presented to the Cabinet, wrote:

> I am afraid that you will never forgive me for bothering you again but this is even more actual than my last plan. It may seem unconstitutional and unorthodox but it is the only possible way of getting one step ahead of the Boche. I know from documents you have already discussed this matter and that certain steps have been taken but it is all too incomplete. There is such a strong feeling in the country that an effective and reassuring organization is necessary.[66]

The plan for the Auxiliary Units was indeed a pale reflection of the endorsement of Scheme D for the rest of Europe by the War Office and Foreign Office in March 1939.

Members of the Chiefs of Staff Committee and the new Ministry of Defence discussed Davies' proposal to create a resistance under military control in excited confusion, momentarily forgetting the official policy against involving civilians. Davies countered concern over the risk of reprisals by saying that if any guerrilla units were formed to operate behind enemy lines then the Germans were likely to take reprisals on the civilian population, whether the latter were involved or not. He believed that the acceptable rules of warfare had already been changed, and that the country wanted some concrete application of the principles that Churchill had proclaimed in his 'Fight on the Beaches' speech of 4 June. He called for the civilian population to 'resist by all practical means in their power whatever the cost', going on to say 'There is no-one who may not be called to give their life for their country,' and calling on the civilian population to 'place themselves unreservedly in the hands of the military authorities'.[67] Here was the cornerstone of Holland's belief in the conduct of guerrilla warfare.

Repeating MI(R)'s long-standing research, Davies highlighted the nuisance value of guerrilla tactics in India, Ireland and Palestine and the vulnerability of modern warfare to the interruption of lines of communication. As MI(R) had proposed for France, he suggested a Civil Resistance Section of the army Area Commands to organize destruction of stores likely to be of use to the enemy at the time of an enemy landing and demolition of infrastructure (bridges, railways, roads, power stations, etc.) in the event of occupation. Personnel to be enrolled for civil resistance would include selected ARP and police for demolition work, an intelligence service drawn from schoolmasters, priests, women and boy scouts, and guerrillas from local inhabitants and serving soldiers. Davies called for 'constant organized civilian opposition to the invader in the back areas and even in the fighting zone' and believed that the vulnerability of the German lines of supply had not been sufficiently tested in previous campaigns. The War Office firmly rejected any resistance role for the Auxiliary Units but Davies declared that after the occupation 'of any locality, or even of the whole country, some form of resistance and of secret organisation would be essential, which would both tie up large numbers of enemy troops and also preserve the morale of the population'. He was also prepared to raise the unthinkable necessity to consider options 'if the possibility of the government and armed forces leaving for a Dominion were considered' – one of the clearest statements of the possibility of a national defeat of British forces and an evacuation of government.[68]

On 18 June Cornwall-Jones submitted Davies' proposal on the *Need for Civil Resistance* to General 'Pug' Ismay, Churchill's Chief of Staff and a member of the Chiefs of Staff Committee, who in turn forwarded it to Colonel Jo Hollis (Secretary of the Chiefs of Staff Committee) and Victor Cavendish-Bentinck (chairman of the Joint Intelligence Committee). Despite clearly running contrary to official policy, there was a rush of initial enthusiasm. Hollis declared Davies' proposal to be 'forceful and logical' but had to admit doubts on how it could be implemented.[69] Cavendish-Bentinck also had doubts but, caught up in the mood, he proposed that schools for spies and saboteurs should be established in likely areas for invasion.[70] Hollis forwarded the Davies scheme to Lord Hankey, whose enthusiastic suggestions were based on what he knew of SIS plans. He saw the core of saboteurs as previously trained LDV who had been able to merge back into the civilian population after the tide of battle had passed over them. Civilians in 'subjugated areas' could then 'keep the enemy continually on the jump as we were in Ireland'. They would have roles in 1) assassination, 2) sabotage and 3) intelligence (run by SIS). Hankey was enthusiastic about 'Assassination on the Irish model', suggesting the use of an undetectable poison.[71]

On 23 June General Ismay forwarded the plan to General Henry Pownall, now Inspector-General of the Home Guard, and Sir Samuel Findlater-Stewart (Chairman of the Home Defence Executive) with a comment aimed at SIS: 'We here are not, of course, fully in the picture about all that has been done and is being done to organise civil resistance.' Ismay emphasized 'the fundamental question of whether the civil un-uniformed population is to be encouraged to fight' (underlined in original).[72] Pownall and Findlater-Stewart cast the first dampening voices, with Pownall saying that this went beyond his responsibility and Findlater-Stewart querying the availability of resources, pointing out that there were not yet sufficient arms for the new LDV never mind any new venture.[73] The idea was finally quashed on 8 July when the Commander in Chief, Home Forces, General Ironside, and the Secretary of War, Anthony Eden, wrote a firm memorandum to the War Cabinet:

It is the view of the Commander-in-Chief, Home Forces, with which I am in agreement, that actual fighting should be restricted to the military and Local Defence Volunteers, and that no civilian who is not a member of these forces should be authorised to use lethal weapons. Only if this principle is accepted would it be possible to ensure control of military activities by the military authorities.[74]

Davies, chafing at what he saw as a lack of 'drive and direction', joined SOE on 23 September 1940 as personal assistant to Frank Nelson, with the remit of advising on SOE's resources of staff and supplies, and established the programme of SOE training schools.[75] In the autumn of 1941 he became Director of Research and Supply, and held that post until the end of his SOE career.

Iberian Peninsula

By June 1940 the German naval staff were displaying interest in acquiring bases in the Azores, Canaries and Cape Verde, despite Portugal's efforts to maintain a strict neutrality. The strategically important Azores lay across British trade routes and hosted British cable-stations but it was important not to take any steps that might precipitate a German occupation, which would have wider consequences for Portugal. Consequently, in June the ambassador in Portugal refused to accept a mission (Mission 105) to make contact with anti-German elements in the country, although two Advance Intelligence Officers (Walford and Fisher) were sent under cover in the Azores and Canaries to study the morale of local forces, to counter enemy agents and to distribute British propaganda.[76] They were followed by J.R. Blandy in July. In addition, Colonel Vickers and Major Pleydell-Bouverie were asked to visit Portugal on their way to South America with Mission 103.

Also in June MI(R) proposed to send Captain Peter Kemp (who had served for three years with the Nationalists in the Spanish Civil War) to Spain to be attached to the embassy and report on conditions and the potential for paramilitary operations if Spain joined the Axis, or if it was invaded. MI(R)'s proposal was premature and as he was *en route* the ambassador in Spain telegraphed to say that Kemp's presence would be counter-productive. His history was hardly likely to endear him to anti-fascist groups who were now working with Section D.[77] Instead he carried out a survey of the Franco-Spanish border from Pamplona to San Sebastian until returning to England in September.

South and Central America

On 1 June the Joint Intelligence Committee raised the uneven organization and influence of British communities abroad and the need to better organize them against the threat of German 'fifth column' activities and enemy propaganda.[78] Inevitably, on 8 June Holland suggested that any personnel appointed to organize British communities in foreign countries should have a service background.[79] On 5 July the JIC invited the War Office to select suitable officers to visit and report on British communities abroad and twelve days later asked for 'a man of considerable personality and experience, in view of the fact that leading British residents in some of the countries to be visited were people of standing and influence'.[80] They were informed that 46-year-old Charles Vickers, a former major in the Lincolnshire Regiment who had won the Victoria Cross in 1915, had been chosen to lead the South America mission.[81] He had joined MI(R), was recommissioned and sent for a month's training at Lochailort, and was then promoted colonel. He was an international commercial lawyer and had the cachet of his Victoria Cross but had no experience of South America.

Vickers was ably complemented by Bartholomew Pleydell-Bouverie, the son of the Earl of Radnor and an investment banker by profession, who had worked in New York from 1932 to 1934 and had travelled widely in South America on business trips. Pleydell-Bouverie joined MI(R) from the OER and was recommissioned into the Grenadier Guards on 3 July 1940. On 1 August 1940 the two men left London as Mission 103, on a whistle-stop tour to inspect and report on the organization of British communities in South America and encourage local governments to act in British interests and to oppose enemy 'fifth column' activities.[82] They visited Portugal and the Azores on their way and then covered the USA, Venezuela, Brazil, Uruguay, Argentina, Chile, Peru, Colombia and Cuba before returning in November. Vickers reported the results to the JIC in January 1941, recommending a new Centre to oversee the activities of British overseas communities, and briefly joined SOE as an executive to deal with South America, the USA and the Far East. In March he became Deputy Director General at the Ministry of Economic Warfare, in charge of economic intelligence, and had a seat on the JIC.[83] Pleydell-Bouverie also joined SOE and returned to South America. From August 1941 to November 1944 he was Chief Liaison Officer for the British Security Commission in Washington.

Chapter Ten

The Caucasus, the Middle East and Africa

Russia

Communist Russia was the long-standing enemy of British Intelligence and General Archibald Wavell, C-in-C Middle East, confided to the DMI on 30 March 1940 'We shall have to fight Russia sooner or later in this war, and the sooner we start preparations the better.'[1] Air Marshal Sir John Slessor later remembered how the gross underestimate of German strength had led to the view in 1940 that as well as fighting on the Scandinavian, western European and Middle East fronts, Britain could simultaneously engage with Russia which, with hindsight 'really makes one's hair stand on end'.[2] The C-in-C Middle East was therefore instructed to plan for the capture of the oil-rich Caucasus which led to the early recruitment to MI(R) of senior officers with experience in Russia. Colin Gubbins was fiercely anti-communist: 'his suspicions of Soviet motives were far better informed and far more deeply held than those of most of his colleagues'.[3] During his trips to Warsaw and the Balkans in 1939 Gubbins contacted the nationalist 'Promethean League of the Nations Subjugated by Moscow', which sought an independent Ukraine under Polish protection, part-funded by SIS but heavily infiltrated by German Intelligence! Gubbins also contacted other White Russians in Belgrade. Such contacts became more significant during the Hitler-Stalin pact and the Finnish Winter War, when it seemed possible that Britain might actually go to war with Russia. Gubbins was followed into MI(R) by Douglas Roberts, a specialist in the territories bordering South Russia. He had served in the British mission to South Russia in 1919 and then worked in famine relief in Russia and in the mining and timber industries in the Caucasus and Eastern Siberia as an SIS asset. Roberts became head of MI(R)b and later second in command of MI(R) Middle East, aka G(R), and in 1946 head of the SIS anti-Soviet section (Section IX).

In recruiting men with strong anti-Bolshevik sympathies, there was an obvious risk that some would have had earlier dalliances with the fascists, creating strange bedfellows in the war against the Nazis. Peter Kemp had first come to the attention of MI5 in 1932 when, as a 16-year-old schoolboy, he had offered to infiltrate the Communist Party, an idea dismissed as 'amusing'.[4] He fought in Spain during 1936–1938, first for the Carlist militia and then as an officer in the Spanish Foreign Legion, during which time he was implicated in the execution of captured International Brigade prisoners. He was wounded at the Battle of Caspe whilst opposing the British battalion of the International Brigade and again at the Battle of the Ebro in the summer of 1938. Still recovering from his wounds, Kemp was recruited to MI(R) in late December 1939. When Gubbins asked about his service in Spain Kemp remarked 'he at least didn't seem to disapprove of the side I had chosen'.[5] Indeed, Kemp noted that they had friends in common from Spain.[6] Fellow MI(R) officer John D. Kennedy described him as an 'exceedingly nice fellow' but with a drink problem and 'cannot be guaranteed to be completely reliable'. Kemp took part in the *Knife* mission and then became Assistant Fieldwork Instructor at the Lochailort Training School. He later served with the Small-Scale Raiding Force and SOE but remained of interest to MI5 into the 1950s and was considered by them to be 'extremely anti-semitic'.[7]

William Allen was recruited by MI(R) to work on a desktop study of the Caucasus and was discreetly described as a man 'whose past has always been doubtful'.[8] He was the wealthy chairman of David Allen & Sons Ltd, a successful bill-posting company, and in 1931 had left the Unionist Party to support Mosley's British Union of Fascists (BUF). He contributed to the periodical *The Blackshirt* and wrote the pamphlet *Fascism in Relation to British History and Character* (1933) and the book *BUF, Oswald Mosley and British Fascism* (1934) under the pen name of James Drennan. He had even been best man at Mosley's marriage to Diana Guinness at Berchtesgaden. Under MI5 surveillance since 1931, Allen was believed to be involved in the laundering of funds to the BUF from Germany and Italy and his secretary, George Tabor, became Secretary-General of the BUF in 1933.[9] Allen later claimed he was not attracted to the fascist ideology but rather that they supported his belief in rearmament, but MI5 believed that he was amoral and driven primarily by a desire for power and business advantage.[10] Allen broke with Mosley in February 1939, after believing he had been swindled out of a deal with Hitler to obtain a concession to run a commercial wireless station in Nordyke, and was recruited to MI(R) six months later in August 1939 as a well-connected expert on Georgian affairs. The Caucasus region was seen as a likely focus of para-military activity and a Caucasus Bureau was briefly set up in September 1939 under Allen with Dr Malcolm Burr to cultivate anti-Soviet Ukrainian groups and use them as a buffer against any future Soviet incursion against British interests through Iran into India. This brought further MI5 concern with Allen, who introduced his Georgian private secretary, the scholar Dr A. Gugushvili, to dissident Georgians, Armenians and Cossack groups working with MI(R). Gugushvili had been accused by another Georgian group in 1935 of being a Soviet agent, infiltrated into Allen's employment to gather intelligence on British fascists; adding even further complication, Allen was living with Natalie de Korganov, who was also suspected of being a Soviet agent. MI5 monitored MI(R) correspondence involving Allen and he was clearly mistrusted, given only restricted access to files. His colleagues regarded Allen as 'a very strange individual' and there was pressure to get him out of the country.[11] This was not easy. In August and October 1939 Elphinstone rejected Holland's suggestions that Allen should join him in Cairo. Elphinstone described Allen as 'an adventurer of no morals or stability' and someone not to be trusted too far. Nonetheless, Allen was eventually posted to the Household Cavalry in Palestine as part of a 'private arrangement' between Holland and the CO of the regiment. Allen later returned to MI(R) in Ethiopia as Paymaster to Mission 101 and then served as Animal Transport Officer to Gideon Force.[12] In February 1943 Allen was released from the army and joined the Ministry of Information but he continued to be widely viewed with suspicion.

It was vital for MI(R) to be able to work smoothly with Middle East Command, which had oversight over the Caucasus. The C-in-C Middle East from July 1939, Archibald Wavell, had suffered first-hand experience of the Boer commando and had himself embraced the concept of irregular warfare (*see above*, p. 5). He did, however, firmly believe it should be under the strategic control of the theatre commander. As soon as Wavell took up his post, Colonel William Elphinstone was appointed by MI(R) to act as liaison officer and was sent to Cairo on 25 August 1939. A former officer of the Indian Army, Elphinstone had served in Palestine during the First World War and was then an Assistant Political Officer in northern Jazira before serving with the British military mission to the Iraqi Army from 1925 to 1928. His 'special duties' with Wavell were described as being 'in connection with organising guerrilla warfare amongst natives' and launching a scheme for 'Preventative Intelligence in the Arab World'.[13] As a precedent to his later concern to establish local control over MI(R), Wavell wanted to establish 'an MI5 of the Middle East' to control security intelligence.[14] Elphinstone brought to Wavell the results of a wide-ranging discussion on improving Intelligence security in the Middle East and Asia, between the Foreign Office, Colonial Office, India Office and Air Ministry. This led to the creation of SIME (Security Intelligence Middle East) under MI5's Defence Security Officer in Cairo, Colonel Raymond Maunsell, to coordinate existing security organizations across the Middle East and India. As part of this, one of Elphinstone's tasks was to visit Sudan, Iraq and India to arrange the cooperation of the existing Security Intelligence organizations in those countries. By coordinating information on all enemy agents in the region, SIME was to prove highly effective in preventing a coordinated Axis Intelligence network in the Middle

East. Elphinstone's other task of organizing guerrilla warfare was largely concerned with Ethiopia and is discussed below (*see*, p. 155).

In March 1940 (whilst writing his novel *The Flying Visit*) the ever-energetic Peter Fleming was organizing a 'crazy gang' in London comprising a 'gang of toughs with local knowledge' for operations in the Caucasus.[15] This work was interrupted by the Norwegian campaign and Fleming was then fully employed elsewhere, while the whole basis of work in the Caucasus and Middle East was about to change. Wavell wanted to expand the support that MI(R) could offer, but on the clear caveat that any operations should be under his direct control. On 15 March 1940 Colonel Adrian Simpson of MI5, a specialist in signal intelligence (and a former deputy managing director of Marconi), went to Cairo to discuss the formation of an MI(R) Middle East as part of the Intelligence Branch of GHQ Cairo. The new body was to be called GSI(R) or more simply G(R), and was initially intended to collate information on Russia from existing intelligence sources and to organize para-military activities in the Caucasus, along with maintaining supply lines into Poland and Czechoslovakia, rather than work in the Middle East *per se*. Wavell suggested the following summary of tasks for G(R) as regards the Caucasus:

(a) collect and collate all available existing information, including from SIS, without having to refer back to the War Office;
(b) draw up plans of operation based on a);
(c) organize the dissemination of subversive propaganda;
(d) plan and organize para-military operations;
(e) arrange details of cooperation with France and Turkey; and
(f) study the possibilities of action if Turkey refused to cooperate.[16]

G(R) was formed in April, and had offices in Grey Pillars, the Middle East Command HQ building in Cairo. Wavell repeatedly stressed that he expected a 'free hand' in managing G(R) and the DMI, Major General Beaumont-Nesbitt, agreed, confirming that it would be 'entirely under your control and direction' and it would not be seen as an 'off-shoot' of MI(R), although he hoped that there would be close liaison between the two bodies, including the exchange of personnel.[17] In practice, during 1940 MI(R) retained the initiative in creating projects in the Middle East, although they were managed locally by G(R).[18] MI(R) also acted as G(R)'s rear link to the War Office, which still determined the overall brief of G(R). It was Holland and the DDMI, Brigadier Ronald Penney, who established the organization of G(R), and MI(R) negotiated its scale of staff with the War Establishment Committee.[19] There was an original establishment of just three officers, two clerks and a stenographer under Simpson as its head.[20] Gradually the staff was increased as MI(R) continued to recruit Arabic speakers in Britain on its behalf, in anticipation of future operations in the Middle East, but the Cairo HQ, like its London equivalent, remained small.[21] Continuity with MI(R) was provided by the appointment of Douglas Roberts as Simpson's deputy. There was also Guy Tamplin, who had been with the Lockhart mission in Russia during the First World War and had served with the MI(R) mission to Finland in January 1940. He had been sent to Cairo expecting to go to Belgrade as part of the MI(R) 'shadow mission', but when that failed he had been obliged to take a temporary post as a staff officer with the Polish Brigade. There was also George Green, who left G(R) in February 1941 to rejoin the Black Watch and later commanded its 2nd Battalion as part of the Chindit columns.

Reflecting Wavell's pressing needs, G(R) had a minimal input into policy or research, being primarily concerned with administrative and logistical support to missions in the field. There was considerable cross-over with MI(R) and on 26 May 1940, with expectation of war with Italy increasing and after dealing with the aftermath of the débâcle with Blake-Tyler in Hungary, Dodds-Parker transferred from MI(R) to G(R), initially to deal with supply lines into Poland from the Middle East and Balkans. Before he left London, he loaded 6 tons of 'toys' from the magazine in Hyde Park onto a Sunderland flying boat as the basis of the new MI(R)/Section D store to be established at Alexandria.[22] Dodds-Parker later gave training to the early LRDG on destroying fuel stocks and arranged for Section D explosives, designed to look like camel droppings, to be taken out by their patrols and left to be 'found' by the Italians, successfully causing panic and delay over any camel droppings encountered on desert tracks. During a short stay in Cairo, George Taylor, head of the Section D Balkans section, brokered an uneasy working relationship between Section D, G(R) and Wavell's Deputy Director of Military Intelligence, Brigadier Shearer. Taylor agreed that Section D would act as the 'civil and underground side of MI(R) Middle East', working under the direction of the Directorate of Military Intelligence in field operations where there was a clear military interest – but equally making it clear that Section D was responsible only to SIS for general instructions and for its lines of communication. Demarcation disputes were renewed with the formation of SOE and were further complicated by internecine disputes within SOE in the Middle East. A satellite G(R) office was opened in Khartoum to manage Mission 101 (*see below*, p. 155) under Terence Airey with Dodds-Parker and Muchu Chaudhauri (later C-in-C India and High Commissioner in Canada). Airey, who had earlier served as a staff officer in the Sudan, later took over from Simpson in overall charge of G(R), continuing its management as SOE's Director of Special Operations, Middle East, before becoming Director of Military Intelligence in the Middle East. As with MI(R), despite the increase in project workload in the Middle East, the central establishment remained small, comprising a colonel, two majors and three captains in September 1940, but nonetheless it was the controlling administrative department for the Long Range Desert Group, the Middle East Commando and the troops of Mission 101 and Gideon Force.[23]

It was only after the disbanding of MI(R) in October 1940 that G(R) began to initiate its own projects. Following the invasion of Russia by Germany on 22 June 1941 there was a new fear that the oil resources of Iran and the Caucasus could be used against Britain if captured, with additional strain resulting from the pro-Axis revolt by Rashid Ali in Iraq. G(R) made a failed attempt to use Jewish 'toughs' to destroy a fuel dump in Baghdad but successfully sabotaged Iraq's new Northrop aeroplanes. A new G(R) Office was opened in Baghdad during August 1941 to recruit and train Armenians and Kurds from northern Syria and Iraq as G(R) Mission 16, to attack oil targets in Iran and the Caucasus in the event of a Soviet collapse.[24] The Middle Eastern War Council Sub-Committee for Secret Activities quickly concluded that using the Kurds and Armenians would be likely to provoke Turkey and the project was cancelled in November.

G(R) under Terence Airey became part of the battle for control of irregular forces between Wavell and SOE. At first Wavell wanted to bring all SOE operations in the Middle East under G(R) but in a dramatic turnaround G(R) lost its responsibility for military raiding forces and, by focusing on covert infiltration and 'stay-behind' parties, came closer to SOE's orbit and was finally transferred to SOE on 4 September 1941 (although its name continued to be used in correspondence).[25]

The Middle East

Middle East Commando

The Middle East campaign saw the rapid proliferation of special service and commando units, many with a heritage linked to MI(R). As the body responsible for managing military irregular warfare in Middle East Command, towards the end of June 1940 G(R) took administrative control of the new Long Range Desert Group, quickly followed by the approval of Simpson's proposals for a Middle East Commando.[26] It was established by MI(R)'s George Young, still in Egypt with the Royal Engineers after the cancellation of the Romanian oil well scheme. No. 50 Middle East Commando was finally raised in early August, with a total strength of 371 men. They were recruited from the infantry and the 1st Cavalry Division, but tank crews, engineers and men from the technical arms were barred from volunteering, with a limit of ten men from a single battalion. They also contained a contingent of Spanish Republican refugees who had been serving with the French Army in Syria but feared being taken over by Vichy forces. In October No. 51 Commando was formed from Palestinian Jews and Arabs, who had previously served in the

Palestinian Company of the Auxiliary Military Pioneer Corps. No. 52 Commando was formed in early November. Nos 51 and 52 Commandos took part in the successful Ethiopian campaign, but much of No. 50 Commando was lost in the Battle for Crete. The history of the Middle East Commandos was bedevilled by confusion over their purpose, a series of cancelled missions, and wider problems in defining the role of G(R) in managing raiding forces and its relationship to SOE. There followed protracted efforts to distinguish between raiding forces managed by GHQ (i.e. LRDG and SAS) and special service forces under SOE. Wavell failed in his attempt to absorb SOE within G(R) and so take control of all irregular operations. Instead it was G(R) that was absorbed by SOE as the Directorate of Special Operations. The surviving remnants of the Middle East Commando, focusing on covert infiltration and preparation of 'stay-behind' parties, were redesignated as 1st Special Services Regiment, including the short-lived 'Special Interrogation Group' formed from a platoon of German-speaking Jews in No. 51 Commando.

Mission 101 – Ethiopia[27]
The largest, and most successful, project of MI(R)/G(R) was the long-running plan to assist the Ethiopian fighters (the 'Patriots') who had been fighting the Italian occupation since October 1935 (Plate 29 and Fig. 9). In a classic exposition of MI(R) policy, the intention was to encourage local resistance forces by the supply of money and weapons, and provide assistance through a small core of military advisers, but success would ultimately rely on an invasion by regular forces on a timescale dictated by wider British strategy.

In late 1938 Captain Dick Whalley, a former British consul for South West Ethiopia now in the Sudan Defence Force, proposed a mission to Ethiopia as a 'scallywag show' to recruit and arm Ethiopian refugees in Kenya. He asked for 4,000 rifles, 200,000 rounds of ammunition, wireless equipment and 10,000 Maria Theresa silver thalers (*see* Plate 32). He also wanted Wilfrid Thesiger, a former Assistant District Commissioner, to invade further north at Kassala, accompanied by the Ethiopian Crown Prince. Enthusiastically, Whalley declared this as having the potential to 'go down to history as one of the greatest routs ever'.[28] The Governor-General of the Sudan, Sir Stewart Symes, was less impressed and thought the plan 'utterly fantastic' while Victor Cavendish-Bentinck, Chairman of the Joint Intelligence Committee, believed Whalley had dreams of becoming a sort of 'Lawrence of Ethiopia'.[29] Whalley's plan was rejected but the basic concept took root because, if Italy entered a coming war, a revolt against Italian rule might tie up sufficient resources to prevent an attack on the British-held Sudan or Kenya. In early July 1939 a conference at the Foreign Office decided that in the event of war, the War Office, through MI(R), should support a revolt by the tribes in Ethiopia from bases in Sudan and provide the necessary arms and funding.

Figure 9. Outline map of the Middle East and African operations of MI(R).

Wavell arrived in Cairo shortly afterwards as the new C-in-C Middle East and took ownership of the plan.

Wavell selected Daniel Sandford in August 1939 to be recalled from the OER (having been identified through the DMI/MI(R) intelligence list) to become head of the Ethiopian section of the Middle East Intelligence Centre in Cairo. Sandford (*see* Plate 5) was 'a calm, stocky, balding, bespectacled colonel' who was 58, but still had the air of a 'vigorous schoolboy'.[30] In 1910 he had joined the Sudan civil service and had been vice-consul in Addis Ababa. After service on the Western Front in the Royal Artillery during the First World War, in 1919 he became the general manager of the British Abyssinian Corporation. In 1921 Sandford leased a farm in Ethiopia and in

1935 became an adviser to Emperor Haile Selassie on the suppression of slavery, but fled Ethiopia for England in 1936. An Ethiopian revolt would distract the Italians while Wavell directed conventional operations against the Italian empire to north and south, and the C-in-C gave Sandford free rein: 'You are my expert on Ethiopia. I will leave you to get on with it until it comes my way.'[31] Holland tried to force the pace on British planning by organizing the passage to the Sudan of Commandant Salan of the French Army, travelling under the alias of M. Hughes of *The Times*. Salan had been instructed by the French government before the outbreak of war to enter Ethiopia with arms and money to stir up the tribes against the Italians, in the expectation that Italy would declare war immediately with the Germans. The French were persuaded to countermand his orders but, as Holland had probably anticipated, his arrival put pressure on Middle East Command to develop its own plan of action.[32]

In late September 1939 Wavell's Deputy Chief of Staff, Major General Arthur Smith, returned to Britain and presented the CIGS (then General Ironside) with an outline for the liberation of Ethiopia, incorporating 'Native uprisings encouraged by ... guerrilla tactics by British columns and by ... Propaganda.'[33] To achieve this, a 'Guerrilla Commandant' was to be appointed to GHQ Khartoum (where General William Platt was General Officer Commanding Sudan), to develop a campaign 'on the lines of those undertaken by Lawrence of Arabia'.[34] As a hint, Sandford was sent by Wavell to Platt in Khartoum 'to retain at your discretion for work in connection with the Abyssinian project'. He arrived with Elphinstone and copies of the MI(R) pamphlets.[35] On 6 October 1939 Elphinstone, Sandford and Lieutenant Colonel Iltyd Nicholl Clayton (an intelligence officer in Middle East Command, originally sent by Section D) met with Platt, his head of intelligence (Colonel José Penney) and the Governor-General (Sir Stewart Symes) to draw up an outline plan for action once war was declared. Sandford put his faith in supporting an internal revolt in favour of the exiled Emperor but Platt believed a British offensive would ultimately be needed to displace the Italians. The Ethiopian resistance had been known to both the Italians and British alike as 'rebels' but Sandford insisted that they now be called by their Ethiopian name of 'Patriots', in order to give a more positive impression. Logistically this was an MI(R) project, designated Mission 101 and heavily reliant on *Art of Guerrilla Warfare* for its methodology. Seven arms dumps were to be established on the Sudan/Ethiopia border, guarded by a new Frontier Battalion of the Sudan Defence Force (Plate 31), which would also escort arms deliveries to the Patriots. Six mobile wireless stations would also be provided by SIS. An Intelligence Centre would be established at Khartoum under ornithologist Robert Cheesman (aged 61), former consul in the Gojjam province in north-west Ethiopia. Wavell was keen to keep up the momentum and on 19 October 1939 his Chief of Staff wrote to ask if Platt had made a recommendation for the 'Guerrilla Commandant', suggesting Sandford for the post but, so as not to antagonize the Italians, with the proviso that he did not base himself in Sudan until the outbreak of war with Italy.[36] To assert his own role in the plan against the influence of both Wavell and MI(R), Platt replied that Major Hugh Boustead, then District Commissioner in Darfur, had already been selected, although Platt thought Sandford might be useful on the intelligence side. Platt saw Boustead as an experienced soldier who had served in the South African Scottish during the First World War and then the Sudan Defence Force, before joining the Sudan Political Service.[37] Nonetheless, Platt was obliged to admit that Boustead did not have any experience of Ethiopia and in January he finally accepted Sandford to the post. On 26 January 1940 Wavell sent an outline of the plan to the DMI and forwarded Clayton's request that a minimum of £100,000 worth of Maria Theresa silver dollars (as the most acceptable local currency; *see* Plate 32) would be required to support the revolt.[38] This request was passed on to MI(R) and, after first exhausting the supplies of Maria Theresa dollars in the French and London mints, Dodds-Parker organized the minting of up to 2 million dollars in the Bombay mint.[39]

Despite the nervousness of the Foreign Office, during January 1940 Sandford toured the capitals of the British territories bordering Ethiopia to contact Ethiopian refugee groups and then formalized the plan for Mission 101. Its twin aims were to tie up Italian resources in Ethiopia (hindering any Italian attacks on Allied territory) and set the scene for a military invasion into Ethiopia. Support would focus on the existing Patriot forces in Gojjam province, in the heartland of the ruling Amhara ethnic group, and Sandford's plan therefore clearly aligned British interests with those of Haile Selassie. The mission would work to arm and unite rival tribal factions in the region to attack isolated Italian outposts and ambush convoys, using a network of advisory centres to liaise at a local level and act as staging points for the distribution of weapons. This was also a psychological offensive, making Italians fearful of moving outside their posts, risking being killed or captured by the Patriots. In addition, the mission would form battalions of Ethiopian refugees in Sudan and Kenya to enter Ethiopia and 'fend for themselves', although fear of tribal tensions eventually meant that they were attached to British commands to enter Ethiopia as part of a British offensive.[40] Sandford believed the return of Haile Selassie as Emperor was an essential feature of the plan and that any invasion had to be seen as an Ethiopian success rather than as a means of establishing a British protectorate. Former journalist George Steer, who had reported on the Italian occupation of Ethiopia and the Winter War in Finland, would be in charge of the associated propaganda unit, which produced leaflets for air drops and a news sheet for distribution within Ethiopia.

Having been commissioned into the Intelligence Corps, he eventually wrote the official account of the campaign.

Meanwhile, the Foreign Office maintained the deception of the official policy towards Italy and assured the Consul-General in Addis Ababa that there was no '*arrières penseés*' in the British government's recognition of the Italian government of Ethiopia and further, 'emphatic personal assurances' had been given that the British government was not engaged in any subversive activity either within Ethiopia or in the surrounding territories against the Italians.[41] To maintain this fiction, in March 1940 the Foreign Office again pressured Wavell to remove Sandford from his work on the boundaries of Ethiopia. But behind the scenes the Frontier Battalion (under the command of Boustead) was sanctioned in March by the CIGS, along with the advisory centres and the refugee battalions, all on the basis of Establishment Lists produced in London by MI(R).[42] Cheesman was also in place by March 1940 and began identifying sympathetic tribal leaders and producing up-to-date maps and guides for future operations. G(R) was created soon afterwards and took local administrative control of the project but MI(R) continued to liaise with the Foreign Office in London and coordinated the construction of the wireless stations with SIS, who provided Staff Sergeant George Grey (Royal Signals) to organize and maintain them once in Ethiopia. Grey had experience of mule pack wireless stations from service in India with 2nd Indian Division Signals at Quetta and was stationed in Ireland in early 1940, but was ordered in February to the SIS Wireless HQ at Whaddon Hall where he 'became part of the Foreign Office' to take charge of signals for the mission. Six wireless stations were built at Whaddon for Mission 101. The load would be spread between three mules, with one carrying the suitcase set, one the batteries and one the battery charger. This took three months to arrange but in May 1940 Grey took the half ton of equipment by sea to Cairo and, after meeting Sandford, began to train thirteen Ethiopian wireless operators, assisted by three RCS corporals.

In May General Platt produced a circular letter ready to be distributed to sympathetic Amharic tribal leaders once war was actually declared, offering weapons and money. The message announced: 'Peace be unto you. Now the British and Italians are at war. In order to crush our mutual enemy we need all the help we can get. If you need rifles, ammunition, food or money, send to us men and pack animals, as many as you can, to the place where the messenger will show you. Whatever you want we can help you.'[43] It was an optimistic promise. The letters were dispatched by native runners on 11 June, the day after Italy's declaration of war, but on the previous day, Arthur Smith, Deputy Chief of Staff to Wavell, had issued *Operation Instruction No. 1* concerning 'Rebel Activity in Italian East Africa'. The intention was, upon the outbreak of war, 'to spread the revolt over the whole of Italian East Africa and so harass the Italians as to make them expend their resources on Internal Security'. The *Instruction* stressed that the Allies had no colonial ambition in Italian East Africa – only to free the Ethiopian people. Under the orders of the General Officer Commanding Sudan (Platt), Mission 101 was to provide advice to the Patriot leaders, coordinate their activities and act as a channel of communication to C-in-C Middle East. The mission was to cross the border as soon as possible – but only when the Patriots were strong enough to ensure its protection. Sandford was given command of Patriot operations, his authority with local leaders expected to come from his control of the supply of arms. The 'Report and Advisory Centres' would first be established on the Sudanese border and then move forward into outlying rebel HQs, functioning as a link to mission HQ in the interior, and as staging posts in the supply chain from Sudan to the rebel bands. In a staged approach, initial reconnaissance would first assess the state of the rebels and encourage small guerrilla bands that would hinder freedom of movement of the Italian forces. Larger groups would subsequently attack infrastructure such as bridges, tunnels, water supply and storage depots. Only in the third and final stage would larger Italian garrisons be attacked, to divert attention from simultaneous British advances from Kenya and Sudan.[44] By August 1940 the Italians had 371,053 troops in East Africa; against them, Britain guarded the 1,900km-long Sudan frontier with just 9,000 men, and the 1,300km-long Kenya frontier with 8,500 men. In British Somaliland there was a garrison of just 1,475 men.[45] Any means of tying up the substantial Italian forces in Ethiopia was, therefore, very attractive. The appreciation of the Chiefs of Staff in September 1940 was that Ethiopia could become a 'wasting asset' to the Italians:

> If we could increase our scale of attack against Italian East Africa the conditions are present for bringing about a large-scale revolution against Italian control in this area. The Italian control could in any event be weakened if we could stimulate the existing state of unrest.[46]

To organize this campaign, MI(R) won approval for Mission 101 to have an initial establishment of seven officers, four NCOs and eighty-three ORs under a satellite office of G(R) to be established at Khartoum under Terence Airey. Most of the mission staff were recruited from the region, including as Intelligence Officer Captain Ronald Asheton Critchley (13/18th Hussars), who had served in Egypt (1921–1931) before being transferred to India (1931–1938); Major Donald Nott (1st Worcesters in Palestine) as Deputy Assistant Adjutant and Quartermaster; Acting Captain Thomas Michael Foley (RE); and Acting Captain Clifford Drew (RAMC, formerly in the Sudan Medical Service). Later were added Count Arthur William Douglas Bentinck (a major in the Coldstream Guards), who had served in East Africa and had been captured by the Italians in Ethiopia in 1936 whilst serving with the Red Cross; and Arnold Wienholt, a civilian in Aden who was pestering the authorities for a job. The mission had assembled at Khartoum by 20 June but their departure for Gojjam was delayed by diplomatic confusion surrounding the unexpected arrival from England of Haile Selassie, much to the dismay of the authorities in Sudan who had less faith in him as a unifying figure than Sandford. An Italian advance also captured Galabat, at the point where Sandford had envisaged entering Ethiopia. Haile Selassie was disappointed at the small scale of Mission 101 and particularly its lack of heavy weapons and air support. He was perhaps not aware of the weakness of the British position and how the value of the mission to the British at this stage was essentially as a distraction to the Italians.

It was not until 4 August that the mission moved forward to its jumping-off point at Doka (Fig. 9), 80km from the frontier where the Frontier Battalion of the Sudan Defence Force had established a string of supply depots, ready to ferry arms to the guerrilla bases. Wilfrid Thesiger was in charge of one depot, protected in a thorn and wire enclosure. He recorded how 'day after day the patriots arrived at Galabat, sometimes in small parties, sometimes in hundreds' to collect arms and ammunition.[47] Many of the rifles were single shot .303 calibre Martini-Enfields (Plate 39), converted from the Zulu War period Martini-Henry rifles and as supplied to colonial forces before the First World War and later issued to the Arab Revolt. In line with its established policy of supplying outdated weapons to colonial troops in case they should ever rebel, the British preferred to issue these old rifles to the Patriots as 'less troublesome to subsequent administration of country'.[48] The Martini-Enfields were grudgingly accepted and 3,432 had been distributed before the Emperor protested that the Italians were making good propaganda use of their antiquity.[49]

The main party left on 6 August when Sandford, Critchley, Drew and signallers Sergeant Grey and Corporal Whitmore set off with two emissaries of the Emperor, along with eleven Ethiopian signallers and fifty Ethiopian bodyguards and muleteers. The mission carried only fourteen days' rations and would soon have to live off the land. They also had three revolvers, forty-one rifles and six wireless sets, all carried on fifty-four mules and thirty-six donkeys. Sandford crossed the frontier on 12 August and planned to set up a forward HQ at Faguta in the Sakala district of the Chokey Mountains, a former Italian fort abandoned after Patriot attacks in March 1940. For Sandford, this would be the base for a 'Free Ethiopian' government, under the Emperor.[50] To Grey, Sandford was 'a wonderful man', very intelligent and charming, who knew the country and got on well with the Ethiopians.[51] They travelled through the bush on a zig-zag route, trying to avoid Italian spotter planes but were once dive-bombed. It was the rainy season, and they had to cross eight flooded rivers as well as 130km of malaria-infested desert scrub and foothills, then climb a 260m-high escarpment onto the open grass-land of the Gojjam plateau. They reached Faguta on 18 September, now accompanied by 700 local Patriots but having lost many of the mules, as well as one of the wireless sets, in a river crossing. Critchley established a number of agents in the surrounding Italian outposts and a courier system across the Gojjam but, after carrying out a number of gruelling reconnaissance missions (for which he was awarded the MC), an old eye injury flared up and he had to withdraw, eventually to be replaced by Thesiger. From their mountain HQ the mission successfully negotiated alliances between local bands of Patriots and together they attacked small forts and isolated garrisons in local villages. Chief wireless operator Grey rarely had a full night's sleep, working through the night to decipher messages using one-time pads, and undertaking repairs as well as taking shifts as a w/t operator. After six months without respite he collapsed with exhaustion and was flown back to Khartoum on 15 February for two weeks' well deserved rest.[52]

The second team, as Mission 101 North under Bentinck, assisted by demo-lition expert Michael Foley (a former mining engineer in the Sudan), left Doka for the Gondar region on 9 September with forty-six men, twenty-three horses, twenty-four mules and fourteen donkeys to establish a base north of Lake Tana at Armachaho where they would distribute rifles and try to win over the local tribes, cut enemy communications north and west of Gondar and harass passing Italian convoys. They entered Ethiopia on 18 September but Bentinck was still lame from a war wound of 1916 and was in ill health. He focused on sedentary diplomatic efforts with the local tribes while Foley conducted sabotage and ambushes (for which he was awarded the MC). Bentinck's war diary shows clear frustration with the lack of support from Khartoum (a feeling shared by Sandford) and also with the internal politics of local tribal leaders and their ceaseless demands for weapons when he knew that many men then sold their existing captured weapons back to the Italians. On 14 December Bentinck made a perceptive entry in his war diary:

> I am also wondering whether HQ are beginning to realise that the wholesale arming of these unruly and turbulent chiefs will eventually become a serious problem as, unless controlled, the country is bound to become a hotbed of shiftas [bandits] who will be thorns in the side of both the Sudan and Kenya. This may be the reason for the sparing issue of rifles.[53]

A third, smaller, team was dispatched under Arnold Wienholt (aged 62) on 31 August, as much to keep Wienholt out of the way as anything else. This former Australian politician, farmer, Boer War soldier and First World War army scout had created an exaggerated reputation as a guerrilla but was undoubtedly skilled in bushcraft. He was driven by the belief that the Italian occupation of Ethiopia threatened wider British empire interests in Africa and the Middle East. After pestering the authorities in Aden to assist the war effort his chance finally came:

> My good news and orders came through last night [14 June]. Aren't I lucky at 62 years to get the most lovely chance of real service again in this great struggle and just what I wanted for so long. One feels a sense of exhilaration in living in Armada days. I feel full of confidence for the future. I always felt it had to come so that we British could get a chance to save our souls – so we will and our own and other countries at the same time.[54]

Sandford appointed him Assistant Intelligence Officer at the Doka base, and Critchley described Wienholt as a 'strange, excitable figure'.[55] Sandford had wanted to give him the protection of a commission and even insisted he wore the uniform of a second lieutenant but despite reminders, Wienholt did not bother to complete his paperwork and consequently continued to serve the mission as an unpaid civilian. He disliked army discipline and wished to preserve his independence to criticize British policy towards Ethiopia. After one outburst Platt was obliged to write to him on 4 August:

> the Major-General Commanding wishes you clearly to understand that no information which may in any way influence or prejudice the armed forces can be communicated by letter or word by a member of His Majesty's forces without the possibility of such person rendering himself liable to trial by Court Martial. I am further instructed to add, that no officer or soldier is permitted to take part in speaking in public or publishing or distributing literature in furtherance of any political purpose or his own political views.[56]

Now a self-declared expert on Ethiopian matters, Wienholt was likely given to Mission 101 in order to contain him, but he was then detached from the main force so that his rebellious streak could not be a liability. Wienholt was sent towards Kwara to collect intelligence and link up with the Patriot leader Ras Wubneh Tessema, but the value of his mission was lessened (according to Bentinck) by not speaking the local Amharic or even Arabic. He left with just three armed Ethiopians and eight donkeys loaded with stores and salt. Unfortunately Wienholt ignored warnings to avoid the area around the garrison of Mutabia and his camp was surprised on 10 September by an enemy patrol. Wienholt was wounded and staggered off into the bush, never to be seen again. He was officially commissioned posthumously in order to provide his widow with a pension.

In addition to the three main teams, Captain Dick Whalley was running arms into south-west Ethiopia from the Boma plateau in Sudan where the

Patriots were trying to cut the road networks and isolate Maji.[57] With the teams in the field, in September Dodds-Parker handed over his other duties to Guy Tamplin and joined the Khartoum office of G(R), to strengthen the organization of the advisory centres. Sandford was 58, Cheesman 61, Bentinck 57 and Wienholt 63. For W.E.D. Allen, 'They were the chiefs among a fine team of older men in the guerrilla racket who between them fairly laid the ghost of "young men first".'

The Secretary of State for War, Anthony Eden, visited Middle East Command in October eager for any sign of a British victory, and tried to appease the Emperor over the delays in mounting a liberation of Ethiopia; he held a Ministerial Conference at Khartoum on 28–31 October. The first meeting concluded that the rebellion should be escalated and confirmed Haile Selassie as a rallying point (despite doubts about his acceptability to all the Ethiopian tribal groups) and that a limited offensive should be launched to recapture Gallabat. A meeting on the next day (attended by Haile Selassie) had to admit to a furious Eden that only 5,073 of the 10,000 rifles promised to the Patriots had actually been supplied and were mainly the antiquated Martini-Enfields.[58] Eden's show of anger in front of Haile Selassie obscured a more machiavellian game by the Foreign Office as, although the official government position was 'to use the Emperor as a centre-piece of revolution, to eject the Italians from Ethiopia, Eritrea and Somaliland', they had agreed to leave the question of Haile Selassie's re-accession to the throne as a matter for the Ethiopians to decide.[59]

Haile Selassie's suspicions seemed to be confirmed by the arrival of MI(R) Mission 107 in Kenya, led by Lieutenant Colonel Henry Brocklehurst. He had served with the Royal Flying Corps in Egypt, Palestine and Tanganyika during the First World War and worked as the chief game warden in Sudan from 1922 until his retirement in 1931. Helen Rodriguez described him as a tall, raw-boned man who 'resembled a fictional hero from some schoolboy's adventure book'.[60] Brocklehurst had been recruited to Section M of MI5 in the autumn of 1939 but left in August 1940 to join MI(R), recruited both for his local knowledge of East Africa and his recently developed skills in political warfare. With eight officers and eight other ranks, his task was to organize anti-Italian activities in Southern Ethiopia but, despite the agreement in founding G(R), the mission's controversial parameters had not been agreed with the C-in-C Middle East before their rushed departure from London on 3 October, so as to circumvent the closure of MI(R). The Foreign Office, having recognized that support for Haile Selassie was not universal, had concluded that if the tribes in south-west Ethiopia were hostile to the Emperor, 'this need not prevent our using them against the Italians but not for the Emperor'. Mission 107 was therefore to pursue an 'independent' attitude.[61] Wavell objected, fearing the impact of such a policy on the Gojjam revolt centred on the Emperor but the Foreign Office was not dissuaded. In a telegram of 12 November, *after* Eden's Middle East conference, the Foreign Office suggested that the 'Galla' (mainly Muslim Oromo majority) might be coaxed towards revolt against the Italians by Britain indicating that it would support them having some form of local autonomy from the Emperor.[62]

Whereas Sandford's background had been with the Amharic aristocracy that supported Haile Selassie, Brocklehurst's experience had been with the Oromo 'Galla', or 'outsiders', in southern Ethiopia. Brocklehurst, supported by Robert Hamilton from Mission 106 in Aden, flew to a conference of MI(R)/ G(R) mission leaders in Khartoum to press the Foreign Office-supported agenda of Mission 107, including offering the 'Galla' a promise of autonomy from Haile Selassie. As a concession, Wavell proposed on 17 December that the Emperor issue a proclamation assuring the non-Amharic population that their rights would be protected and that they would have a full role in government.[63] Now wavering in their attitude, this compromise was rejected by the Foreign Office but reports of the tone of the discussions reached Haile Selassie, for whom the prospect of British support being given to opposing tribal groups was worrying. It was more important than ever for Haile Selassie to enter Ethiopia and unequivocally stake his claim to power. On 24 December he appealed directly to Churchill and, on the argument that being pro-Oromo meant being anti-Amharic and therefore pro-Italian, accused Brocklehurst of being pro-Italian and refused to meet him.[64] When the Foreign Office tried to excuse the delay in allowing Haile Selassie to cross into Ethiopia on the grounds of difficulties in recruiting a suitable bodyguard (of 3,000 to 5,000 men), Churchill huffed, 'One would think the Emperor would be the best judge of when to risk his life for his Throne.' The Foreign Office was clearly irritated by Churchill's intervention, believing it was being 'stampeded' into arranging his return, and an exasperated G.H. Thompson of the Foreign Office added a comment to the bottom of Churchill's minute, pointing out that the Emperor was 'very obstinate and difficult to deal with' and the timing of his return should be left to General Wavell.[65] Nonetheless, the Foreign Office finally accepted defeat and withdrew support for Brocklehurst's scheme to raise the Oromo. Having reassured Haile Selassie that a separate mission would not be sent to the 'Galla', Brocklehurst was offered up as a convenient scapegoat to conceal the Foreign Office scheming and was transferred to duties in Kenya.[66] Orde Wingate (*see below*, p. 166) even sent a signal to his GSO2, Major Tony Simmonds, joking 'On encountering Lt Col. Brocklehurst you will shoot him.'

Sandford bemoaned that by 1 December still only a thousand rifles and no money, explosives or mortars had reached Gojjam province. The Frontier Battalion of the Sudan Defence Force had escorted a few small-arms convoys but the first large convoy, comprising 300 men, 220 camels and 40 horses, bringing money, 100 rifles and some Lewis guns, did not leave until 27 November. In the north, Bentinck warned of a suspicion of British duplicity amongst the Patriots and reported that some of the weapons that had been supplied had even been traded with the Italians.[67] Such reports had a discouraging effect in Khartoum and both Eden and Wavell accused Platt of a consequent lack of enthusiasm for the mission. The campaign was now refocused away from a guerrilla campaign towards the more conventional military offensive as always envisaged in *Operation Instruction No. 1*. Thus the recruitment of Ethiopian refugee battalions would be accelerated – but trained as regular troops ready for the conventional final assault.

One of the most significant decisions of the October conference with Eden had been that, as Sandford was in the Ethiopian interior, a new staff officer should be appointed to the G(R) office in GHQ Khartoum to be in charge of recruitment, mobilizing the advisory centres and liaising with Haile Selassie on the Sudan side of the border. Orde Wingate, a *protégé* of Wavell, was appointed to the post, having been banned from Palestine; he arrived in Cairo in July after being suggested for a 'small show on his own' where he would not antagonize too many people (although no post was actually offered until after the October conference).[68] As it was, the main role of Dodds-Parker (who became Wingate's GSO3) over the coming months in Khartoum, seems to have been to pacify the rising number of senior officers that Wingate insulted! Wingate arrived in Khartoum on 6 November. By force of personality he extended his role, but his contribution to the subsequent campaign has been over-blown by his later legend. The egocentric Wingate was dismissive of the achievements of Mission 101, but, as intended, Sandford's efforts (as much political as military) had successfully set the scene for the final assault by containing the equivalent of four Italian brigades and thereby gave Generals Cunningham and Platt greater freedom of movement to enter Ethiopia in the final campaign.[69] Significantly, the official history of the campaign, written by George Steer and published in 1942 before Wingate achieved fame with the Chindits and his untimely death, devotes a whole chapter to Sandford and Mission 101 but Wingate is only described in passing as a 'staff officer'.[70]

Wingate flew out for his first meeting with Sandford on 20 November, two weeks after having been appointed. Ten 'Report and Advisory Centres' were finally being formed, but Wingate had modified their role. Redesignated 'Operational Centres', each would be based around a core of British or Dominion officers, with four sergeants and accompanied by thirty Ethiopians from the 1st Ethiopian Battalion and 100 Sudanese troops.[71] They would infiltrate into Ethiopia and attach themselves to the Patriot guerrilla groups, to act not only as coordinators and advisers but now having a combat role. Sandford agreed this strengthened the original concept but the two men disagreed over the distribution of the stores to the Patriots. Sandford still saw the Mission 101 operations on the Gojjam plateau as the focus of a 'Free Ethiopia' which could expand outwards towards the national borders. Yet the mission had exposed the reluctance of many sections of the populace across Ethiopia to join a popular revolt and Bentinck's successor in Mission 101 North, Major Tony Simmonds, reporting an apathy in northern Ethiopia against taking action against the Italians, claimed that the locals had even asked him to leave the area.[72] In southern Ethiopia Mission 107 had also found the Galla and Amhara more interested in fighting each other rather than the Italians. It is therefore hardly surprising that there was a growing reluctance in Khartoum to arm the Patriots and in early February Wingate finally forbade the issue of weapons other than to those willing to come under the direct orders of the new Operational Centres.[73] Wingate fundamentally disagreed with MI(R)'s pragmatic policy of buying support and supplying arms, although it had been an unavoidable consequence of overstretched British resources at the time. Wingate explained after the campaign that 'to raise a real fighting revolt you must send in a *corps d'élite* to do exploits and not pedlars of war material and cash' to local tribesmen.

The Operational Centres would now be used to demonstrate that the British would not only fight *alongside* the Ethiopians but *in front* of them to provide a psychological lead, becoming fighting units divided into ten guerrilla squads.[74] Yet rather than being a revolutionary concept, Wingate's tactics were firmly rooted in *Seven Pillars of Wisdom* and *Art of Guerrilla Warfare* and Fleming had suggested the same methodology as a principle for MI(R) strategy in supporting the Chinese guerrillas. Wingate insisted on a high level of training for the Ethiopian guerrillas in the Centres, using battle drill and set-piece simulations. Such training had been sorely lacking in MI(R)'s early efforts but was an aspect which the Lochailort Training School was now rectifying. The first Operational Centre entered Ethiopia in late December 1940 and, together with the Frontier Battalion and 2nd Ethiopian Battalion, became Gideon Force, thereafter sidelining Mission 101 to a supporting role in the final offensive. Dodds-Parker praised the bravery and endurance of No. 1 (Australian) Operational Centre but noted that:

> I had one other difficulty with them. Months later a letter arrived from the Game Warden's Office, saying that they had shot, without a licence, a giraffe with a Bren gun and an elephant with a Boys anti-tank rifle. The fine was £5.14.

The final offensive from 19 January 1941 was more of a conventional campaign than a guerrilla war and even Wingate's pioneering use of Long Range Penetration Units in Gideon Force, a precedent for his later Chindits, was organized on near-conventional lines (its practical value to the campaign remaining a matter of debate). The offensive was enabled by the collapse of

Italian forces in North Africa from December 1940, allowing British forces in Sudan and Kenya to be reinforced ready for a three-pronged offensive against Ethiopia. General Platt advanced from the north into Eritrea while General Cunningham attacked from Kenya into Italian Somaliland and southern Ethiopia. Wingate's Gideon Force of two battalions moved into the Gojjam, and the Emperor was finally allowed to enter the country with him, the force supplied by regular flights to its forward supply base and supported by the ten operational centres. The Patriots were in a supporting role as scouts and sources of intelligence.

Wingate revisited Sandford's camp on 4 February 1941, having already written to Platt suggesting that the roles of mission and military commanders should be separated and he be appointed 'Commander of British and Ethiopian Forces in the field'.[75] This was agreed on 8 February. Although Sandford was promoted to brigadier and appointed principal military and political adviser to Haile Selassie, he retained only a nominal overall control of operations. On 15 February Wingate linked up with the Mission 101 HQ at Faguta and Mission 101 was finally absorbed into Gideon Force, which then made contact with Cunningham's force and both headed for Addis Ababa, which fell on 5 April, the Emperor finally entering his capital on 5 May.

Mission 102 – Libya

In late September 1939 Lieutenant Colonel David Bromilow, former CO of the 20th Lancers in India, who had retired from the army in 1934, was recalled and sent by MI(R) as a staff officer to General Wilson, commanding British troops in Egypt, to organize para-military activities in Libya as Mission 102. The intention was to distribute funds for subversive activities by the Senussi tribes and provide training for exiles in the Western Desert, liaising with the Egyptian Frontier Force.[76] After Italy's entry into the war, Wilson formally invited the Libyan leader Sayyid Idris to ask his followers to participate in the formation of a Senussi force organized by Bromilow, who in August 1940 became Commanding Officer, Libyan Arab Force [Egypt]. Five battalions were formed and trained for guerrilla warfare, becoming the core of the new Libyan Army which took part in the Western Desert Campaign. From August 1941 to 1944 Bromilow was head of the British Advisory Military Mission and Inspector-General to the Iraq Army.

Mission 106 – Aden

Mission 106 was formed with the intention of using Somali refugees in Aden as the basis of organizing sabotage across the Gulf of Aden in the captured French protectorate of Djibouti (Fig. 9). It was led by 37-year-old Robert Hamilton (later Lord Belhaven), who had been commissioned into the Royal Scots Fusiliers in 1924 but was seconded to the Aden Protectorate Levies in 1931 and commanded the Camel Troop. He retired from the army in 1934 and became a political officer in the Colonial Service in Aden. Hamilton was recommissioned and promoted to acting lieutenant colonel to lead the mission in August 1940, but, like Mission 107, it was not dispatched until October. By Hamilton's account, in August 1940 he was summoned to the Colonial Office in London whilst on sick leave (having accidentally shot himself in the foot in 1937, causing a wound that never properly healed) and was told that the War Office had requested its help in mounting irregular operations against the Italians in Africa. As Hamilton happened to be in England, and knew the region, they thought he might be able to help. Recruited to MI(R), he was then sent to Lochailort for a modicum of training (given his disability). Here he was able to seek advice from William Stirling and Lieutenant Commander Geoffrey Congreve and produced a scheme for armed dhows that might raid trading vessels in the Barrows and two companies of native commandos to raid the 320km-long coast of Eritrea, Djibouti and captured British Somaliland. Hamilton sent this outline to Wavell, in London at the time, who sent a brief response: 'I want this.'[77] Congreve devised a means of fitting a naval 2-pounder QF gun to a dhow and instructions were sent to Aden to buy and suitably equip four vessels in readiness for the arrival of the mission. Stirling suggested officers from those at Lochailort and they were a mixed bag. George Musgrave was an explosives instructor, who had worked in the oil industry in Bahrain and been responsible for anti-sabotage measures there in 1939 before being commissioned into the Royal Artillery. George Gilbart-Smith, another oil engineer and a former nightclub owner, had also worked in Bahrain, and had been commissioned in March 1940 into the Buffs, winning an MC in June when the troopship *Lancastria* had been sunk at St Nazaire. Both Musgrave and Gilbart-Smith later joined SOE. There was also Gordon Waterfield, a journalist who had been at school with Hamilton, tall, quiet but humorous, with no apparent military experience, although commissioned in July 1940 when he joined MI(R). Why he was originally selected for MI(R) is not clear but his journalistic background makes it conceivable that he had been involved with SIS. After the team was selected, Hamilton consulted with the MI(R) office and one of its secretaries, Cyrilla Binns, was added to the team for administrative support (and later married Hamilton).

Despite Musgrave's explosives expertise, it was the militarily-inexperienced Waterfield, with only the Lochailort course behind him, who was selected to leave in advance of the rest of the mission and cross the Gulf of Aden, enter Ethiopia and sabotage the Addis Ababa–Djibouti railway.[78] On 21 September he left for the Middle East but on arrival at Cairo, *en route* for Aden, his orders were countermanded by a mystified Middle East Military Intelligence, who declared, 'But we don't want the Djibouti railway blown up, and if we did we could blow it up ourselves, without the War Office flying someone out from

London!'[79] Instead, Waterfield went to Aden to prepare the way for the main mission, which did not arrive until November. As well as arranging accommodation, which included the necessity of providing five sets of toilets (native troops, native officers, British NCOs, British officers, ladies), he secured the assistance of R.G. 'Somali' Smith of the Somaliland Administration, who had commanded Somali irregulars in the opening stages of the Italian attack and now assisted in recruiting a company for the mission comprising half Somali refugees and half local Arabs. There was no shortage of eager volunteers from the local tribes who appeared each day at the gates of their compound just outside Aden, as the pay offered was good at 1 rupee per day. Smith had already put ashore some Somalis to get intelligence on the Italian garrisons and one night Smith and Waterfield sailed to the enemy-held coast in a dhow to pick them up and 'exchanged shots' with their Lewis gun. It was a disaster; not only did they fail to pick up the earlier party, but they also left behind four additional Somalis, who had paddled ashore in a canoe to rendezvous with the original team.[80] Hamilton later recalled such escapades: 'I forget what purpose they had, but any excuse would do for bothering the Italians, and they had enjoyed themselves.'[81] Holland would have been horrified at this casual approach to raiding (*see above*, p. 130).

In the London MI(R) office Brigadier Wyndham had been naturally concerned over Hamilton's fitness – the latter could only guarantee getting the team to Aden and carrying out preliminary seaborne research for a period of three months, after which he would pass over the command to a fitter man. The main mission sailed from Liverpool to Cape Town and then travelled by train to Durban, flying boat to Uganda and down the Nile to Cairo, arriving at Khartoum on 6 November and thence to Aden. The mission was met with some local suspicion and resentment. They brought Bren guns and Thompsons that were in short supply with the local troops and the idea of bringing in an amateur team from London to train local Somalis, without using the expertise of the Somaliland Camel Corps or exiled Somaliland police officers, seemed ridiculous. Waterfield later pointedly criticized the War Office practice of relying on 'local experts' to organize irregular missions and believed they had roles only as advisers.[82] Lieutenant Commander Cardell-Ryan, an eccentric red-bearded Irishman who dressed in Arab clothing and professed to being Muslim (but who nonetheless drank alcohol) and called himself 'Haji Abdullah', was in charge of the armed dhows on which he installed a small menagerie as camouflage. Cardell-Ryan named the flagship the *Cowpat* and Admiral Murray, whilst supportive of the mission, would not permit the distinctly un-naval dhows to fly the White Ensign. Instead they flew the St Patrick's flag of Ireland!

The purpose of the mission was confused and its cover name of 'Mobile Force' was soon amended locally to the 'Mobile Farce'. Hamilton warned that this was a suicide enterprise but Waterfield's first suggestion of landing a picked party of Somalis on a deserted part of the coast of Italian Somaliland and basing themselves in the mountains to raid Italian positions was immediately rejected. Morale was poor and after Hamilton's first reconnaissance his officers took the extraordinary step of asking to resign from the mission, citing Hamilton's bad temper. There was one further reconnaissance mission with Waterfield but by then Hamilton's promise to serve for three months had expired and the difficulty in mission discipline was solved by him being declared medically unfit and returning to London (where eventually his leg had to be amputated). On 1 March 1941 Musgrave took command of what became G(R) Aden. He was known by the local troops as *Shaitain* (the Devil) because he was dark, silent and unemotional. Reorganized as a guerrilla company of five platoons, and with Waterfield as intelligence officer, G(R) Aden finally achieved success and took part in the retaking of Berbera later in March, which formally surrendered to Waterfield in the town square. It thereafter operated in British and Italian Somaliland, supported by an RAF flight of Vincent bombers and three armoured cars. The mission was finally disbanded in August 1941 and Musgrave and Gilbart-Smith were transferred to the Mission 204 Bush Warfare School in Burma (*see below*, p. 180). Musgrave went on to train the SAS and Jedburgh teams.

West and Central Africa

German operations in East Africa during the First World War had tied up disproportionate Allied resources and a British fear in 1940 was that if the Axis succeeded in occupying Egypt and advanced southwards towards Central Africa and eastwards towards Iraq and Iran, then Britain risked defeat through its resources being so overstretched. There was, however, a reluctance in the War Office to divert supplies of arms and troops urgently needed in the Middle East and Britain to any contingency planning. The Joint Planning Committee (JPC) consequently requested that MI(R) centres should be established in Africa to provide training in guerrilla warfare with refugees recruited to versions of the Independent Companies and pro-Allied propaganda distributed on a wide basis. By such means, Britain sought to forestall any German or Italian seizure of territory, especially encouraging the Belgian and French colonies that it was in their best interests to support the free governments in exile in Britain. In the colonial attitude of the times, the JPC maintained that 'the natives of Africa will follow any white leader, and are easily swayed by persuasion'.[83] This patronizing attitude led to an MI(R) mission to assist the Belgians to 'control the native population in the Congo'.[84]

Francis Rodd (Lord Rennell), Saharan explorer, diplomat and latterly merchant banker, had been commissioned into the Royal Artillery in 1914 and then served as an intelligence officer in Italy and a liaison officer with the

Arab Revolt. In September 1938 he joined the OER and was included in the MI(R) list of potential intelligence officers. In early 1939 Rodd visited West Africa and on his return he proposed to the DMI, Major General Beaumont-Nesbitt, the formation of a mobile defence force in Nigeria, to protect the country in the event of war. There was no immediate response and in the summer of 1939 Rodd joined the intelligence department of the Ministry of Economic Warfare as a civilian, working primarily on encouraging Italian trade with Britain as a means of dissuading Italy from allying with Germany. He did not get on well with Hugh Dalton and resigned on 3 June 1940 to join MI(R). Commissioned as a captain, he was immediately sent to West Africa to advise the Governor-General of Nigeria on para-military activities and to recruit expatriate officers for possible guerrilla action in Nigeria, Gold Coast, Sierra Leone and Gambia. On the way there he was also expected to report on morale in French Morocco and West Africa.

As the one-man 'Rodd Mission', he set up an intelligence-gathering network based around Kano and Lagos but the Free French coup in French Equatorial Africa (Republic of the Congo) in late August 1940 caused a change in direction. Rodd flew to Brazzaville to meet the Free French leader, General de Larminat, for discussion on Anglo-French cooperation in the region and Rodd became 'economic and financial advisor' to the new Free French administration. Rodd returned to London in early 1941 and then became financial adviser to the Political Branch Headquarters in Cairo, helping to establish the Overseas Enemy Territory Administrations in the newly freed Italian colonies.

The MI(R) mission to Central Africa was on a much larger scale. The Belgian Congo had followed strict neutrality in the first months of the war, to the frustration of the British Consul-General, E. James Joint.[85] When Belgium fell in May 1940, the Belgian Congo remained governed by the Governor-General, Pierre Ryckmans, who, in a difficult constitutional situation, had to deal with complex tensions between those in the colony who wished to remain neutral and those who wanted to join the Allies in the war. There was some panic amongst the white colonial population over the threat of Italian invasion and several industrial concerns wanted to preserve the neutrality of the colony in order to maintain their trade links with Germany and Italy. There was also a pro-German and pro-Italian element in some districts. Colonel Gilliaert, the commander of the *Force Publique* (Belgian Army of the Congo), fearful of Axis strength in the region and neighbouring Vichy Congo, also for a time urged neutrality but the majority of his officers wanted to take a more active role in the Allied war effort in the Middle East. Ironically, this enthusiasm had to be contained by the British, who wanted the *Force Publique* to concentrate on home defence to protect the colony's economic assets.

Immediately after the German invasion of Belgium the Governor-General announced 'I follow the King' and German residents were interned. Before it was realized that King Leopold III would surrender the country, this was regarded positively, assuming that Belgium would join the Allies and allow the Congo to be occupied and used as a route through to Sudan.[86] But by 27 May the loyalty of the Belgian Congo to the Allies was in doubt and the following day the Belgian government in exile in London repudiated the action of their king and released officials from their oath of allegiance.[87] Would the government in the Belgian Congo follow their king or the government in exile? The British Consul-General remained confident of the loyalty of the colony to the Allies but Whitehall had its doubts.[88] Ultimately, the British were prepared to invade the territory to protect its valuable strategic resources, such as rubber, industrial diamonds and uranium; Mission No. 19 to the Belgian Congo was dispatched to collect the necessary military intelligence for this option. Its public brief was one of liaison with the Belgian authorities, giving advice in countering German infiltration and propaganda, surveying industrial assets to protect them against sabotage and reconnoitring the border to identify likely routes for German infiltration into the country. Under other circumstances, these were standard MI(R) objectives but here the ultimate purpose, in case the Belgian administration surrendered, was to prepare for British invasion and 'establish, then support, any national committee in the Congo that was established there'.[89] The obvious sensitivity of this task meant that the true purpose of Mission 19 could not be shared with the local Belgian administration or even with the British consular staff.

Mission 19 was led by Lieutenant Colonel Frederick McKenzie, a civil engineer who had been commissioned into the London Territorial Royal Artillery in 1923. Although not a professional soldier, he was believed by the British Consul-General in the Congo to have been briefly an assistant military attaché in Brussels, and this unusual appointment for a Territorial Army officer suggests he might have had an SIS connection. McKenzie joined MI(R) and was appointed GSO1 on 'special employment' as acting lieutenant colonel on 29 June 1940. He did not, however, have any experience of Africa. The sheer size of the mission raised local suspicion as to its real intention as, in all, the mission comprised nine officers and fifteen other ranks, accompanied by a fleet of lorries, cars, wireless equipment and motorcycles. McKenzie was assisted by Major Cecil Forde, a former Regular army officer serving with 1st Reserve Field Regiment, Royal Artillery (and who later joined SOE), with the Belgian lieutenant Jacques Van Hoegaerden as adviser and translator. Van Hoegaerden was commissioned on to the General List and almost immediately transferred to the Intelligence Corps in July 1940.[90] Other officers included Captain Handley from the South African Army and Captain William Sandison from the 8th Punjab Regiment of the Indian

Army. Lieutenant W.A. Duncan-Smith was the Intelligence Officer, transferred from General List to Intelligence Corps in mid-July 1940, and Lieutenant D. Hubble was Cypher Officer. Lieutenant Miller RAMC was the Medical Officer. Mr P.G. Harris, British Senior Resident in Nigeria, was attached to the mission as political adviser until 22 October.

The mission left London for the Congo on 4 July via South Africa and finally arrived in late August. McKenzie began to send back a stream of intelligence reports on the state of the Belgian Army in the Congo, plans of fortifications, lines of communications from Sudan and Uganda, a survey of the Congo river, a guide for pilots and a series of photographs of local landmarks and strategic installations (*see* Plate 33). He also liaised closely with neighbouring Commands in the Middle East, Nigeria and South Africa. The mission established wireless stations for the benefit of the Belgian *Force Publique* and to allow better communication with East Africa Command, and had a particular task of promoting the substantial war effort of South Africa. A great deal of work was done to build links with pro-Allied elements in the *Force Publique* and the usual MI(R) rationale would be to use these contacts to assist in creating guerrilla units against the possibility of future invasion. In this case MI(R) had to control the desire for a pro-Allied coup against the existing administration which, if carried out prematurely, would have been disastrous for Britain's reputation in the region. It was obvious from its size and composition that the official purpose of the mission concealed a more sinister intent beyond mere liaison and McKenzie described the initial atmosphere with the Belgian Governor-General, Pierre Ryckmans, as frigid, with McKenzie also misinterpreting the Belgian's need to balance the activist and neutralist factions of the colony as being a lukewarm enthusiasm for the war effort. Suspicious of McKenzie's real purpose, in early September the Governor-General asked leading industrialists to share no more than general economic information and, through Colonel Gilliaert, ordered army officers to maintain a reserve towards the mission, both officially and socially. A more overt economic mission led by Lord Hailey, essentially to advise the British government on what to buy from the Congo in order to keep it on the side of the Allies, arrived on 5 September and was able to improve the atmosphere by the practical promise of improved trade. The tension eased by early October and McKenzie then began to build up a good rapport.[91] Even so, some in the Belgian administration still considered the mission (reasonably enough) to be spies.[92]

The British Consul-General, E. James Joint, also resented the arrival of the mission. Joint had played a key role with the Governor-General in keeping the Belgian Congo in the war; his opinion was well respected in London but he now felt side-lined by the War Office. Before the fall of Belgium Joint had enjoyed close personal contacts with the Belgian General Staff but thereafter a succession of liaison officers arrived from the British Commands in the Sudan and East Africa and seemed to displace his influence, which culminated in the arrival of Mission 19. In June 1941, after the dissolution of the mission, Joint submitted a bitter report which Roger Makins at the Foreign Office dismissed as 'posthumous mud-slinging' full of 'tittle-tattle and personal prejudice', whilst admitting the Foreign Office had been well aware of the shortcomings and occasional 'wildness' of the mission.[93] Joint complained that both he and the Governor-General had been 'entirely without information as to the composition or objects' of the mission, although he believed it was vaguely to do with countering German propaganda (which he said did not exist), surveying the route to East Africa (which he said could be done from London) and 'something to do with using the Catholic Missions'.[94] He complained McKenzie had never shown him his full instructions or shared his telegrams to London and remained mystified why the mission had such a large number of staff and vehicles. The security of the mission had evidently been well maintained by McKenzie! Joint's most reasonable complaint was that only one officer had been in Africa before or had a good knowledge of French. Joint had initially tried to assert his authority but McKenzie had equally been keen to establish his independence and refused to carry out instructions that Joint gave him, insisting that he was under the direct orders of the War Office. McKenzie was also accused of spending too much time flying between South Africa, Cairo, Khartoum, Nairobi and Lagos; Joint had not comprehended McKenzie's delicate liaison role with neighbouring Commands – which precluded using wireless communication. Duncan-Smith was accused of going on unauthorized shooting trips in Stanleyville province, but was actually using such trips to collect intelligence. Most damning of all, Joint accused the mission of being 'improperly dressed' – McKenzie had visited the Governor-General in 'an open-necked shirt and shorts'.[95]

Relations with Joint remained sour but those with the Governor-General improved from October 1940 and McKenzie established a good relationship with local pro-Allied officials in the Congo, balancing encouraging enthusiasm for the war effort in the country without taking forces away from home defence or fostering independence.[96] Thus, McKenzie encouraged pilots to join the British, Rhodesian or South African Air Force but dissuaded efforts to create a Belgian Air Force independent of the RAF. The Intelligence Officer, Duncan-Smith, inveigled himself into the confidence of the 'malcontented' Colonel Mauroy and the *Ligue D'Action Patriotique* which sought a more active participation in the war. The mission encouraged Mauroy's enthusiasm for the war effort but he wanted to go further than the despised 'government of weaklings' in Leopoldville, with its 'mentality of defeat', and planned a coup. The Foreign Office was worried when McKenzie advised of the possibility of the army taking power in the eastern provinces, the Kivu and

Rwanda-urundi, while speaking in negative terms towards the Governor-General. London mistakenly took this as a sign of support for the coup, leading to the comment 'I understand all the Depts. agreed in abhorring Col. McK. leanings toward a dissensionist movement in the Congo.'[97] The mission also cultivated the head of the *Force Publique* Intelligence department who similarly disliked the cautious stance of the Governor-General and who passed on a proposal from the army on 1 October that the mission should be seconded to the *Force Publique*, so that the dissidents could communicate directly with London.[98] Recognizing that a coup would only bring instability and chaos, the mission maintained that it had been 'politely evasive' in requests to support the rebels.[99] Moreover, they helped forestall the coup on 19 November by passing on information gleaned from Mauroy and prevented the commanding officer of the *Force Publique* (Colonel Gilliaert) from being seized by the rebels at Stanleyville airport. Gilliaert was going to be arrested when his plane landed on a scheduled visit but Duncan-Smith gave Mauroy an arrival time that was three hours late and the rebel forces were not in position on the airfield or on the road to Mauroy's HQ. When Gilliaert landed he was accompanied by McKenzie and they were able to drive directly to confront Mauroy and persuade him to stand down. McKenzie then helped Gilliaert restore the confidence of his officers by stressing that the Governor-General had the support of the British government. To diffuse the situation, the mutineers were transferred to British Army units rather than being imprisoned.

There was less gratitude for the intervention of the mission than might have been expected. In January 1941 the Belgian Minister of the Colonies M de Vleeschauwer expressed 'strong disapproval' of the mission, in particular political reports being sent to London based, as he claimed, on inaccurate data. The British Consul-General also emphasized 'the danger of permitting military personnel to intervene in [the] political sphere'. This was despite the fact that their penetration of the dissident organization had potentially saved the government. There was, indeed, some puzzlement in the Foreign Office as to the exact complaint against McKenzie![100] In February Joint made a tour of the colony and sent back a report on the work of the mission complaining that 'throughout my tour I have heard unfavourable reports as to the activities of the Military Mission', and recommended that it be withdrawn as soon as its essential military work was completed, leaving just two liaison officers.[101] The Foreign Office thought the dispatch was provocative and decided not to forward it to the War Office. The complaint seemed to be based on misinformation provided by the Belgian Minister for the Colonies that 'your Officers had something to do with fomenting the Mauroy movement' and there were rumours of this circulating in Costermanaville, Watsa and Stanleyville.[102]

To counter complaints from the Belgian Governor-General and the Minister for Colonies over the size of the mission and continued accusations that they were spying on the Belgian civil and military community, in March 1941 the mission was reduced to McKenzie, a cypher officer and an intelligence officer in Leopoldville, with a wireless station, intelligence officer and cypher officer in Bunia. In the light of the earlier complaints, the War Office had assumed McKenzie should be recalled as part of the reduction but then confusingly learned that the Governor-General (just one month after Joint's damning report) had made a special request that McKenzie should remain because of his expertise and the fact that he was well liked in the colony![103] The main work of the mission would now be to liaise with the Belgian administration over the transit of Empire troops through the Congo to the Middle East but in June the mission was finally dissolved and substituted by a small liaison staff of just two officers under GOC West Africa. McKenzie was to remain as senior liaison officer but now there were concerns that McKenzie was working too closely with the local administrations who were demanding a greater say in organizing defence, rather than relying on negotiations between the government in exile and the War Office in London.[104] In return, Sir Edward Spears pointed out, 'I doubt if London realises the dislike and contempt felt by the active war party in the Belgian Congo for Belgian ministers in London who are believed to be half-hearted in prosecuting the war and to be more concerned with husbanding material assets with a view to post-war reconstruction.'[105]

Chapter Eleven

Asia, the Far East and Australia

China

One of GS(R)'s earliest interests in 1939 was towards China, then fighting a guerrilla war against the Japanese. When Japan declared war on 7 December 1941 against the United States of America and Britain, one of the justifications was that the latter had supported the Chinese in their resistance to the Japanese invasion of 1937. In that year Mao Tse-Tung published *On Guerrilla Warfare* and in early 1939 GS(R) produced an analysis of the war in China as *Considerations from the wars in Spain and China with regard to certain aspects of Army Policy*.[1] Meanwhile, in February 1938 Peter Fleming, adventurer and travel writer, author of *News from Tartary* (1936), which described his 5,600km trek between Peking and Kashmir, had set off on his fourth visit to China as a war correspondent for *The Times*. By then Japan had captured large swathes of Eastern China and he reported the war from Hankow, which was the temporary headquarters of the Chinese government, and from Chungking, where Britain had an embassy. Fleming made frequent visits to the 2,400km-long battle front, sending back daily reports to *The Times*, and also interviewed the Chinese commander-in-chief, Chiang Kai-shek. It seems highly likely that Fleming, a former supplementary reserve officer with the Grenadier Guards, had also been asked to act as an unofficial 'honourable correspondent' with SIS to provide intelligence on the war. Fleming returned to Britain in July 1938 and later contacted MI2 (the section responsible for collecting geographic information) offering his assistance. As a result, on 31 January 1939 he had a meeting with the DMI, Major General Beaumont-Nesbitt, but the process of his recruitment to military intelligence was protracted.[2] In May 1939 he rejoined the Grenadier Guards reserve and trained with the regiment but then worked for a month with MI2. Finally, on 1 August he was telephoned by a 'shadowy colonel' – probably Holland. They met and Fleming was asked if he would return to China to lead a mission to encourage the Chinese guerrillas. He had clearly anticipated the approach and quickly submitted *Notes on the Possibilities of British Military Action in China*, in which he proposed a multi-tasking British mission to China, with its HQ liaising with Chiang's HQ at Chungking, including a propaganda component, technical training for the Chinese, advisory teams in the field, and 'sub-missions' including junior officers who would 'organise and, where possible ... *lead personally* local offensive action against the enemy'.[3] In many respects this became the model for Mission 101 and Gideon Force. He also borrowed from Mao Tse-Tung and proposed the creation of a British, Indian or Australian cavalry force in the Mongolian Corridor north-west of Beijing, arguing that the terrain was ideal for irregular warfare, allowing a small force to have a substantial impact. Fleming met with two MI(R) officers on 8 August and it was proposed to form a joint bureau with Viscount Bearsted of Section D, with Fleming leading a reconnaissance mission to China accompanied by Martin Lindsay, under cover of working for the Ministry of Information and as part-time journalists for *The Times*. They were to explore, 'in an entirely non-committal way', means of helping the Chinese if Britain became involved in a war with Japan. When in China it was anticipated they could work with Lindsay's brother Michael (an economist at Yenching University who was already working with the communist guerrillas) and Fleming's friend A.J. Keswick of the Jardine Matheson & Co. business empire. In preparation for this, Holland wrote on 15 September requesting that Keswick be commissioned by the British Embassy in Shanghai as a captain in MI(R).[4] At this stage, with MI(R) sharing offices with Section D, Fleming mused 'I seem to be under but not of the War Office.'[5] The diplomatic risks of sending such a mission before any declaration of war with Japan were obvious and having been given just a week's notice of the imminent departure of the mission, both the Foreign Office and Ministry of Information raised objections on 20 September 1939. This led to an agreement that the project should be postponed until at least November, before finally being shelved.[6] The plan was eventually revived as Mission 204.

In April 1941, with fears that the Japanese were likely to attempt to cut the Burma Road and starve China's main supply line from South East Asia, the C-in-C Far East, Air Chief Marshal Sir Robert Brooke-Popham, revived the MI(R) concept on a suggestion from General L.E. Dennys (military attaché in Chungking). In anticipation of a Japanese declaration of war, a corps of Chinese guerrillas was to be formed, consisting of fifteen companies of Chinese formed in China but advised by officers from the Indian and British Armies, including demolition experts.[7] The latter would be trained at a new guerrilla school in Burma. While Britain was not to be officially involved in China and was to avoid confrontation with Japan until a declaration of war, the Chinese would prepare the demolition of key sites in southern China, infiltrate saboteurs into areas adjoining Burma, and open smuggling routes across the Himalayas.[8] If discovered in China, the British advisers would be dismissed as being 'volunteers' akin to the US 'Flying Tigers'.[9]

Chiang Kai-shek agreed to the proposal and in early May 1941 General Wavell, C-in-C Middle East, was asked if he had any suitable personnel to spare for what was now labelled Mission 204 of G(R). Eventually, 10 officers and 125 other ranks were transferred from the former Missions 101, 106 and 107 and the commando Layforce, including Bentinck, Brocklehurst, Musgrave and Gilbart-Smith. In addition, Michael Calvert, former instructor at Lochailort, was transferred from the Mission 104 training school in Australia (*see below*). Five Chinese guerrilla battalions of 850 men were to be raised in China, each of which would eventually have three Mission 204 advisory squads (one officer and fifteen other ranks, with a Chinese liaison officer), reminiscent of the earlier Mission 101 operational centres. Brocklehurst (ex Mission 107) and Bentinck (ex Mission 101) would coordinate operations at the nearest HQs of the Chinese Army. The Mission 204 guerrilla training school for advisers and instructors at Maymyo, Mandalay, was given the cover name of 'Bush Warfare School' and would eventually formed the kernel for Wingate's Long Range Penetration Groups (Chindits).

Unsurprisingly, Sir Frank Nelson, head of SOE, suggested in March 1942 that Mission 204 should be amalgamated with its No. 101 Special Training School in Singapore, formed shortly after the Maymyo Training School by the new SOE Oriental mission (created after an exploratory mission by Alan Warren, formerly of MI(R)) and intended to organize 'stay-behind' guerrillas for Malaya and the Dutch East Indies.[10] Here too, there was a strong former MI(R) influence under its CO Jim Gavin, and Freddy Spencer-Chapman. The old demarcation disputes continued and it was agreed that SOE would operate covertly in civilian dress in the period before formal hostilities broke out with Japan, while Mission 204's uniformed British officers would work with Chinese guerrillas only after war was declared. The arrival of SOE's Oriental mission had been deeply resented by the British command in Malaya and Burma but SOE proposed forming a Chinese commando unit in Chungking to help deliver the Dennys plan. To avoid the British government ban on British personnel being used directly in China against the Japanese, Danish refugees were recruited by SOE from August 1941 and trained in Malaya, under the cover of working for the Madsen Corporation. They finally moved into China in February 1942 and established a training base at Chungking, its chief executive officer being A.J. Keswick of the original Fleming plan, who had joined SOE and had been sent in December to head the SOE China mission. There was, however, ambiguity as to how far the new force was to be under Chinese direction or how far it would be controlled by SOE. Keswick tried to take full command of the Chinese Commando Group and complained of Chinese interference in its management but Chiang Kai-shek believed this reneged on the original agreement with SOE and smacked of British imperialism. Consequently, the Chinese Commando Group was disbanded in April 1942, even as the first training course was completed. Its explosives and other stores were transferred to Mission 204, which had sent a team of more than 100 men into China and established training bases in Kwangsi and Chekiang provinces but had not excited the same Chinese ire. Keswick was finally ordered to leave the country in 1943 and was transferred to Lord Mountbatten as a liaison officer with the Southeast Asia Command.

Wingate arrived in India in March 1942 and immediately visited the Mission 204 Bush Warfare School, where he struck up a close rapport with Calvert. However, based on earlier experience in Ethiopia, both Brocklehurst and Bentinck refused to serve again under Wingate. This was Wingate's opportunity to develop the principles behind Gideon Force and he proposed the formation of Long Range Penetration Groups with a G(R) mission to direct their tactical operations, recruitment and training established at Corps HQ, all under the strategic direction of the corps commander. He envisaged two operational groups of four columns each, totalling four infantry battalions in all. Borrowing from Holland's 1940 vision and his own experience in Ethiopia, they would be dependent on resupply by air drops and able to penetrate 160km or more behind enemy lines to attack strategic targets in support of a general Allied offensive. Mission 204 was then incorporated into Wingate's Chindits, finally bringing an independent MI(R)/G(R) to an end.

Australia

One of the last missions of the original MI(R) was to Australia and was partly a spin-off of the Lochailort Training School. Mission 104, under Australian John Charles Mahwood, was to create 'a specially trained body of men for hazardous overseas service' on the model of the Independent Companies. Mahwood, briefly a former MI5 officer, was also to extend the remit of the ISSB to evaluate Australia's internal security intelligence system, at the time wracked with interservice rivalry. Mahwood, Mike Calvert and Spencer-Chapman left Britain in October 1940 amongst the wave of project teams that departed to beat the disbandment of MI(R) and arrived in November 1940, where they oversaw the establishment of a commando school (No. 7 Infantry Training School) at Tidal River, Wilson's Promontory, Victoria. Here, three Australian Independent Companies were formed and trained. The original intention of the War Office in London was to use them to reinforce operations in Western Europe but the Australian General Staff needed the new Independent Companies for operations nearer to home and deeply resented Mahwood's interference into their security system, tapping his telephone and eventually demanding his recall. The problems with the Australian intelligence system were not resolved until after the war. Mahwood became head of New Zealand's security intelligence service before returning to England in 1943. Spencer-Chapman and Calvert went on to Singapore and formed SOE's training school, STS 101.

Chapter Twelve

MI(R) and SOE

He [Jo Holland] could, if he had wished, have regarded himself as the man who began it all. [Joan Bright][1]

In April 1939 few in government had known of the Section D/MI(R) blueprint for war against the Nazis using sabotage, subversion and black propaganda. After the outbreak of war Section D and MI(R) took separate offices, and the vision of Jo Holland and Laurence Grand for an integrated plan of civilian resistance and para-military intervention began to disintegrate. Then, in the panic following the *blitzkrieg* in the Low Countries and France, the need for economic blockade, raids, subversion and propaganda became the core of strategic planning for what was still optimistically expected to be a short war. At the end of May Gladwyn Jebb of the Foreign Office still predicted the collapse of the German home front within weeks.[2] Hugh Dalton, the new Minister for Economic Warfare, similarly predicted that within six months Europe would be faced with 'famine, starvation and revolt, most of all in the slave lands which Germany had overrun,' and declared that the Nazi pall would soon dissipate 'like the snow in Spring'.[3] This was the context for Churchill's enthusiasm in expanding the concept of irregular warfare in July 1940 with the rash slogan of 'Set Europe Ablaze'; covetous eyes began to be cast towards MI(R) and Section D.

There had long been a consensus that there needed to be better coordination of irregular warfare and that its management should be given higher status within government, but there was little agreement on how this might be achieved. In March 1940 the DMI (Beaumont-Nesbitt) suggested the formation of the Inter-Services Project Board (ISPB) to coordinate irregular warfare, with representatives from the three fighting services and SIS reporting to the Joint Intelligence Committee (JIC) of the Chiefs of Staff which would assign the most appropriate body to carry out a project.[4] But there was disagreement as to the power to be given to the Board. Beaumont-Nesbitt proposed that Lord Hankey might take ministerial responsibility for the Board but this was considered as impinging on the authority of the War Office minister.[5] In a conciliatory move, Stewart Menzies, Chief of SIS, suggested that instead of creating a new bureaucracy, MI(R) could take on the role of coordinating projects, reporting to the JIC but making clear that responsibility for project execution would remain with 'MI6 or whichever other Department was most appropriate'.[6] Eventually, the ISPB was set up in April as a relatively low level advisory group, under the chairmanship of Jo Holland, with MI(R) also providing the secretariat. The ISPB had no executive powers but would try to ensure there was no overlap in planning the projects, and encourage the best use of irregular activities in regular operations. Where a project affected only a single department the ISPB would merely be informed of its existence. If it was more wide-ranging, there would be consultation with the service Directors of Intelligence (already sitting on an existing committee with Sir Alexander Cadogan, Permanent Under-Secretary for Foreign Affairs), who would determine the lead body, although the responsibility of sending agents abroad would remain largely with SIS.[7] In the event of dispute the matter would go to Lord Hankey or the Chiefs of Staff Committee. It is not surprising that this ponderous arrangement soon became moribund and a more authoritative level of coordination was required.[8] On 25 May, with the fall of France imminent, the Chiefs of Staff concluded that 'A special organisation will be required and plans to put these operations into effect should be prepared, and all the necessary preparations and training should be proceeded with as a matter of urgency.'[9]

Jo Holland advised the DMI on the way forward and could not hide his frustration; for Joan Bright 'He was too outspoken to be liked by the majority of his colleagues, and to us he could be very rude indeed.'[10] At times this extended to his dealings with senior officers. Although Holland's core belief was the need to coordinate irregular warfare with military strategy under the General Staff, he was clearly not convinced of their current capabilities. Having been shown a draft proposal by Beaumont-Nesbitt for the establishment of a new directorate in the War Office to oversee irregular warfare, on 4 June Holland, clearly in a foul mood, drafted a memo in which he described the General Staff as wrong 'to an amount that almost amounts to criminal negligence' over their predictions of the course of the war. He believed that without the right man in charge, the proposed directorate 'is likely to be as pathetically ineffective as most of the ideas of the General Staff'. Fortunately for his career, this memo was never sent.[11] His final, more temperate, version proposed Beaumont-Nesbitt as the director of this new directorate, delegating his routine DMI duties elsewhere, and on 5 June Beaumont-Nesbitt formally proposed the idea.[12] General Ismay, Churchill's Chief of Staff, naturally agreed to the idea of a new directorate, declaring with typical War Office self-belief, 'As I see it, the War Office would normally be the predominant partner in any sabotage business or other form of irregular warfare.'[13] Yet Beaumont-Nesbitt had to admit that in practical terms the contribution of the War Office to such operations had so far been on a small scale.[14] On 13 June 1940 Holland met with Lord Hankey (Churchill's adviser on intelligence), Stewart

Menzies (head of SIS) and Laurence Grand (head of Section D), where the two SIS representatives managed to push back against the idea of War Office control. Holland was obliged to agree that a small coordinating committee, comprising just one representative of the three fighting services, presumed to be the DMI in the War Office (with Naval and RAF officers attached to him), SIS and Electra House (managing propaganda to enemy countries), should be formed with direct access to a minister (presumably Hankey). Crucially, this proposal left existing operational organizations intact.[15]

Hugh Dalton, the Labour Minister for Economic Warfare, eager to restore the flagging credibility of his Ministry, also had ambitions to win the ministerial coordinating role over the work of Section D, MI(R) and Electra House. His Ministry was being widely criticized in the press and parliament as the 'Ministry of Wishful Thinking' and he needed to restore his reputation.[16] Dalton used his party political relationship with Clement Attlee to persuade Churchill that he was the man to lead any new organization, arguing that as the proposed work would include the incitement of strikes and subversion, the main allies were likely to be among the European Left, making a Labour minister the obvious choice to lead such a movement.[17] Dalton was widely disliked, not least by Churchill, and Gladwyn Jebb described him as a poor organizer, energetic but regarded by many as heavy-handed and a bore.[18] Success seemed to be in the offing when, on 21 June, Dalton recorded that Sir Alexander Cadogan, Permanent Under-Secretary at the Foreign Office, was considering a scheme whereby Dalton and Eden would share responsibility (as ministers for MEW and the War Office) for a new organization with civilian and military branches.[19] Dalton wanted sole control and received an unexpected boost when he saw Davies of MI(R), 'who makes a good impression on me ... [he] says there has been a lack of drive and direction. He obviously wants me to begin to supply these deficiencies.'[20] On 28 June Cadogan moaned about 'Dalton ringing up hourly to try to get a large finger in the sabotage pie' but he was not convinced and circulated a paper echoing the Holland/Beaumont-Nesbitt plan of earlier in the month, believing that Section D and MI(R) should be amalgamated and 'placed under military authority as an operation of war ... the whole thus coming under control of the DMI'. Not surprisingly, Dalton was fiercely opposed to this plan. 'It proposes to give too much to [the] DMI,' he wrote in his diary. Worried that the tide was turning against him, Dalton decided: 'I concert counter-measures and invoke the aid of Attlee.'[21]

On 1 July 1940 (the day that the German Army occupied the Channel Islands) there was a high-level meeting with Lord Halifax (Foreign Secretary) in the chair. Present were Lord Lloyd (Secretary of State for the Colonies), Lord Hankey (Minister without Portfolio), Hugh Dalton (Minister for Economic Warfare), Major General Beaumont-Nesbitt (DMI), Stewart Menzies

(CSS) and Desmond Morton (representing the Prime Minister), with civil servants Sir Alexander Cadogan and his private secretary, Gladwyn Jebb. There was considerable support for putting irregular warfare under the control of the DMI, no doubt helped by the precedent agreed on 3 June by which Section D and MI(R) Middle East (G(R)) was to act under the instruction of the Director of Military Intelligence in Middle East Command, forming 'virtually two halves of the same body'.[22] Dalton complained that he wanted an organization to promote 'chaos and revolution – no more suitable for soldiers than fouling in football or throwing when bowling at cricket', holding that there was a clear distinction between 'war from without' and 'war from within' and that the latter was more likely to be better conducted by civilians than by soldiers.[23] The paucity of practical success from MI(R) seemed to confirm Dalton's opinion but, unsurprisingly, Holland dismissed this conclusion as being 'amateurish' and it soon proved not to be sustainable.[24] The meeting could only reach a vague agreement that a coordinator of existing departmental activity was required at a ministerial level but Dalton saw potential for his future ambition in the decision that 'Whether any reform of the existing machinery was required could safely be left to him [the ministerial coordinator] to decide, after he had some experience of its working.'[25] This was the licence that allowed Dalton to later develop SOE as an independent body. He wasted no time and on 3 July suggested himself to Attlee and Halifax as the coordinating minister.[26] The War Office continued to argue that Section D and Electra House should come under DMI direction through an MI(R) paper of 4 July and Dalton feared that he might be outflanked; he therefore stepped up the pressure by urging members of the Cabinet to support his bid.[27] The War Office could not compete with this political manoeuvring and on 10 July Dalton recorded 'There has been a great to-do today. Beaumont-Nesbitt has been pulling every string. Chiefs of Staff Committee – always apt to be girlish – and Ismay threatening to resign.'[28]

Despite the best efforts of Holland and Beaumont-Nesbitt, the decision had already been made as on 7 July Halifax and Churchill (despite the latter's reservations) had agreed that Dalton be given ministerial oversight of MI(R), Section D and Electra House. On 22 July Neville Chamberlain's draft Charter for the Special Operations Executive (SOE) was approved by the War Cabinet.[29] Dalton was to chair a body 'to co-ordinate all action by way of subversion and sabotage, against the enemy overseas' and direct which organization would carry out a particular project. This decision was not envisaged as affecting the structure of the three existing bodies which 'will, for the time being, continue to be administered by the Ministers at present responsible for them'.[30] In a desperate move to consolidate MI(R)'s status and the bargaining position of the War Office, Holland raised with the JIC aspirations to organize its own 'fifth column' and sabotage operations under the cover of 'Welfare of British Communities Abroad'![31] But Holland had to recognize defeat, commenting in the MI(R) War Diary for 22 July: 'It looks a little as though the Army has missed the bus, so to speak, and has allowed para-military activities to be carried on outside its jurisdiction.'[32] He was still determined that MI(R) should not be lost and on 24 July, just two days after the formal creation of SOE, the DMI met Dalton and expressed the view that MI(R), as a branch of the General Staff, would not be taken over.[33] The pressure was maintained when Holland and Kenyon met directly with Dalton on 29 July and the latter seemed to concede that MI(R) would remain with the War Office – for the present.[34] George Taylor of Section D (soon to be Chief of Staff in SOE) reported that 'MI(R) is furious at the new arrangement and are fighting it in every possible way.'[35] To strengthen their position, a series of progress reports were quickly produced to inflate the achievements of MI(R), including the fiction that it advised on the methodology of Section D through MI(R)c.[36] Nonetheless, the arrival of SOE had highlighted the need for tighter coordination of what had become a rambling Directorate of Military Intelligence and on 2 August the DMI requested authority to appoint a Deputy Director of Military Intelligence (Research) to coordinate the work of MI7, MI9, MI10 and MIL – and to re-evaluate the role of MI(R).[37] Acting Brigadier the Honourable Everard Humphrey Wyndham, the existing DDMI, was appointed DDMI(R) on 15 August. He had served in the First World War with the Life Guards and had been Assistant Adjutant-General, Northern Command before joining the Directorate of Military Intelligence. Wyndham launched a review of the function and future of MI(R) 'as a detached observer' and whereas Holland was polite and described him as 'a nice man doing an unpleasant job in an extremely nice way', the MI(R) War Diary, compiled by his ever-loyal secretary Joan Bright, was less kind and commented that whilst in Northern Command Wyndham had been 'about as much use as a sick headache' and that his arrival was 'unfair' on Holland.[38] Henceforth Wyndham not only took control of discussions regarding the function and future of MI(R) but began to take a more active role in MI(R) projects, edging out a clearly disillusioned Holland. Consequently, when Hamilton visited the MI(R) offices in September to formalize Mission 106 to Aden, he believed MI(R) was under the command of Wyndham. The future of MI(R) was being taken out of Holland's hands and this must have been galling to its founder, who began to look for ways of re-establishing the original research focus of GS(R). According to the MI(R) War Diary, 'There then followed a disheartening period when MI(R) were unable to put into effect any of their plans or projects' and an erased clause blamed this, perhaps unfairly, on the arrival of Wyndham.[39]

Dalton did not give up easily and three days after Halifax finally agreed that SOE should take over responsibility for Section D, likely having heard whispers of the review of MI(R) in the War Office, on 19 August Dalton asked that the subversive functions of MI(R) be transferred to SOE. In the report 'The Fourth Arm' he wrote: 'It is hardly for me to make recommendations of the future of a section of the War Office, but there is no doubt in my mind that, up to now, the functions of MI(R) and of D have seriously overlapped.' Although this was exaggerated, he concluded 'there will be no place for two bodies engaged upon the same work'.[40] Dalton accepted that the military operations of MI(R) should remain within the War Office but wanted its subversive functions to devolve upon what he was still describing as 'the reformed D Organization' and 'If certain of the particularly gifted junior officers of MI(R) could gravitate towards the latter, nobody would be more pleased than I.' As with his machinations to remove the heads of Section D (Laurence Grand) and Electra House (Campbell Stuart), this clearly rejected any role for the likes of Holland.[41] But while the Chiefs of Staff gave general approval to Dalton's proposal (noting that Wyndham's review was likely to come to the same conclusion of absorbing much of MI(R) into the operations side of the War Office), they also ensured that there would be little else left structurally for SOE to commandeer. On 26 August Wyndham made clear that the MI(R) initiative of inserting assistant military attachés into legations must remain within the War Office and disingenuously claimed 'Obviously it would be entirely improper for him [the AMA] to take part in subversive activities although they can, of course, gather information on conditions which may lend themselves to such outbreaks.'[42] He similarly maintained that all military missions should remain with the War Office as being conducted by uniformed officers. The main concern of the War Office remained the mantra of MI(R) that irregular warfare had to be subordinate to the main war strategy and, with the new realization that the German occupation of Europe was going to last until at least late 1942, issued a warning against Churchill's appealing, but dangerous 'Set Europe Ablaze' soundbite:

> Subversive operations must not be an end in themselves. They should conform with military operations ... It will be important to ensure that subversive movements should not be allowed to break out spontaneously in areas that individually become ripe for revolt. No appreciable results can be expected in the early future and we should organise these activities on a large scale so that they are timed to mature in relation to regular operations undertaken as part of our general policy.[43]

Instead, success would depend on 'Adequate preparations to supply the necessary material and physical assistance and support of the revolts ... A carefully prepared scheme of propaganda ... [and] A clear policy as to the economic and political future of Europe.'[44]

Wyndham's draft review of MI(R), submitted on 26 August 1940, seems to have been largely compiled by Holland.[45] It repeated Holland's frustrations, complaining about the discouraging lack of clear guidance from the General Staff, the reluctance of the Foreign Office to engage with subversive warfare and their 'dismal' failure to reply to MI(R)'s proposals. Wyndham also repeated Holland's contention that, wherever possible, irregular warfare tactics should be incorporated into War Office operations as a matter of course, within modernized existing branches, rather than proliferating new organizations. But Wyndham admitted that 'The pursuit of para-military activities has been added to the labours, without being properly fitted into the framework, of the General Staff.' Accepting that existing departments were by no means equipped to accept this new form of warfare, Wyndham nonetheless believed 'It will however clearly be best to adhere to them and endeavour to cure their ills rather than to scrap them and start again. The shattering effect on morale of the latter alternative would more than outbalance any advantages which might be gained.' In defence of MI(R) he went on: 'It is, however, important to stress the discouraging effect that the lack of clear guidance has inevitably had on the staff officers responsible for much hard work in preparation for this form of warfare.'[46] Wyndham's draft report saw MI(R) as being retitled the 'Special Operations Branch' under the Directorate of Military Operations and Planning (DMO&P), creating a distinct section for research where it would encourage 'original thought' as well as maintaining its existing operational functions and a new section providing the link between the War Office and SOE. The report was, however, rejected by DMO&P, and the eventual decision was made to simply disperse MI(R) functions to other War Office branches. A final report to the Vice Chief of the Imperial General Staff was submitted on 12 September when DMI concluded: 'So far as MI [Military Intelligence] is concerned, this will mean the disappearance of MI(R), some of the officers concerned being absorbed into other branches of the Directorate, others becoming available for appointment elsewhere.'[47] The final product of MI(R) HQ was a comprehensive report on the organization of Nazi subversive operations across the world, written by Lionel Kenyon and circulated on 19 September.[48]

On 26 September 1940 it was announced that the reorganization of MI(R) was settled, to be implemented on 1 October, although in practice it was still dispatching the last of its missions (Missions 104, 106, 107) on 3 October. By then most of the fourteen officers on the establishment had been transferred to other branches of the Directorate of Military Intelligence. In the short term, SOE absorbed only a small number of individual members of MI(R), making it almost entirely dependent on the former Section D. Davies was one of the few MI(R) officers to transfer to SOE directly (on 23 September) but many other individuals would gravitate towards SOE over the coming year.[49] MI(R)a

(Projects and Planning) and MI(R)b (Personnel section) transferred to MO9. The technical section, MI(R)c, was initially intended to transfer to the Ministry of Supply but eventually, although administered by the latter, functionally it became MD1 in the new Ministry of Defence. It was a dispersal that the philosophical Holland, never a personal empire-builder, saw not as cause for regret but merely as part of the process of evolution:

> A great deal of the work hitherto done by MI(R) has been taken away for these new organizations [Directorate of Combined Operations, SOE and MO9], and I do not myself see any objection or cause for regret in what I see as the normal process of evolution. As I have said, MI(R) was never intended in itself to be anything more than a small branch of the General Staff dealing with one of the leading features of the present war [irregular warfare], and enabling the General Staff itself to take some lead in that particular aspect of the war.[50]

Holland had always seen MI(R) as a free-thinking research and advisory body and had resented its limited resources being increasingly drawn directly into managing operations simply because there was no existing alternative. Even before Wyndham's review, in August 1940 he was seeking a way of re-establishing the earlier research basis of GS(R); freed by Wyndham's increasing role in day-to-day matters, he began to develop ideas that went far beyond the current concepts of irregular warfare, looking to evolve ideas for 'blue sky' thinking that were increasingly out of place in a war that looked for short-term solutions. He believed that 'If we are, in the long run, to be successful, we must urgently set going a search for tactical and mechanical conceptions that will surprise the enemy and put us ahead of the game.' Holland argued that by such study, 'irregular warfare carried to its highest form may be our only means of winning the war'. Rather than leave irregular operations to a specialist branch, he believed that irregular tactics 'should in future become the normal tactics and strategy of the British Army'.[51] As examples, Holland cited the revolutionary potential of autogyros, helicopters and short take off/landing aircraft, and wanted to explore the problems of maintaining morale in a large army and the means of making the best use of women in the services.[52] In particular Holland wanted to direct MI(R) into researching the technical and tactical aspects of what he saw as a new air cavalry 'since out of this may come a way, perhaps the only way, of supporting subversive movements in Europe, to say nothing of the possibilities in African territories'.[53] With little faith in the ability of the existing army to appreciate or develop the tactical use of such troops he wanted to use the Independent Companies in training at Lochailort to experiment with the tactical doctrine.

There was, however, to be no place for Jo Holland in the reorganization that led to SOE; his name was submitted for reposting to the Royal Engineers as early as 23 September.[54] As with Laurence Grand, the opportunity to return to regular soldiering was probably a relief and he had no interest in serving in Dalton's SOE. Joan Bright commented, 'He had never sought personal aggrandisement in the work he had begun, and the fact that it had outgrown the conventional garb in which he had hoped for it did not inspire him to continue in it.'[55] After a final lunch for the original members of MI(R) on 2 October, Holland returned to the Royal Engineers, but his health was still delicate and he remained at the War Office. Here he had a major role in the strategy for lend-lease, and then continued his exploration of the use of Royal Engineer units in MI(R) by developing the concept of assault engineers (as implemented by Percy Hobart and his 79th Armoured Division), which had a major impact on the success of D-Day. It was not until September 1944 that he was posted abroad to Italy. Sadly, renewed illness obliged him to return after only a few months. He finally retired in 1951 as a major general but died in 1957.

In the Middle East G(R) under Terence Airey continued to maintain a separate identity from SOE and in June 1941 Dalton was still complaining that Wavell expected G(R) and SOE in the Middle East to both act under his direction.[56] A robust reply from Wavell repeated many of the arguments concerning the control of Section D and MI(R) in 1940.[57] Wavell argued that G(R) operated under the orders of regular formations and that all subversive activities in operational areas should be coordinated with the military.[58] A memorandum circulated to Dalton and the War Office summarized the operational division of labour between SOE and G(R) in familiar terms. SOE would promote subversive movements against the enemy and undertake sabotage and covert propaganda. G(R), under the control of GHQ Middle East, was responsible for organizing all irregular and guerrilla activities that could be carried out by uniformed personnel. Nonetheless, SOE finally won the battle on 4 September 1941 when it absorbed G(R) in the Middle East. In the period before Colin Gubbins became its head, SOE was uncomfortable with inheriting a department which had maintained the military perspective of Jo Holland, and Lord Glenconner was appointed head of SOE Middle East in August 1942 with part of his remit 'To expel the G(R) influence – the tendency to become para-military rather than subversive'.

MI(R) in SOE

MI(R) did not provide a structural basis for SOE in the same way as Section D or Electra House but F.T. 'Tommy' Davies soon established a small core of former MI(R) officers in the training and policy sections of SOE and became the original Director of Training, as well as personal assistant to the Executive Director of SOE (Frank Nelson). Davies carried much of the early responsibility for organizing supplies and services and on 12 October he produced a report on training and the establishment of training schools. A training section was consequently established under John Wilson (joined later by other former MI(R) officers Peter Wilkinson and Harold Perkins). Wilson had been in the MI(R) mission to Yugoslavia in 1939 and had joined the Lochailort Training School on 31 July 1940, teaching counter-espionage techniques.

Other former MI(R) officers began to join from late 1940. The most important was Colin Gubbins, who joined on 18 November 1940 from the Auxiliary Units, when the immediate threat of invasion was over. He brought with him as his secretary Lesley Wauchope from MI(R). Gubbins was seconded to SOE at the personal request of Dalton because, although the latter had been disparaging over the role of the regular army in irregular warfare, he had been obliged to accept that the new SOE needed a senior military figure to improve relations with the War Office.[59] Gubbins had made a favourable impression on Dalton when the two had met at a dinner given at the Polish Embassy in November 1939, where Gubbins had railed against the bureaucracy that had held up delivery of Hawker Hurricanes to the Poles before the invasion. He brought his expertise in training from MT1 and MI(R), his reputation as a decorated commander from the Norwegian campaign and his more recent experience in forming the Auxiliary Units, but it was in SOE that Gubbins found his metier as an organizer and politician. Finally restored to his rank of acting brigadier, Gubbins was made Director of Training and Operations and Kim Philby recorded the shock of the arrival of Gubbins and his military cohort, 'who barked at each other and at us', at the former Section D training school at Brickendonbury.[60] His initial role was less than Dalton had intimated and he was not even given offices in the new HQ at 64 Baker Street. Instead he was relegated to two gloomy family flats in the Berkeley Court apartment block, opposite Baker Street station.[61] Although Dalton had promised him the title of Director of Operations, in practice the situation was confused as George Taylor from Section D had overall responsibility for operations and had specific responsibility for most of the few on-going projects, while Sir Charles Hambro had responsibility for operations in Scandinavia. Gubbins' power base lay in the Polish and Czech Sections but it was not until November 1941 that additional country sections (French, Belgian, Dutch, German and Austrian) would be grouped under him.[62]

Peter Wilkinson (who joined at the same time as Gubbins) maintained that Gubbins' decision to enter SOE was surprising because 'he had little confidence in sabotage and subversion as such'.[63] Such negativity may have been due to his frustrating experiences with Section D but Wilkinson concluded that Gubbins' decision to join SOE was to continue the work of Jo Holland and 'can only be attributed to a conviction that, if properly coordinated with regular operations, guerrilla warfare on the mainland of Europe might prove decisive in what might otherwise be a single-handed struggle against Hitler ... Gubbins may well have believed that with his unique MI(R) background this is where his duty lay, at any rate for the time being.'[64] The new SOE now seemed an opportunity to finally put into practice the principles he had preached in *Art of Guerrilla Warfare*. But under the influence of Dalton and the former SIS executives there was an early bias against the para-military philosophy of MI(R)/G(R) and it was not until Sir Charles Hambro resigned as head of SOE in September 1943 (rather than accept theatre commander control of operations) that Gubbins could bring SOE more into the mainstream with a military focus. At last it seemed that Holland's vision was finally coming to fruition and at least partially justified Joan Bright's assessment. Already in early 1942 SOE had taken on a shared responsibility with Combined Operations HQ for the new Small Scale Raiding Force (SSRF). In July 1942 Gubbins had first raised the concept of the Jedburgh units – multinational teams of three men parachuted into occupied France in uniform to feed-back intelligence and coordinate the resistance and maquis after D-Day. From January 1944 their training base at Milton Hall, Cambridgeshire, came under the command of George Musgrave, formerly of Mission 106 in Aden, who had gone on to command the Special Service Battalion under Military Mission 204 and the 3rd SAS Training School. The insertion of the Jedburghs and the SAS Brigade made a decisive guerrilla contribution to D-Day and was the final vindication of Holland's vision of para-military units to organize and mount irregular operations in direct support of a conventional offensive.

Many other former members of MI(R) drifted into SOE during the course of the war. The bonds created by their early service in MI(R) remained firm, and Hazell, Dodds-Parker, Wilkinson and Perkins worked with Gubbins at the end of the Second World War to try to secure a post-war role for SOE, independent of SIS. This was not to be and, after being given responsibility for absorbing or dissolving SOE, Menzies took revenge on Gubbins for his earlier attacks on SIS. Gubbins was firmly told there was no job for him and he was obliged to retire on the pension of his substantive rank of colonel. Some members of SOE were retained within SIS and formed the core of its 'Special Operations Units', whose function was later taken over by the shadowy 'Increment', linked to the SAS.

Conclusion

MI(R) held a unique position in British Intelligence during its short existence but struggled to find a niche as uniformed warriors trying to operate in secret whilst in 'conventional garb', and for its officers it became an exercise in 'repressed frustration'.[1] Not created as an operational service where its achievements could be measured by success in the field, it was intended as 'a clearing house for bright ideas', focused first on countering the threat of the newly labelled 'fifth column' against British interests abroad and then in developing a para-military interpretation of guerrilla warfare.[2] Jo Holland's vision was to incorporate irregular warfare into the existing structures of the War Office and, evangelically, into the methodology of foreign General Staffs. This was all predicated in the firm belief that the purpose of irregular warfare was to support conventional campaigns and that it should mainly be undertaken by uniformed officers rather than by what was widely seen in government and the War Office as the distasteful 'cloak and dagger' secret agents of SIS.

One of MI(R)'s main achievements was in providing the War Office with a consistent doctrinal approach to guerrilla warfare during 1939–1940, in a period of considerable flux, and establishing the longer-term potential of air-supplied, and even helicopter-borne, special forces.[3] It was not able to codify its doctrine in the comprehensive Field Service Regulations that Holland had originally envisaged, but the essence was contained in Gubbins' pamphlets (translated into at least seventeen languages) and widely used throughout the war, while Holland's flow of briefs for his superior officers ensured that his philosophy became the bedrock of the War Office perspective on irregular warfare and its faith in British leadership through specialist 'advisers'. MI(R)'s officers were, in the main, backroom warriors and their discrete contribution to operational security through the ISSB and in establishing the escape organization MI9 should not be underestimated. Based on the traditional role of intelligence officers, MI(R) also collated information, often from desk-based studies, to supply assessments to other parts of Military Intelligence and Operations. Some of this work duplicated the long-standing intelligence-gathering of SIS (as in Yugoslavia) but the General Staff were deeply frustrated by the official policy of SIS to exclude the Chiefs of Staff Committee from knowledge of their operations. In 1940 MI(R) also filled a vital gap, albeit on a small scale, in reconnaissance, deploying advance security officers in Norway and reconnoitring the potential for a British invasion of the Belgian Congo. In some respects, it was a forerunner of the future Intelligence Corps as intelligence analysts and indeed Gerald Templer, the founder of the Corps in July 1940, had worked closely with MI(R).

MI(R) proved to be a significant reservoir of wartime talent for the intelligence services, SOE and the future special forces, not least through the index it compiled of potential recruits; many officers in those bodies served their apprenticeship in MI(R). MI(R) also advised the DMI on the development of general intelligence training and the Cambridge 'Gauleiters' course was innovative in teaching political warfare, while the Lochailort Training School provided a model for future commando training. Lochailort brought together men who would have a key role in the development of Britain's special forces; instructors included three commanding officers of the future SAS, the 1st Special Service Brigade and the Chindits. As a clearing house for the ideas of others, thousands of Allied servicemen had reason to be grateful to MI(R) in its role in establishing the escape and evasion service of MI9, under Norman Crockatt. The technical section of MI(R)c under Millis Jefferis operated more or less independently and produced a range of innovative material, designed primarily for the regular army rather than the clandestine market. As such it was retained in MD1 rather than being passed to SOE like its Section D equivalent. Even here, Jefferis followed the somewhat academic approach of Jo Holland, his interest being primarily in the inventions *per se*, with little interest in the practicalities of production of his inventions, leaving that to Stuart Macrae.

By launching a partnership with Laurence Grand of Section D in March 1939, the character of GS(R), as it was then called, was changed from a small desk-bound research unit to a department operating across the world. Scheme D gave MI(R) the funding it needed for expansion and offered the potential for an integrated clandestine service combining civilian and military operations, but Holland was more constrained by the War Office and Foreign Office than was Section D, which took advantage of the traditional distancing of SIS from normal government. The head of SIS, Stewart Menzies, had explained to the Hankey Inquiry in March 1940 'that from the earliest days S.S. [SIS] had, for vital reasons of secrecy, deliberately been kept aloof from regular Government committees such as the Committee of Imperial Defence and the Chiefs of Staff organization'.[4] MI(R) therefore remained focused on being a semi-legitimate advisory service, using the traditional mechanism of military missions, while Section D threw itself into the field of sabotage and subversion with gusto – leaving MI(R) behind. After the outbreak of war the War Office became desperate to re-establish its leadership and, much to Holland's frustration, the small MI(R) was obliged to take on operational responsibilities for which it was neither trained nor properly resourced, relying instead on the contemporary arrogance of the British military establishment in believing their inherent superiority in all forms of warfare.

Its most effective field operation in Europe was arguably the conventional logistical support provided for the Finnish campaign, but it struggled to repeat this operational success other than with Mission 101 in Ethiopia. The War Office wanted MI(R) to work in at least a semi-official way with the General Staffs of target countries, meaning it could not operate in a completely covert manner, and tried to contain the potential for embarrassment by limiting the use of regular officers or foreigners as advisers. In line with this conventional military approach, the first choice for any demolition plan was to delegate to the Royal Engineers (as in the Low Countries, France and Romania) rather than following SIS in recruiting local agents. For Macrae MI(R) was 'a more or less legitimate outfit ... not to be confused with saboteurs'.[5] MI(R) officers were chosen as organizers and liaison officers and few had practical experience in the skills they were supposed to be teaching, although there were perhaps more former SIS intelligence officers than the War Office cared to admit. Other than Mission 101, few became personally involved in organizing sabotage and MI(R)'s efforts never delivered its full promise.[6] Some officers seemed chosen primarily for their enthusiasm, and a number of those chosen for the Middle East missions were known to be infirm and were unable to complete their tasks.

The most famous member of MI(R) is Colin Gubbins, due to his later leadership of SOE. He was recruited in April 1939, largely for his expertise in training, after the division of labour with Section D had been agreed. He had a different perspective from Holland, more driven by personal ambition. The restrictions on MI(R)'s ability to become an operational organization became deeply frustrating, especially when he discovered that at almost every turn Section D had already begun operations and that MI(R) was reliant on Section D both for funding and for its supply chain. While Section D could deliver the government imperative to support the economic blockade by sabotage on the supply network (albeit on a small and uneven scale), MI(R) could deliver little in practical terms and its attempts to emulate Section D often proved a dismal failure. Gubbins wildly oversold the contribution that MI(R) could make to the Polish and Czech resistance in order to create a power-base and left confusion in his wake. Despite this, after the war Gubbins and his devoted staff, disappointed by his treatment by SIS, created a mythological back-story for his role in SOE, suggesting that MI(R) was somehow more practical than Section D, and this has been followed unquestioningly by most later writers. This legend also presented Gubbins as an innovator in guerrilla warfare that is not supported by the evidence, although he undoubtedly was important in collating existing methodologies into his pamphlets.

The rapidity of the *blitzkrieg* in Europe prevented MI(R) from developing its remit of encouraging foreign General Staffs to take up guerrilla warfare and there was not the time to properly embed its military missions. Instead, MI(R) discovered, to its chagrin, that in the face of apparent German invincibility foreign generals were not necessarily prepared to take its 'Johnny come lately' advice other than as a price for being supplied with funds and weapons. MI(R)'s claim to expertise, based largely on its production of the 1939 pamphlets and the products of MI(R)c, was somewhat exaggerated and it admitted that its staff would have to be installed with minimal or no training. In truth, the Poles and Czechs had far more practical experience in such warfare. MI(R) could offer too little, too late and its Mission 13 in Norway, despatched in the final stages of the campaign, was largely ignored while, in a typical War Office bureaucratic fashion, MI(R)'s response to the invasion of France was to suggest raising a committee to investigate the potential of guerrilla warfare.

Unfortunately, when the opportunity arose to showcase MI(R)'s ideas in the British Army, the Independent Companies had to be deployed to Norway without adequate training and in circumstances where they were obliged to operate as conventional light infantry rather than as guerrilla units. Yet despite their failings, they proved to be an important stepping-stone for the creation of the Commandos. With the utmost irony, the first attempt to organize a military guerrilla force in Britain was undertaken in June 1940 by General Thorne of XII Corps, independently of MI(R) and based on an East Prussian concept. The GHQ Auxiliary Units were then formed as a more respectable and legal military alternative to the Section D Home Defence Scheme, but despite MI(R)'s long-standing efforts to offer advice abroad, it took Gubbins a month to arrive at their final format. Even then, it can be argued that the Auxiliary Units were a strategic failure and the antithesis of Holland's vision of guerrilla troops able to operate in support of conventional operations, largely because there was no means of communicating with them once they had 'gone to ground'.

Following the collective failure of Independent Companies, the attempts at sabotage in Romania, the military mission in Norway, the Davies mission to the Netherlands, and the dismissal by Churchill of Warren's French mission as a 'silly fiasco', it is not surprising that in June 1940 Hugh Dalton believed that the Directorate of Military Intelligence was not the body to organize irregular warfare. In a last-ditch defence, MI(R) produced a number of reports that inflated its achievements and the degree of work in progress. Yet even as it was being disbanded, the MI(R) vision finally achieved success in the Middle East where, in line with Holland's philosophy, G(R) provided logistical support, administration and advice, but practical control of the missions was in the hands of the theatre commander. Its efforts to create a raiding force in Aden with Mission 106 was another disaster and Mission 107 to south Ethiopia ended in confusion, but Mission 101 finally showed the potential of its military advisers. Sandford's HQ in the Gojjam province of Ethiopia would form the model for future SOE advisory missions.

MI(R) was a male preserve other than the three specially appointed secretaries. Joan Bright took on wider administrative duties and later compiled the MI(R) War Diary. She became especially well known through her presence at interview panels, where she was a deliberate distraction to recruits, and as holder of the 'bag of gold' from whom officers received funds invisible to the War Office auditors. A woman with such roles was highly unusual in the War Office at the time and therefore attracted much attention and legend, although in sharing offices with Section D of SIS, who employed female SIS officers in senior positions, the employment of female officers may have come to seem more normal to Holland.[7] As a result, Holland saw an exploration of the role of women in the forces as a future priority for MI(R).

It is over-simplistic to say MI(R) was absorbed by SOE and its component parts slipped quietly into other sections of the Military Intelligence Directorate and the new Ministry of Defence. The early SOE was essentially a reworking of Section D with a few individuals from MI(R), although many former officers drifted into SOE from late 1940 onwards. The most significant recruit was Colin Gubbins who, when head of SOE, ensured that this accepted the basic philosophy of MI(R) and was subject to the demands of theatre commanders, an idea despised by both the original minister, Hugh Dalton, and Gubbins' predecessor, Charles Hambro. As the estimates for the length of the war extended from the optimism of early 1940 it had become difficult to maintain the initial advice that resistance forces in occupied territories should not engage in premature sabotage, risking large-scale civilian reprisals, until they would be needed to support an Allied invasion. Activists understandably wanted to demonstrate opposition to occupation and fulfil Churchill's careless mantra to 'Set Europe Ablaze' but this came at considerable cost. By 1942 Gubbins was already trying to revitalise MI(R)'s focus on specialist military guerrilla units to support invasion, with plans for what became the Jedburgh teams, and SOE took on a more para-military aspect when he took charge in 1943. By D-Day the insertion of the uniformed Jedburgh teams and the SAS Brigade lay at the heart of the Allied guerrilla strategy. Meanwhile, in the Far East Wingate's Chindit columns similarly leaned heavily on the methodology established by MI(R). At last, the pioneering vision of Jo Holland was being fulfilled.

If the practical successes of MI(R) during 1939–1940 were limited, after the war its history was distorted to support the reputation of Colin Gubbins and his role in the mythology of SOE. As a consequence, MI(R) was presented as a more active and practical body than its partner/rival Section D of SIS (whose reputation was systematically destroyed). Thus M.R.D. Foot, relying heavily on Gubbins as a source, considered the exploits of Davies in Amsterdam as being more successful than those of Chidson, despite the pessimistic assessment of Davies himself (*see above*, p. 133). In his biography of Gubbins, Linderman reinforces this assessment, unfairly claiming 'Holland was thinking up clever projects and the men of Section D were chasing ghosts,' and credits Gubbins with the more practical role.[8] Claims of duplication of effort and rivalry between Section D and MI(R) were exaggerated and chiefly blamed on Laurence Grand, with no attention paid to the divisive role played by Gubbins. Yet Grand and Holland, whilst very different characters, complemented each other very well and, for them, the demarcation of responsibilities was clear. Problems only arose when MI(R) ceased to be the military arm of Section D and moved back to the War Office, and Colin Gubbins was allowed the independence of the Polish missions to test the boundaries of responsibilities and build his own power-base. It is arguable that Gladwyn Jebb, no fan of Grand, reversed the story when he claimed Section D 'spent much of its time conducting subversive operations less against the enemy than against a rather similar outfit operating under the War Office known as MI(R)'.[9] The argument has tended to be one-sided due to the control that Gubbins and his allies had in orchestrating the post-war telling of the story. Sadly, Holland and Grand never published their own version of events after the war.

MI(R) was the creation of Jo Holland, an intelligent and imaginative leader who, despite his famous bursts of frustrated temper at the War Office (which contrasted with his reputation as a good-humoured raconteur at home), inspired great loyalty among his staff. His time as a secret warrior was less than two years in a long and distinguished career, but he was sadly hampered by his poor health resulting from disease contracted in the First World War and the mysterious wounding by the IRA in 1921. Yet it was this accident of fate that brought him to MI(R). By August 1940, disheartened by the War Office losing the initiative in irregular warfare to the new SOE, Holland was already seeking a return to the longer-term research perspective of the original GS(R) but in October, like Laurence Grand before him, he was relieved to escape the politics and in-fighting and returned to the Royal Engineers. Holland became Deputy Chief Engineer, Northern Command before returning to the War Office in April 1942, where his capacity for strategic thinking was invaluable in establishing the priorities for Lend-Lease and, as Deputy Engineer-in-Chief, he continued his focus on the specialist use of the Royal Engineers championing the concept of assault engineers, which were used to great effect on D-Day. Promoted major-general in 1943, in September 1944 he finally had a chance to serve abroad, becoming Chief Engineer, Mediterranean, at Allied HQ in Italy until another bout of illness again obliged his return. More staff appointments followed and in 1948 he became Deputy Quartermaster General at the War Office. He would have been promoted to his dream of Quartermaster General but was again taken ill and finally retired in December 1951. Holland died just five years later and sadly never wrote his own memoir of irregular warfare in the Second World War, which would surely have contained some pithy observations. However, as with Laurence Grand, it is likely that he would never have dreamed of revealing his secrets at that time and these two pioneers slipped into obscurity.

The full implementation of Holland's vision for irregular warfare was yet to come. His military missions evolved into the small teams of special forces 'advisers' discreetly deployed around the world and, as he predicted, helicopters became an invaluable tool for delivering and supplying troops. His foresight was remarkable and although he opposed the creation of the short-lived SOE, taking a longer perspective there is some justification in Joan Bright's claim for him as 'the man who began it all'.[10]

Notes

Introduction

1. See Atkin (2017) for a detailed history of Section D.
2. 'Irregular Tactics and Strategy', J.C.F. Holland to DMI, August 1940: TNA HS 8/256.
3. Hailsham (1990), p. 144.
4. Gubbins (1948), p. 221.
5. Gubbins' address to the Danish/English Society in Copenhagen, 29 April 1966: Gubbins papers 4/1/20, IWM. He made no acknowledgement of the SIS intelligence networks already in place on the continent, the efforts of Section D in Norway to insert agents, and wireless and the already sizeable inventory of special equipment provided by Section D and MI(R).
6. Linderman (2016), p. 106.
7. Mackenzie (2000), p. 54.
8. Mackenzie (2000), p. 54.
9. Foot (1966), p. xii.
10. Anglim (2005).

Chapter One: The Formation of MI(R)

1. Dunsterville (1920); MacLaren (1976), p. 9.
2. 'General Staff Research', MI(R), 23 August 1940: TNA HS 8/258.
3. 'War Diary of MI(R) from 3 September 1939 to 2 October 1940' (report): TNA HS 8/263.
4. House of Commons Debates, 10 March 1938: Hansard, vol. 332 c. 213.
5. Broomhall (1957), p. 302.
6. Astley (2007), pp. 19, 30.
7. *Ibid.*, p. 30.
8. Foot (1970), p. 41.
9. His later claim for compensation gives the date as 8 January but an entry in the List of British Casualties for 1921 in the Irish Military Archives (A/0614), gives the date as 9 January 1921. I am grateful to Ger Murphy for sharing this record.
10. Obituary in W.M. Broomhall (1957); 'The Interview in Bath History XI: some notes', *The Survey of Bath and District*, no. 23, October 2008; correspondence with Elizabeth Holland (daughter), November 2018.
11. Thanks to Ger Murphy for providing these references and discussion about the incident.
12. TNA T 160/146/6.
13. TNA LCO 53/55.
14. 'Comments on Foot's Book', Gubbins papers 3/2/57, IWM.
15. *Ibid.*; Gubbins, 'The Underground Forces in Britain 1940–1944', lecture given to the Cerne Abbas Discussion Club, Dorchester, 1973: Gubbins papers, 4/1/42, IWM.
16. Astley (2007), p. 41.
17. Foot and Langley (1979), p. 31.

18. 'Functions and Organisation of MI(R)', Holland to DDMI(O), 20 December 1939: TNA HS 8/258. I am grateful to Elizabeth Holland for discussion on her father's influences and character.
19. Fox-Davies to Wavell, 1 October 1935, quoted in Fergusson (1961), p. 25.
20. 'CG's Comments on Foot's Book': Gubbins papers, 3/2/57, IWM; Report No. 8, *Investigation of the possibilities of Guerrilla Activities*, 1 June 1939: TNA HS 8/260 and Appendix 2.
21. 'Duties of the New Branch', J.C.F. Holland, 3 April 1939: TNA HS 8/256.
22. *Official History of VTC*, 1920.
23. Lawrence (1929).
24. Gubbins, quoted in Wilkinson and Astley (1993), p. 35.
25. Atkin (2017), Chs 1, 2.
26. Astley (2007), p. 21.
27. 'Scheme D', 20 March 1939: TNA HS 8/256.
28. Astley (2007), pp. 20–2; information from Lady Bessborough, with thanks.
29. 'Comments on Foot's Book,': Gubbins papers 3/2/57, IWM.
30. Mackenzie (2000), p. 8.
31. *Ibid.*, p. 9.
32. 'Section D', Laurence Grand, 20 March 1939: TNA HS 8/256.
33. D Scheme: TNA HS 8/256.
34. *Ibid.*
35. *Ibid.*; Atkin (2017), Appendix 1.
36. *Ibid.*; Atkin (2017), Appendix 1.
37. 'Report No. 8: Investigation of the possibilities of Guerrilla Activities', 1 June 1939: TNA HS 8/260; 'General Staff Research', MI(R), 23 August 1940: TNA HS 8/258.
38. D Scheme, 20 March 1939: TNA HS 8/256 and Atkin (2017), Appendix 1.
39. Notes and Lessons by Laurence Grand, 1946: TNA HS 7/5.
40. 'Report on MI(R) Mission to Romania', 19 December 1940, R. Watson: TNA HS 8/261.
41. Astley (2007), pp. 20–1.
42. 'Duties of MI(R)', 2 June 1940: TNA HS 8/256.
43. Astley (2007), p. 20.
44. Wilkinson and Astley (1993), p. 34.
45. Minute of 18 April 1939: TNA HS 8/256. The meeting on 13 April led to the production of GS(R) Report No. 8 of 1 June 1939.
46. 'Draft Agenda for meeting to settle the future of GS(R) and certain connected questions', 16 June 1939; 'Minutes of meeting to settle the future of GS(R) and certain connected questions', 27 June 1939: TNA HS 8/256.
47. TNA HS 8/256.
48. 'Report on the organisation within the War Office for the conduct of para-military activities', Brigadier Wyndham, 25 August 1940: TNA HS 8/258.
49. *Ibid.*
50. George Larden personnel file: TNA HS 9/890/2.
51. Maschwitz (1957), p. 130.
52. Wilkinson (2002), p. 87.
53. Wilkinson to PCO, 4 February 1940: TNA HS 4/31.
54. Record of an interview of 13 April 1939 with CIGS with regard to the duties of D/M, 13 April 1939: TNA HS 8/256.
55. *Ibid.*
56. 'General Instructions', J.C.F. Holland, 13 April 1939: TNA HS 8/256; repeated in GS(R) Report No. 8 and 'Duties and Responsibilities of MI(R)', J.C.F. Holland, 22 July 1940: TNA HS 8/256.

57. Letter of 19 April 1939 to military attachés: TNA HS 8/256.
58. 'General Instructions', 13 April 1939: TNA HS 8/256.
59. Gubbins to Foot, 28 April 1964: Gubbins papers, 3/2/57, IWM.
60. Eric Mockler-Ferryman to Joan Bright Astley, 7 December 1976, Gubbins papers 12/2, IWM.
61. Macrae (1972), p. 71.
62. *Ibid.*, p. 24.
63. Astley (2007), p. 23.
64. Wilkinson and Astley (1993), p. 34.
65. Astley (2007), pp. 21–2.
66. Wilkinson and Astley (1993), p. 102.
67. Young (1980), p. 100.
68. *Ibid.*, p. 259.
69. Quoted in Ward (1997), p. 58.
70. Astley (2007), p. 23.
71. *Report No. 8: Investigation of the possibilities of Guerrilla Activities*: TNA HS 8/260.
72. *Ibid.*
73. From Holland's service history, courtesy of Elizabeth Holland.
74. Memo by J.C.F. Holland, 29 June 1939: TNA HS 8/256.
75. *Art of Guerrilla Warfare:* TNA HS 8/256.
76. 'Organisation and Duties of MI(R)', J.C.F. Holland, 3 September 1939: TNA HS 8/256.
77. 'War Diary of MI(R) from 3 September to 2 October 1940' (report), 10 December 1940: TNA HS 8/263.
78. 'General Instructions', J.C.F. Holland, 13 April 1939: TNA HS 8/256.
79. 'Record of meeting held in the War Office to settle the future of GS(R) and certain connected questions', 27 June 1939: TNA HS 8/256.
80. Wilkinson and Astley (1993), p. 35.
81. 'Progress of Para-Military Preparation', 10 July 1939, MI(R): TNA HS 8/260.
82. 'Progress up to date and action if war breaks out early', 8 August 1939, MI(R): TNA HS 8/260.

Chapter Two: The Outbreak of War

1. 'Progress up to date and action if war breaks out early', 8 August 1939, MI(R): TNA HS 8/260.
2. 'Report No. 8: Investigation of the possibilities of Guerrilla Warfare: Appendix III', 1 June 1939: TNA HS 8/260.
3. 'Progress up to date and action if war breaks out early', 8 August 1939, MI(R): TNA HS 8/260.
4. DMI note, 22 August 1939: TNA HS 8/260.
5. 'Organisation and Duties of MI(R)', J.C.F. Holland, 3 September 1939: TNA HS 8/256.
6. 'Report No. 8: Investigation of the possibilities of Guerrilla Warfare', 1 June 1939: TNA HS 8/260.
7. 'Organisation and Duties of MI(R)', J.C.F. Holland, 3 September 1939: TNA HS 8/256.
8. Memo of Holland to Wyndham, undated. Repeated in 'Suggested line of demarcation between War Office and "D"', Wyndham, 25 August 1940: TNA HS 8/258.
9. 'Establishment and Personnel of MI(R)', J.C.F. Holland, 5 September 1939: TNA HS 8/257.
10. TNA HS 8/257.
11. 'Establishment and Personnel of MI(R)', J.C.F. Holland, 5 September 1939; DCIGS to PUS, September 1939: TNA HS 8/257. At the time the 'Intelligence Corps' was a loose

collection of officers and the Intelligence Corps proper was not consolidated as a badged unit until July 1940. Little provision had been made for Intelligence provision prior to the outbreak of war in 1939 and such work as was done in the first year was as a result of the personal initiative of Major (later Field Marshal) Gerald Templer and the retired Captain F.C. Davis MC. The latter trained the thirty-one Field Security Sections of the Military Police in Intelligence duties. When the Intelligence Corps was formed on 19 July 1940, these FS Sections were transferred to the new Corps.

12. Thanks to Elizabeth Holland for her many insights into the Holland family circle.
13. Functions and Organisation of MI(R), J.C.F. Holland, 20 December 1939: TNA HS 8/256.
14. *Ibid.*
15. DMI to VCIGS, 5 June 1940: TNA GS 8/256.
16. Holland to DDMI(O), 2 February 1940: TNA HS 8/256.
17. Note by DDMI(O), 3 February 1940: TNA HS 8/256.
18. Astley (2007), p. 30.
19. 'Duties and Responsibilities of MI(R)', J.C.F. Holland, 22 July 1940: TNA HS 8/256.
20. 'Duties of MI(R)', DMI, 11 February 1940: TNA HS 8/256.
21. Beaumont-Nesbitt to Wavell, 17 April 1940: TNA WO 201/2864.
22. 'Functions and Organisation of MI(R)', J.C.F. Holland, 20 December 1939: TNA HS 8/256.
23. MI(R) War Diary: TNA HS 8/263; Dodds-Parker (1983), p. 35.
24. 'Functions and Organisation of MI(R)', J.C.F. Holland, 20 December 1939: TNA HS 8/256.
25. Dodds-Parker (1983), p. 40.
26. *Ibid.*, p. 50.
27. *Ibid.*, p. 57.
28. Atkin (2017), p. 128.
29. History of SOE in Greece by I. Pirie, p. 16: TNA HS 7/150.
30. 'Projects', Major Kenyon, 5 April 1940: TNA HS 8/258.
31. Beaumont-Nesbitt to Ismay, 3 March 1940: TNA CAB 21/1425.
32. TNA CAB 127/376; West and Tsarev (2009), p. 201.
33. Hankey Report, TNA CAB 63/192, f.66.
34. 'Extent of MI(R) activities in the past, at present, and possibilities for the future', April 1940; 'Duties of MI(R)', 2 June 1940: TNA HS 8/258.
35. Order No. M/I/1, J.C.F. Holland, 12 April 1940: TNA WO HS 8/257.
36. MI(R) No. 155/40, 24 April 1940: TNA WO 8/257.
37. Holland to HD1, 3 June 1940: TNA WO 8/257.
38. Dodds-Parker (1983), p. 39.
39. *Ibid.*, p. 44.
40. DMI to VCIGS, 5 June 1940: TNA HS 8/258.
41. Appendix A to Aide-Memoire on the Co-Ordination of Subversive Activities in the Conquered Territories: TNA HS 8/259.
42. 'The Co-ordination of all Irregular Operations and Special Operations' (brief prepared for DMO for COS meeting of 7 June 1940), J.C.F. Holland, 6 June 1940: TNA HS 8/259.
43. Minutes of Chiefs of Staff meeting, 13 June 1940: TNA CAB 80/13.
44. J.D. Kennedy to DRO, 28 June 1940: TNA WO 8/257.
45. Meeting of War Establishment Sub-Committee, 2 July 1940: TNA WO 8/257.
46. Minutes of JIC, 17 July 1940: TNA CAB 81/8.
47. Minutes of Chiefs of Staff Committee, 'Future Strategy', 4 September 1940: TNA 66/11/42.

48. 'An Appreciation of the Capabilities and Composition of a small force operating behind the enemy lines in the offensive', 7 June 1940: TNA HS 8/259.
49. *Ibid.*

Chapter Three: The Technical Section

1. Holland (1935).
2. Astley (2007), p. 22.
3. Macrae (1972), p. 90.
4. *Ibid.*, p. 5.
5. *Ibid.*, p. 137. The caveat is that this conclusion came from Macrae himself, whose account of MI(R)c is egocentric.
6. 'Activities in the past, at present and possibilities for the future', 5 April 1940: TNA HS 8/263.
7. 148. Macrae (1972), p. 12.
8. *Ibid.*, p. 26.
9. *Ibid.*, p. 61.
10. Astley (2007), p. 40.
11. Macrae to T. Korda (Oldhams Press), 23 September 1939: TNA T 166/125/13.
12. Macrae (1972), p. 7.
13. 'Resumé of MI(R)c Activities from April 1939 to November 1940': TNA HS 8/263.
14. Macrae (1972), p. 75.
15. *Ibid.*, pp. 76–7.
16. 'The extent of MI(R)'s activities in the past, at present and possibilities for the future', April 1940: TNA HS 8/258.
17. Macrae (1972), p. 82.
18. Churchill to Eden, 10 November 1940: TNA CAB 120/372.
19. Munthe (1954), pp. 37–9.
20. Macrae (1972), p. 6.
21. *Ibid.*, p. 11.
22. TNA T 166/125/2.
23. Macrae (1972), p. 148.
24. *Ibid.*, p. 150.
25. VCIGS to DMI, 26 August 1940: TNA HS 8/263.
26. Wyndham to DMI, 27 August 1940: TNA HS 8/263.
27. TNA T 166/125/5.
28. Macrae (1972), p. 36.
29. *Ibid.*, pp. 37–42.
30. *Ibid.*, p. 51.
31. *Ibid.*, p. 98.
32. ACIGS to Eden, 11 June 1940: TNA WO 185/1.
33. Churchill to Ismay, 16 June 1940: TNA CAB 120/372.
34. Carr to Jacob, 17 June 1940: TNA CAB 120/372.
35. Carr to Ismay, 18 June 1940: TNA CAB 120/372.
36. Ismay to Churchill, 18 June 1940: TNA CAB 120/372.
37. Minute of 19 June 1940: TNA WO 185/1.
38. Report by D of A on trial of Sticky Bomb on Hangmoor Range, 22 June 1940: TNA CAB 120/372.
39. Churchill to Ismay, 24 June 1940: TNA CAB 120/372.
40. Ismay to Churchill, 29 June 1940: TNA CAB 120/372.
41. Carr to Ismay, 24 June 1940; Ismay to Churchill, 27 June 1940: TNA CAB 120/272.

42. Churchill to Eden, 7 August 1940: TNA CAB 120/372.
43. Memo to Ismay, 26 November 1940, Jacob to Ismay 7 February 1941: TNA CAB 120/372.
44. Macrae (1972), p. 125.
45. Jefferis to Jacob, 13 November 1940: TNA CAB 120/372.
46. Jefferis to Jacob, 15 December 1940: TNA CAB 120/372.
47. Macready to Jacob, 5 February 1941: TNA CAB 120/372; Macrae (1972), p. 126.
48. Ismay to Churchill, 26 June 1941: TNA CAB 120/372.
49. Macrae (1972), p. 157.
50. *Ibid.*, p. 78.
51. Blacker to Holland, 14 August 1940: TNA HS 8/262.
52. Mobility of Spigot Mortars, 12 May 1942: TNA WO 199/363.
53. Macrae (1972), p. 84. Farrant became deputy assistant director of MD1. He was eventually promoted major general and became President of the Ordnance Board.
54. *Ibid.*, p. 120.
55. C-in-C Home Forces to Under-Secretary of State for War, 3 May 1941: TNA WO 199/3249.
56. 'An Appreciation of the Capabilities and Composition of a small force operating behind the enemy lines in the offensive', 7 June 1940: TNA HS 8/259.
57. Holland to DMI, August 1940: TNA HS 8/256.
58. 'Irregular Tactics and Strategy', J.C.F. Holland to DMI, August 1940: TNA HS 8/256.
59. MI(R) War Diary for 23 September 1940: TNA HS 8/263.
60. Macrae (1972), pp. 68–72.

Chapter Four: Recruitment and Training

1. Elliott (1998), pp. 25–34.
2. Ogden (2019), p. 9.
3. *Manual of Military Intelligence in the Field*, para. 10.
4. 'War Diary of MI(R) from 3 September to 2 October 1940' (report), 10 December 1940: TNA HS 8/263.
5. 'Duties of the new branch', J.C.F. Holland, 13 April 1939: TNA HS 8/256.
6. Templer was responsible for the creation of the Intelligence Corps in July 1940.
7. Astley (2007), p. 24.
8. John Brunyate's comments on 'Appendix H: Review of the Activities of the Personnel Section of MI(R)', 10 December 1940: TNA HS 8/263.
9. Munthe (1954), p. 24.
10. Dodds-Parker (1983), p. 39.
11. Kemp (1958), p. 11.
12. Household (1958), p. 98.
13. *Ibid.*, p. 100.
14. Wilkinson (2002), p. 63.
15. 'Regular and Irregular Warfare: Problems of Co-Ordination', lecture by Gubbins at University of Manchester, 29 November 1967, Gubbins papers 4/1/27, IWM.
16. Wilkinson and Astley (1993), p. 26.
17. *Record of the Rebellion in Ireland*, Vol. IV: Record of the 5th and 6th Divisions and Dublin District, p. 68: TNA WO 141/93/5.
18. *Notes on Guerrilla Warfare in Ireland*, War Office; *Record of the Rebellion in Ireland*, Vol. IV: Record of the 5th and 6th Divisions and Dublin District, Appendix XXVI: TNA WO 141/93/5.
19. *The Art of Guerrilla Warfare*: TNA HS 8/256.
20. *Record of the Rebellion in Ireland*, Vol. IV, Part 1, Ch. 4, p. 40: TNA WO 141/93/5.

21. Griffiths (1961), pp. 96–7.
22. *The Art of Guerrilla Warfare*: TNA HS 8/256.
23. *Notes on Guerrilla Warfare in Ireland*, War Office: *Record of the Rebellion in Ireland*, Vol. IV: Record of the 5th and 6th Divisions and Dublin District, Appendix XXVI: TNA WO 141/93.
24. D Plan, 20 March 1939: TNA HS 8/256; Atkin (2017), Appendix 1.
25. *The Art of Guerrilla Warfare*: TNA HS 8/256.
26. Mackenzie (2000), p. 41, n. 1.
27. Gubbins, quoted in Wilkinson and Astley (1993), p. 34.
28. Wilkinson and Astley (1993), p. 36; Wilkinson (2002), p. 63.
29. 'Report No. 8: Investigation of the possibilities of Guerrilla Warfare: Appendix III', 1 June 1939: TNA HS 8/260.
30. Dodds-Parker (1983), p. 35.
31. 'Duties and Responsibilities of MI(R)', J.C.F. Holland, 22 July 1940: TNA HS 8/256.
32. 'War Diary of MI(R), 3 September 1939 to 2 October 1940' (report), 10 December 1940: TNA HS 8/263.
33. *Ibid.*
34. 'The extent of MI(R)'s activities in the past, at present and possibilities for the future', April 1940: TNA HS 8/258; 'Report on the Organization within the War Office for the Conduct of Para-Military Activities', Brigadier Wyndham, 25 August 1940: TNA HS 8/258.
35. 'War Diary of MI(R), 3 September 1939 to 2 October 1940' (report), 10 December 1940: TNA HS 8/263.
36. Dodds-Parker (1983), p. 45.
37. Lovat (1978), p. 162.
38. 'War Diary of MI(R), 3 September 1939 to 2 October 1940' (report), 10 December 1940: TNA HS 8/263.
39. MI(R) War Diary: TNA HS 8/263.
40. Kemp (1958), p. 25.
41. Kemp (1990), p. 146; MI(R) War Diary: TNA HS 8/263.
42. 'Duties and Responsibilities of MI(R)', J.C.F. Holland, 22 July 1940: TNA HS 8/256.
43. Interview with James Merrick Lewis Gavin, IWM Sound Archive 12308, Reel 1, 1983.
44. 'War Diary of MI(R), 3 September 1939 to 2 October 1940' (report), 10 December 1940: TNA HS 8/263.
45. Macpherson (2010), pp. 47.
46. Iain Thornber (2010), *The former military camp at Lochailort: a photographic record*: www.librarylink.highland.gov.uk.
47. Spencer-Chapman (1949), p. 6.
48. Davies to Mayfield, 31 July 1940: TNA HS 9/1605/3.

Chapter Five: Escape, Evasion and Deception

1. Holland to Beaumont-Nesbitt, 14 October 1939: TNA 8/263; Foot and Langley (1979), p. 32.
2. Minutes of ISSB Meeting, 14 February 1940: TNA WO 283/1.
3. Minutes of ISSB Meeting, 30 April 1940: TNA WO 283/1.
4. Minutes of ISSB Meeting, 14 February 1940: TNA WO 283/1.
5. Minutes of ISSB Meeting, 27 February 1940: TNA WO 283/1.
6. *Ibid.*
7. Minutes of JIC Meeting, 6 March 1940: TNA CAB 81/89.
8. Minutes of ISSB Meeting, 16 April 1940: TNA WO 283/1.

Chapter Six: Central and Eastern Europe

1. Wilkinson and Astley (1993), p. 128.
2. 'Report for DCIGS No. 8 – Investigation of the Possibilities of Guerrilla Activities, Appendix I: Preliminary Report on a Tour to Poland, Baltic States, and Romania', Gubbins, 1 June 1939: TNA HS 8/260.
3. *Ibid.*
4. 'CG's Comments on Foot's Book', Gubbins papers 3/2/57, IWM.
5. In fact, between 25 and 27 July French and British cryptanalysts met with Polish counterparts who shared their knowledge of the Enigma code machine. Britain sent two cryptanalysts from GC&CS and the head of the Royal Naval Y Service to the meeting and as a result the Poles freely handed over a replica Enigma machine each for the British and French. The transfer of the machine to Britain was then organized by William Dunderdale of SIS.
6. 'Progress of para-Military Preparation: Report No. 1', 10 July 1939: TNA HS 8/260.
7. 'Resumé of discussions with Polish General Staff regarding para-military activities', July 1939: TNA HS 4/193.
8. Atkin (2017), pp. 137, 148.
9. 'Protocols of conversations held in Warsaw from 14–16 August with Lt. Col. Gubbins', Colonel Smolenski, 19 August 1939: TNA HS 4/224; *Art of Guerrilla Warfare*, para 34: Appendix 2.
10. 'Progress up to date and action if war breaks out early', 8 August 1939, MI(R): TNA HS 8/260.
11. *Ibid.*
12. Wilkinson and Astley (1993), p. 38.
13. 'CG's Comments on Foot's Book', Gubbins papers 3/2/57, IWM.
14. Dorril (2000), p. 261.
15. SOE personnel file: TNA HS9 1186/5.
16. Wilkinson (2002), p. 65.
17. *Ibid.*, p. 68.
18. Household (1958), p. 100.
19. Gubbins, address to Anglo-Polish Society, 18 November 1972, 2, Gubbins papers 4/1/41, IWM.
20. Holland to MI1(b), 19 January 1940: TNA HS 4/224.
21. Gubbins to Holland, ?5 September 1939: TNA HS 4/224.
22. 'Report on Military Mission', F.T. Davies, 5 September 1940: TNA HS 4/224.
23. MI(R) to Gubbins, 10 September 1940: TNA HS 4/224.
24. Wilkinson (2002), p. 82.
25. 'Duties and Responsibilities of MI(R)', J.C.F. Holland, 22 July 1940: TNA HS 8/256.
26. 'Present Organization as Regards Irregular Activities in SE Europe', Gubbins, 26 March 1939: TNA HS 8/258.
27. 'Duties of MI(R)', 2 June 1940: TNA HS 8/257.
28. Gubbins to Holland, 2 January 1940: TNA HS 4/193.
29. TNA HS 4/31; 'War Diary of MI(R) from 3 September to 2 October 1940' (report), 10 December 1040: TNA HS 8/263.
30. 'War Diary of MI(R) from 3 September to 2 October 1940' (report), 10 December 1940: TNA HS 8/263.
31. *Ibid.*; Gubbins to Holland and comments from DMI, 25 January 1940: TNA HS 4/193.
32. 'The extent of MI(R)'s activities in the past, at present and possibilities for the future', April 1940: TNA HS 8/258.

33. *Ibid.*
34. 'Note on Present Polish Organization', Gubbins, 16 October 1939: TNA HS 4/193.
35. Wilkinson and Astley (1993), p. 47.
36. 'Present Organization as Regards Irregular Activities in SE Europe', Gubbins, 26 March 1939: TNA HS 8/258.
37. Gubbins to Watson, 27 January 1940: TNA HS 4/193.
38. Atkin (2017), pp. 109–13; TNA HS 9/160/6; Watson to Gubbins, undated but January 1940: TNA HS 4/193.
39. Harris-Burland to Gubbins, undated but January 1940: TNA HS 4/193.
40. 'War Diary of MI(R) from 3 September 1939 – 2 October 1940' (report), 10 December 1940: TNA HS 8/263.
41. Wilkinson (2002), p. 88.
42. *Ibid.*, p. 89.
43. 'Questionnaire', S.E. Carlton, undated: TNA HS 4/193.
44. 'Stores delivered to Poles up to 1 April 1940', 21 April 1940: TNA HS 4/193.
45. Gubbins to Wilkinson, 28 January 1940: TNA HS 4/31.
46. Gubbins to Kwiecinski, 1 January 1940: TNA HS 4/193.
47. Gubbins to Sutton-Pratt, 7 April 1940: TNA HS 4/193.
48. Wilkinson to Gubbins, 29 January 1940: TNA HS 4/193.
49. 'Polish Underground Activity and its possible inclusion in Allied War Plans', MI(R), 4 February 1940: TNA HS 4/193.
50. Gubbins to DMI, 12 April 1940: TNA HS 4/193.
51. Wilkinson and Astley (1993), p. 49.
52. Astley (2007), p. 23.
53. 'Present Organization as Regards Irregular Activities in SE Europe', Gubbins, 26 March 1939: TNA HS 8/258. Ironically, Naval Intelligence was responsible for the greatest disaster of irregular warfare in the region – *see* Atkin (2017), pp. 109–13.
54. 'Present Organization as Regards Irregular Activities in SE Europe', Gubbins, 26 March 1939: TNA HS 8/258.
55. *Ibid.*
56. Gubbins to Holland, 3 February 1940: TNA HS 4/193.
57. Dodds-Parker (1983), p. 41.
58. Harrison to Goodwill and Wilkinson, 11 March 1940: TNA HS 9/612.
59. Report of Harrison, 14 April 1940: TNA HS 9/612.
60. Witkowski had commanded an anti-tank unit armed with long anti-tank rifles nicknamed 'muskets'.
61. Wilkinson to de Chastelain, 28 May 1941: TNA HS 4/198.
62. 'Czech Para-Military and Political Organization', July 1939: TNA HS 4/31.
63. 'Record of an interview with Colonel Kalla', Greg, 23 August 1939: TNA HS 4/31.
64. 'Meeting between Colonel Gubbins and Colonel Kalla', 11 October 1939; 'Czech Organization', 11 October 1939: TNA HS 4/31.
65. Meeting between Gubbins and Inger, 14 October 1939: TNA HS 4/31.
66. TNA HS 4/31; 'War Diary of MI(R) from 3 September – 2 October 1940' (report), 10 December 1940: TNA HS 8/263.
67. Record of a meeting between Gubbins and Fisera, 18 November 1939: TNA HS 4/31.
68. Record of a meeting between Gubbins, Greg and Wilkinson with Fisera, 22 November 1939: TNA HS 4/31.
69. Record of a meeting between Wilkinson and Greg with Fisera, 30 November 1940: TNA HS 4/31.

70. Record of meeting between Holland and Wilkinson with Moravec and Fisera, 5 January 1940: TNA HS 4/31.
71. Gubbins to Wilkinson, 2 February 1940: TNA HS 4/31.
72. William Strang to Beaumont-Nesbitt, 17 January 1940: TNA HS 4/31.
73. Beaumont-Nesbitt to Strang, 1 February 1940, based on a memo of Holland to Beaumont-Nesbitt, 22 January 1940: TNA HS 4/31.
74. Wilkinson to Hanau, 29 February 1940: TNA HS 4/31.
75. Record of a meeting of Holland, Gubbins, Wilkinson, Fisera and Moravec on 5 January 1940, made on 22 January 1940: TNA HS 4/43; Langley to Wilkinson, 2 April 1940: TNA HS 4/31.
76. Beaumont-Nesbitt to Gubbins, 4 March 1940: TNA HS 4/31.
77. MI(R) to MIL(s), 12 March 1940: TNA HS 4/31.
78. Gubbins to Barclay, 5 October 1939: TNA HS 4/193.
79. Note by Wilkinson, 31 January 1940: TNA HS 4/31.
80. *Ibid.*; see Atkin (2017), pp. 132–7 for Section D operations in Hungary.
81. He was promoted lieutenant colonel on 20 January 1941. In 1942 he became First Secretary at the British Embassy in Washington DC, USA.
82. MI(R) War Diary for 22 April 1940: TNA HS 8/263; 'The extent of MI(R)'s activities in the past, at present and possibilities for the future', April 1940: TNA HS 8/258.
83. Duncan to Taylor, 16 May 1940: TNA HS 9/458/2.
84. *Ibid.*
85. MI(R) to M.A. Budapest, 21 May 1940: TNA HS 4/193.
86. M.A. Budapest to DMI, 23 May 1940: TNA HS 4/193.
87. Harris-Burland to Gubbins, undated but January 1940: TNA HS 4/193; M.A. Budapest to DMI, 24 May 1940: TNA HS 4/193.
88. Wilkinson (2002), p. 92.
89. Memo re Blake-Tyler and D, by Dodds-Parker, 25 May 1940: TNA HS 4/193.
90. *Ibid.*
91. MI(R) War Diary: TNA HS 8/263.
92. M.A. Bucharest to DMO&I, 31 May 1940: TNA HS 4/193.
93. MX (Wilkinson) to M (Gubbins), 27 April 1941: TNA HS 4/198.
94. *Ibid.*
95. Atkin (2017), pp. 136–7.

Chapter Seven: Romania and the Balkans

1. Letter of 19 April 1939 to military attachés: TNA HS 8/256.
2. 'Report for D.C.I.G.S. No. 8 – Investigation of the Possibilities of Guerrilla Activities, Appendix I: Preliminary Report on a Tour to Poland, Baltic States, and Romania', Gubbins, 1 June 1939: TNA HS 8/260.
3. Deletant (2016), p. 69.
4. MI(R) War Diary: TNA HS 8/263.
5. Davidson-Houston (1949), p. 153.
6. 'War Diary of MI(R) from 3 September 1939 – 2 October 1940' (report), 10 December 1940: TNA HS 8/263.
7. Deletant (2016), p. 198, note 32.
8. Gubbins to Holland, 22 September 1940: TNA HS 4/224.
9. E.A. Berthould to HM Minister Bucharest (Hoare), 28 October 1940: TNA HS 5/830.
10. Pearton (2000), pp. 194–5.
11. MI(R) War Diary: TNA HS 8/263.
12. Davidson-Houston (1949), p. 162.

13. *Ibid.*, p. 166.
14. Pearton (2000), p. 194.
15. Household (1958), p. 106.
16. 'MI(R) Project: Romania': TNA HS 8/263.
17. 'Polish Assistance – Oil Fields Plan', MI(R), 9 February 1940: TNA HS 4/193.
18. Watson to Wilkinson, 5 April 1940: TNA HS 4/193.
19. Gubbins to Broad (FO), 28 March 1940: TNA HS 4/193.
20. Household (1958), p. 107.
21. *Ibid.*, p. 120.
22. *Ibid.*, p. 121.
23. Wedlake SOE personnel file: TNA HS 5/498.
24. De Chastelain history of SOE in Romania: TNA HS 7/186; letter from Broad to Brittain, 26 November 1940: TNA HS 5/830.
25. With thanks to Elizabeth Holland, October 2019.
26. Summary report of Yugoslav Mission by Sir John Shea, 19 December 1939: TNA FO 371/25033.
27. Yugoslav Shadow Mission by F.T. Davies, 10 May 1940: TNA FO 371/25033.
28. Davies to Butler, 12 May 1940: TNA FO 371/25033.
29. Atkin (2017), pp. 85–102.
30. Amery (1973), p. 179.
31. Elliott (1998), pp. 171–9; Dorril (2000), p. 175.
32. Atkin (2017), pp. 114–17.
33. Glen to Bailey, 15 July 1940: TNA HS 5/60; Minute of 22 July 1940 from '797' to D/H, H/H2 and D/HR: TNA HS 5/60.

Chapter Eight: Scandinavia

1. Dodds-Parker (1983), p. 42.
2. 'Functions and organisation of MI(R)', J.C.F. Holland, 20 December 1939: TNA HS 8/256.
3. MI(R) War Diary: TNA HS 8/263.
4. 'War Diary of MI(R) from 3 September 1939 – 2 October 1940' (report), 10 December 1940: TNA HS 8/263.
5. 'Report on a visit to Finland' by Whittington-Moë, 31 January 1940: TNA HS 8/261.
6. Minutes of JIC Meeting, 6 March 1940: TNA CAB 81/89.
7. Kotakallio (2014), p. 233.
8. de Wiart (2007), p. 165.
9. MI(R) War Diary: TNA HS 8/263.
10. Croft (1991), pp. 144–9.
11. Munthe (1954), pp. 50–119; McKay (1993), pp. 76–8. Thanks also to Helge Lockert Hansen for sharing his unpublished research in the Norwegian archives on Munthe.
12. Atkin (2017), p. 167.
13. Hart-Davis (1987), p. 222.
14. *Ibid.*, p. 223.
15. de Wiart (2007), p. 166; Hart-Davis (1987), p. 224.
16. Fleming to Admiralty, 15 April 1940: TNA WO 106/1916.
17. Fleming to MI(R), 14 April 1940: TNA WO 106/1916.
18. Fleming to MI(R) (by telephone), 14 April 1940: TNA WO 106/1916; MI(R) War Diary: TNA HS 8/263.
19. 'General Report', April 1940, Peter Fleming: TNA HS 8/261.
20. Hart-Davis (1987), p. 231.

21. 'Preliminary narrative – Namsos 1940', pp. 115–25; Appendix 40: TNA CAB 44/73.
22. Shakespeare (2017), Appendix, pp. 413–15.
23. Atkin (2017), pp. 169–77.
24. MI(R) War Diary: TNA HS 8/263.
25. Mackenzie (2000), p. 50.
26. 'Subsidiary Report on No. 13 Mission to Norway' by Captain Readhead, July 1940: TNA HS 8/261.
27. MI(R) War Diary: TNA HS 8/263.
28. Macrae (1972), p. 66. Macrae mistakenly assumed that Jefferis was not able to accomplish anything in Norway.
29. 'Report of No. 13 Military Mission to Norway', A.W. Brown: TNA HS 8/261; Diary of Major Jefferis's Duty in Norway, 29 April 1940: TNA HS 8/261.
30. Minutes of Meeting of War Cabinet, 1 May 1940: TNA CAB 65/7/1.
31. 'Report on the organisation within the War Office for the conduct of para-military activities', Brigadier Wyndham, 25 August 1940: TNA HS 8/258.
32. Astley (2007), p. 31.
33. 'Irregular Tactics and Strategy', Holland to DMI, August 1940: TNA 8/256.
34. Melville (2004), pp. 123–6.
35. Minutes of ISPS meeting, 30 April 1940; UPT to Regional Commands, 20 April 1940: TNA WO 106/1889.
36. 'Report on the organisation within the War Office for the conduct of para-military activities', Brigadier Wyndham, 25 August 1940: TNA HS 8/258.
37. Prendergast (1979), p. 118.
38. DMO to OOCs, Regional Commands, 24 April 1940: TNA WO 106/1889.
39. Instructions to Lt. Col. Gubbins, 2 May 1940: Derry (1952), pp. 257–9.
40. War Office UPT to Regional Commands, 20 April 1940: TNA WO 106/1889.
41. Riley (2006), p. 47.
42. SD9(a) to OS2, P.W. Kennedy, 2 May 1940: TNA WO 106/1889.
43. War Office to Flag Officer Narvik, *Rupertforce*, repeated to Gubbins, 7 May 1940: TNA WO 106/1944; War Office to *Rupertforce*, 11 May 1940: TNA WO 106/1944.
44. DMO&P to HQ 5 Corps, 5 May 1940: TNA WO 106/1889.
45. Administrative Headquarters Group, *Scissorforce* (TNA WO 106/1889).
46. Riley (2006), p. 46.
47. Garner (2018), pp. 68–74.
48. DMO to OOCs, Regional Commands, 24 April 1940: TNA WO 106/1889.
49. *Ibid.*
50. War Diary of 2nd Independent Company: TNA WO 168/106.
51. IWM Sound Archive 10231 (1988) with Sir Ronald Swayne.
52. Parker (2000), p. 11.
53. War Diary, *Scissorforce*, report by Captain J.H. Prendergast: TNA WO 168/103.
54. Prendergast (1979), p. 116.
55. *Ibid.*, p. 114; *Scissorforce* to War Office, 14 May 1940: TNA WO 106/1944.
56. The special long-range transmitter (Special Set No. 2) incorporated a commercial National HRO receiver and was rushed into production soon after the outbreak of war by the Signals Experimental Establishment (SEE) to provide communications from expeditionary forces back to Britain.
57. 'Scissor Signals – Notes': TNA WO 106/1889. Thanks to Louis Meulstee for discussion on the likely types of set used in Norway.
58. War Diary, *Scissorforce*, report by Captain J.H. Prendergast: TNA WO 168/103.
59. War Diary, 1st Irish Guards, 24 May 1940: WO 168/57.

60. Connell (1959), p. 113.
61. Instructions to Lt. Col. Gubbins, 2 May 1940: Headquarters, *Scissorforce*: TNA WO 106/1889 and WO 168/57.
62. Massy to OC 1 Independent Company, 30 April 1940: TNA WO 106/1944.
63. War Diary of No. 1 Independent Company: TNA WO 168/105.
64. Gen. Massy to Officer Commanding, No. 1 Independent Company, SS *Orion*, 30 April 1940: TNA WO 106/1889 and TNA WO 168/105.
65. 'Independent Companies', 6 May 1940: TNA WO 106/1944.
66. Admiralty to Mohawk, 2 May 1940: TNA WO 106/1944.
67. Cork to Admiralty, 4 May 1940: TNA PREM 3/328.
68. Admiralty to Flag Officer Narvik, 5 May 1940: TNA WO 106/1845.
69. Admiralty to Cork, 7 May 1940: TNA WO 106/1945; War Office to *Rupertforce*, 7 May 1940: WO 106/1944.
70. War Office to *Rupertforce* and Gubbins, 8 May 1940: TNA WO 106/1944.
71. Instructions to Lt. Col. Gubbins, 2 May 1940, reproduced in Derry (1952), pp. 257–9.
72. War Office to Flag Officer Narvik, 7 May 1940: TNA WO 106/1944.
73. War Office to Flag Officer Narvik, 9 May 1940: TNA WO 106/1944.
74. Prendergast (1979), p. 125; War Diary, *Scissorforce*, report by Captain J.H. Prendergast: TNA WO 168/103.
75. TNA ADM 199/485.
76. Admiralty to Flag Officer Narvik, 9 May 1940: TNA WO 106/1944.
77. Fell (1966), p. 48.
78. *Ibid.*, p. 49.
79. Croft (1991), p. 154.
80. Fell (1966), pp. 51–2.
81. NWEF to War Office, 15 May 1940: TNA WO 106/1944.
82. IWM Sound Archive 10231 (1988) with Sir Ronald Swayne, p. 14.
83. 'Points', Gubbins notes: TNA WO 198/8.
84. Derry (1952), p. 182.
85. War Diary of 1 Independent Company: TNA WO 168/105.
86. *Rupertforce* to War Office, 11 May 1940: TNA WO 106/1945.
87. *Scissorforce* War Diary: TNA WO 168/103.
88. Croft (1991), p. 153.
89. Auchinleck to Fraser, 13 May 1940, NWEF Operational Instruction No.1: TNA CAB 106/1156; IWM Mackesy Papers, PJM Box 3, quoted in Kiszely (2017), p. 261.
90. Auchinleck to Gubbins, 16 May 1940: IWM Gubbins Papers 2/3, quoted in Kiszely (2017), p. 261.
91. Connell (1959), p. 119.
92. 'Report on the operations in North Norway', Auchinleck, 19 June 1940, in Grehan and Mace (2015), p. 95.
93. Riley (2006), p. 51.
94. 'Certain Points', Gubbins' notes quoted in report by Dowler, 27 May 1940: TNA WO 198/8.
95. Notes on Visit to Bodø, 21/22 May, Dowler: TNA WO 198/8.
96. War Diary *Scissorforce*, 18 May 1940: TNA WO 168/103.
97. Quoted in Connell (1959), p. 122.
98. Wilkinson and Astley (1993), pp. 58, 61, quoting Fraser's wartime diary.
99. Quoted in Connell (1959), p. 123.
100. *Ibid.*, p. 125.
101. *Ibid.*, p. 119.

102. Notes on visit to Bodø, 22 May 1940, Colonel Dowler 1940: TNA WO 198/8.
103. *Ibid.*
104. War Diary, *Scissorforce*, situation report by Gubbins, 21 May 1940: TNA WO 168/103.
105. Notes on visit to Bodø, 22 May 1940, Colonel Dowler: TNA WO 198/8.
106. *Ibid.*
107. *Ibid.*; War Diary of 24th (Guards) Brigade: TNA WO 168/24; NWEF to War Office, 23 May 1940: TNA 106/1944.
108. Trappes-Lomax was eventually promoted to brigadier and served as a staff officer in Southern Command in India.
109. Stockwell served with the West Africa Frontier Force before becoming an instructor at the Small Arms School and then brigade major to 158th (Royal Welch) Infantry Brigade in the 53rd (Welsh) Division. He was promoted to lieutenant colonel and passed No. 2 Independent Company to the command of Tom Trevor.
110. Kyle (2011), p. 176.
111. Riley (2006), p. 56.
112. Fell (1966), pp. 53–5; TNA ADM 199/485.
113. Croft (1991), p. 157.
114. Wilkinson and Astley (1993), pp. 55–64.
115. MI(R) War Diary: TNA HS 8/263.
116. 'Irregular Activities in Norway', report of ISPB to COS Committee, 8 May 1940: TNA CAB 80/10.
117. Atkin (2017), pp. 169–77.
118. Draft Memo of Holland to Beaumont-Nesbitt, 4 June 1940; 'Comments by Colonel Holland on the DMO&P draft', J.C.F. Holland, 4 June 1940: TNA HS 8/263.
119. 'Report on the organisation within the War Office for the conduct of para-military activities', Brigadier Wyndham, 25 August 1940: TNA HS 8/258.
120. 'Duties and Responsibilities of MI(R)', J.C.F. Holland, 22 July 1940: TNA HS 8/256.
121. Astley (2007), p. 42.
122. 'Report on the organisation within the War Office for the conduct of para-military activities', Brigadier Wyndham, 25 August 1940: TNA HS 8/258.
123. *Ibid.*
124. Dalton Diary for 22 July 1940, p. 62.

Chapter Nine: Western Europe and the Americas

1. War Diary of MI(R), 3 September 1939 – 2 October 1940 (report), 10 December 1940: TNA HS 8/263.
2. Atkin (2017), Ch. 6.
3. Wilkinson to Gubbins, 29 January 1940: TNA HS 4/193.
4. Minutes of JIC, 29 September and 2 October 1939: TNA CAB 81/87.
5. War Diary of Kent Fortress Company: TNA WO 166/3549.
6. Report by R.L. Mayler, undated: TNA HS 8/261.
7. For the Section D operations see Atkin (2017), pp. 74–8. For the MI(R) mission see 'Report on visit to Amsterdam', F.T. Davies, 16 May 1940: TNA CAB 63/132; War Diary of MI(R) for 13 May 1940 and Appendix A/2: TNA HS 8/263; TNA ADM 1/10607, p. 13; Report by Commander Goodenough: TNA M 010752/40. Note there is a discrepancy in dates in these sources. Thanks to Darron Wadey for discussion on Davies mission.
8. 'Organisation of Civil Resistance in France and Belgium', MI(R), 23 May 1940: TNA CAB 21/1476.
9. MI(R) Report VIII, July 1940: TNA HS 8/214.

10. 'Great Britain's Only Successful Experiment in Total Warfare', Laurence Grand, August 1940: TNA HS 7/5; Turner (2011), p. 60; Atkin (2017), pp. 69–73.
11. Warren was not, as claimed in his biography (Skidmore 1981, p. 7), Holland's second in command. Warren refers to recruiting Hodges and Sinclair direct from public school after a letter in *The Times* by Lt Col. Ralph Bingham, CO of No. 168 OCTU, Aldershot, complaining about the entry of middle- and lower-class candidates. This incident did not occur until February 1941 and MI(R) files refer to the subalterns being recruited from Camberley OCTU: Skidmore (1981), p. 9; TNA HS 8/256.
12. 'Duties and Activities of MI(R)', J.C.F. Holland, 22 July 1940: TNA HS 8/256.
13. Churchill to Secretary of State for War, 23 July 1940: *The Second World War* (Cassell, 1950), p. 572.
14. Atkin (2015), Ch. 11.
15. Chiefs of Staff report to War Cabinet, *British strategy in a certain eventuality*, 25 May 1940: TNA CAB 66/7.
16. War Diary of MI(R): TNA HS 8/263; Atkin (2019), pp. 7–9.
17. 'Organisation of Civil Resistance in Belgium, France, UK and Ireland', 23 May 1940. Document from unknown source provided by FCO SOE Adviser 1997, with thanks to Stephen Sutton for making it available to this author. Version as 'Organisation of Civil Resistance in Belgium and France' at TNA CAB 21/1476; See Atkin (2015), Ch. 4 for a detailed account of the HDS.
18. 'Mobilisation of National Resources, moral, physical and material, to deny to the enemy the advantages obtained by his methods of invasion', ISPB, 27 May 1940: TNA CAB 63/167, f. 71; TNA CAB 21/1476.
19. 'Mobilisation of National Resources, moral, physical and material, to deny to the enemy the advantages obtained by his methods of invasion', ISPB, 27 May 1940: TNA CAB 63/167, f.72.
20. *Ibid.*
21. Lindsay (1987), p. 109.
22. Fleming (1957), p. 269.
23. Chiefs of Staff report to War Cabinet, *Urgent measures to meet attack*, 19 June 1940: TNA CAB 66/8/43.
24. Conclusions of War Cabinet, 17 June 1940: TNA CAB 65/7/65 f.321.
25. Wilkinson and Astley (1993), p. 70.
26. *Ibid.*, pp. 68, 76.
27. *Ibid.*, p. 69.
28. MI(R) War Diary for 17 June 1940: TNA HS 8/263. The War Diary was compiled from notes in November 1940.
29. Peter Wilkinson interview in Sutton, S., *Farmers or Fighters. Dissertation on the existence and function of Britain's 'secret army'. Auxiliary Units in southern England during 1940–44.* Unpublished BA dissertation 1995, Canterbury Christchurch College.
30. The same might be said of the Intelligence wing of the Auxiliary Units, the Special Duties Branch (SDB), which operated on parallel but separate lines from the Operational Branch with a continuing SIS influence. See Atkin (2015), Chs 9, 10.
31. Wilkinson and Astley (1993), p. 72.
32. DMI to Ismay, 24 June 1940: TNA CAB 21/1473; Atkin (2017), pp. 188–91.
33. D Section Early History to September 1940, pp. 17–18: TNA HS 7/3.
34. Gubbins to LDV Area Commanders, 5 July 1940: TNA CAB 120/241.
35. *Ibid.*
36. Gubbins to Colonel Hall, Southern Command, 20 September 1940: TNA WO 199/2151; Atkin (2015), p. 69.

37. TNA CAB 120/241.
38. Oxenden (2012), p. 1.
39. Fleming (1957), p. 13.
40. Memories quoted on www.kentauxiliaryunits.org.uk. Exercises in 1973, designed to test the effectiveness of similar hides built by 23 SAS in Germany, showed how quickly such hides could be discovered, being especially vulnerable to search dogs. (TNA DEFE 48/279)
41. Calvert (1964), p. 46; Calvert (1954), p. 7.
42. Calvert (1964), pp. 48–9.
43. Oxenden (2012), p. 7.
44. The development of the myth of the Auxiliary Units as a resistance organization is discussed in Atkin (2019), Ch. 4.
45. Oxenden (2012), p. 9.
46. Lindsay (1987), p. 142.
47. This temporarily changed when subsequent COs were able to use the secrecy surrounding the Auxiliary Units to requisition supplies with the minimum of scrutiny. See Wilkinson and Astley (1993), pp. 69, 74; Atkin (2019), p. 67.
48. *Art of Guerrilla Warfare*, para. 34: see on-line Appendix 2.
49. Minutes of ISPB Meeting, 27 May 1940: TNA HS 8/193.
50. Major Jones, June 1944: TNA WO 199/1194.
51. TNA WO 260/9.
52. Sandys/Ismay progress report to Churchill, 8 August 1940: TNA CAB 120/241.
53. Section D: Early History to September 1940, pp. 17–18: TNA HS 7/3.
54. Atkin (2015), Chs 9, 10. The TRD sets used telephony and there was, therefore, no need for training in morse code.
55. Wilkinson (2002), p. 104.
56. Oxenden (2012), p. 7.
57. Pryce-Jones (1975), p. 184.
58. Wilkinson and Astley (1993), p. 74.
59. Progress report on Auxiliary Units for period ending 1 September 1940 by Peter Wilkinson: TNA CAB 120/241.
60. Quoted in Sutton, S., *Farmers or Fighters. Dissertation on the existence and function of Britain's 'secret army'. Auxiliary Units in southern England during 1940–44.* Unpublished BA dissertation 1995, Canterbury Christchurch College, p. 2.
61. Atkin (2015), Ch. 11.
62. Wilkinson (2002), p. 104.
63. Quoted in Sutton, S., *Farmers or Fighters. Dissertation on the existence and function of Britain's 'secret army'. Auxiliary Units in southern England during 1940–44.* Unpublished BA dissertation 1995, Canterbury Christchurch College, p. 3.
64. Ward (2013), p. xxii. See Atkin (2019), Ch. 4 for an analysis of the development of the Auxiliary Units mythology.
65. Minutes of ISPB Meeting, 27 May 1940: TNA HS 8/193.
66. Davies to Cornwall-Jones, 17 June 1940: TNA CAB 21/1476.
67. 'Need for Organization of Civil Resistance', F.T. Davies, 18 June 1940: TNA CAB 21/1476.
68. *Ibid.*
69. Hollis to Ismay, 20 June 1940: TNA CAB 21/1476.
70. Letter of Cavendish-Bentinck to Ismay, 21 June 1940: TNA CAB 21/1476.
71. Letter of H to Hollis, 22 June 1940: TNA CAB 21/1476.

72. Letter of Ismay to Pownall, 23 June 1940: TNA CAB 21/1476.
73. Letter of Pownall to Ismay, 25 June 1940; letter of Findlater-Stewart to Ismay, 26 June 1940: TNA CAB 21/1476.
74. TNA CAB 67/7/27.
75. Dalton Diary for 25 June 1940: Pimlott (1986), p. 65.
76. 'Report on the organisation within the War Office for the conduct of para-military activities', Brigadier Wyndham, 25 August 1940: TNA HS 8/258.
77. Atkin (2017), pp. 66–8.
78. Minutes of JIC Meeting, 1 June 1940: TNA CAB 81/87.
79. Minutes of JIC, 8 June 1940: TNA CAB 81/87.
80. Minutes of JIC, 5 July 1940: TNA CAB 81/87.
81. Minutes of JIC, 17 July 1940: TNA CAB 81/87.
82. 'Duties and Responsibilities of MIR', J.C.F. Holland, 22 July 1940: TNA HS 8/256; MI(R) War Diary for 1 August 1940: TNA HS 8/263.
83. Minutes of JIC, 2 January 1941: TNA CAB 81/88.

Chapter Ten: The Caucasus, the Middle East and Africa

1. Wavell to Beaumont-Nesbitt, 30 March 1940: TNA WO 201/2864.
2. Slessor (1956), p. 270.
3. Wilkinson and Astley (1993), p. 133.
4. Kemp MI5 file: TNA KV 2/4418.
5. Kemp (1990), p. 143.
6. Kemp (1958), p. 11.
7. Kemp MI5 file: TNA KV 2/4418.
8. 'The extent of MI(R)'s activities in the past, at present and possibilities for the future', April 1940: TNA HS 8/258.
9. Reports in TNA KV 2/879.
10. Interview by E.B. Stamp, 9 April 1942: TNA KV 2/880.
11. MI5 report on W.E.D. Allen, 15 December 1940: TNA KV 2/879.
12. MI5 internal memo: 14 March 1940: TNA KV 2/879.
13. Arthur Smith to R. Stone, 13 October 1939: TNA WO 201/271.
14. Maunsell to Head of MEIC, 6 June 1942: TNA KV 4/306.
15. 'MI(R) activities in the Middle East', Elphinstone, 18 March 1940: TNA WO 201/2864. *The Flying Visit* was written during March/April 1940 and is a humorous tale of Hitler accidentally parachuting into England, being captured, and finally being dropped back over Berlin by the RAF.
16. Major General A. Smith (GHQ Middle East) to DMI, 25 March 1940: TNA WO 201/2864.
17. Wavell to DMI, 30 March 1940: TNA WO 201/2864; DMI to Wavell, 17 April 1940: TNA WO 201/2864.
18. 'Duties of MI(R)', 2 June 1940: TNA HS 8/258.
19. DMI to Wavell, 17 April 1940 and Simpson to Cawthorn, 14 April 1940: TNA WO 201/2864; GSIx to Simpson, 18 October 1940: TNA WO 201/2864.
20. Smith to DMI, 28 March 1940: TNA WO 201/2864.
21. DMI to Wavell, 17 April 1940: TNA WO 201/2864; Appendix G to Report on Para-Military Activities: Briefing for DMO to COS Meeting of 7 June 1940: TNA HS 8/259.
22. Dodds-Parker (1983), p. 45; D Section Early History to September 1940: TNA HS 7/4.
23. 'Quasi-Military Organisation and Activities: Appendix E', 19 September 1940: TNA HS 8/261.

24. 'Middle Eastern War Council Sub-Committee for Secret Activities, Suggested activities bearing on the situation in the Caucasus', Lt Colonel Simpson, 15 August 1941: TNA AIR 40/2605, paras 1–5, 11.

25. Quoted in Mackenzie (2000), p. 186; 'Special Operations Executive: Report by Joint Planning Staff ', 9 August 1941, in TNA CAB 84/33.

26. See Messenger (1988) for a full history of the Middle East Commando.

27. The most exhaustive accounts of Mission 101 are contained in Anthony Mockler (1984), *Haile Selassie's War*, and David Shirreff (2009), *Bare Feet and Bandoliers*, although both focus on the personalities and make little mention of the organizational role of MI(R)/G(R).

28. Whalley to Cavendish-Bentinck, 21 February 1939: TNA FO 371/23377.

29. Symes to Cavendish-Bentinck, 9 April 1939: TNA FO 371/23377; Comments on letter of Whalley to Cavendish-Bentinck by Cavendish-Bentinck, 2 May 1939: TNA FO 371/23377.

30. Allen (1943), pp. 35, 47. He claims he was appointed Paymaster on the basis of six months spent as a chartered accountant, twenty-five years before. Not surprisingly, this ignores his role as financial adviser to the BUF and maintainer of their secret bank accounts.

31. Quoted in Shirreff (2009), p. 23.

32. Arthur Smith to Platt, 28 September 1939: TNA WO 201/271.

33. Smith to Platt, 28 September 1939: TNA WO 201/271.

34. *Ibid*.

35. Wavell to Platt, 29 September 1939: TNA WO 201/271.

36. Smith to Stone, 19 October 1939: TNA WO 201/271.

37. Stone to Smith, 25 October 1939: TNA WO 201/271.

38. Wavell to DMI, 26 January 1940: TNA WO 201/271.

39. Dodds-Parker (1983), p. 43.

40. Planex correspondence, 5 October 1940: TNA WO 201/271.

41. G.H. Thompson to G. MacKereth, 28 February 1940: TNA FO 371/24639/637.

42. Incorporated in 'The fomentation of Rebellion Against Italian Rule in Abyssinia', Appendix A–C, undated (August 1940 or later): TNA WO 201/271.

43. Mockler (1984), p. 220.

44. *Operation Instruction No. 1*, Arthur Smith, 10 June 1940: TNA HS 8/261 and WO 201/271; Mideast, Cairo to Kaid, Khartoum, 24 July 1940: TNA WO 201/271.

45. Playfair (1954), pp. 92–7, 189.

46. 'Future Strategy: appreciation by the Chiefs of Staff Committee', 4 September 1940: TNA CAB 66/11/42.

47. Thesiger (1987), p. 314.

48. GOC Sudan (Platt) to War Office, 25 April 1939: TNA FO 371/23377.

49. 'The Fomentation of Rebellion Against Italian Rule in Abyssinia', August or later 1940: TNA WO 201/271.

50. 'Notes on Plans for Abyssinian Campaign', Sandford, 10 October 1940: TNA CAB 106/934.

51. Grey interview: IWM Sound Archive 7390, reels 1 and 2 (1984).

52. *Ibid*.

53. War Diary of Mission 101 North, 14 December 1940: TNA WO 178/36.

54. Wienholt to Ellen Lawrence (cousin), 15 June 1940, UQFL 121 Box 1: quoted in Siemon (2005), p. 285.

55. Siemon (2005), p. 289.

56. Platt to Wienholt, 4 August 1940: quoted in Siemon (2005), p. 291.

57. 'Ethiopia', Chapman-Andrews, TNA FO 371/2643.

58. Record of a meeting at Khartoum, 29 October 1940: TNA FO 371/24639.

59. 'Ethiopia – Policy of HMG from 18 October to 31 March 1941': TNA WO 230/24.

60. Rodriguez (1983), p. 36.
61. 'Ethiopia – Policy of HMG from 18 October to 31 March 1941': TNA WO 230/24.
62. *Ibid.*
63. TNA WO 230/24.
64. Haile Selassie to Churchill, 24 December 1940: TNA FO 371/27516.
65. Churchill to Eden, 31 December 1940: TNA FO 371/27516.
66. TNA WO 230/24, p. 2; Report by Major Neville, commanding G(R) Mission 107: TNA WO 201/90.
67. War Diary of Mission 101, Northern Section: TNA WO 178/36.
68. Leo Amery to General Sir Robert Haining (DCIGS), 24 August 1940: Churchill Archive Amery Papers AMEL 2/1/31 quoted in Anglim (2010), p. 126.
69. War Office and MOI (1942), p. 13.
70. *Ibid.*, p. 60.
71. Dodds-Parker (1983), p. 57.
72. Simmonds to Wingate, 12 February 1941, IWM Wingate Abyssinian Papers, Box II.
73. Wingate to G(R), 7 February 1941, Wingate to Sandford, 9 March 1941: IWM Wingate Abyssinia Papers, Box II, quoted in Anglim (2010), p. 137.
74. Wingate, 'The Ethiopian Campaign August 1940–June 1941', pp. 6, 13: IWM Wingate Abyssinian Papers, quoted in Anglim (2010), p. 129.
75. Minutes of a conference held at HQ, Troops in Sudan, 12 February 1941: IWM Wingate Abyssinian Papers, quoted in Anglim (2010), p. 134.
76. 'MI(R) in the Middle East', Elphinstone, 18 March 1940: TNA WO 201/2864.
77. Belhaven (1955), p. 227.
78. MI(R) War Diary for 11 August 1940: TNA HS 8/263.
79. Waterfield (1944), p. 11.
80. *Ibid.*, pp. 20–1.
81. Belhaven (1955), p. 233.
82. Waterfield (1944), p. 24.
83. 'Report on the organisation within the War Office for the conduct of para-military activities', Brigadier Wyndham, 25 August 1940: TNA HS 8/258.
84. *Ibid.*
85. Consul-General to Foreign Office, 5 June 1940: TNA FO 371/24282/6687.
86. Consul-General to Foreign Office, 10 May 1940: TNA FO 371/24282/6687.
87. Note on message from Consul-General to Foreign Office, 27 May 1940; Foreign Office to Consul-General, 28 May 1940: TNA FO 371/24282/6687.
88. Consul-General to Foreign Office, 5 June 1940: TNA FO 371/24282/6687.
89. War Office telegram, 8 July 1940: TNA FO 371/24282.
90. Van Hoegaerden transferred to the RAFVR in March 1942 and became a naturalized British subject in 1947.
91. Mission 106 Report: TNA WO 178/3.
92. R. Makins (Foreign Office) to Carlisle (War Office), 29 Jan 1941: TNA FO 371/26347.
93. Note by R. Makins, 24 June 1941: TNA FO 371 26347.
94. Joint to Roberts (Foreign Office), 27 June 1941: TNA FO 371/26347.
95. *Ibid.*
96. Mission 106 Report: TNA WO 178/3.
97. Vanderlinden (1988), p. 44; TNA FO 371/24282/169.
98. Mission 106 Report: TNA WO 178/3.
99. *Ibid.*
100. Joint to Foreign Office, 22 January 1941: TNA FO 371/26347.
101. Joint to Foreign Office, 26 February 1941: TNA FO 371/26347.

102. Notes for Colonel McKenzie, 26 February 1941: TNA WO 371/26347.
103. McKenzie to War Office, 26 February 1941: TNA FO 371/26347.
104. Col. Percival (War Office) to R. Makins (Foreign Office), 14 June 1941; War Office to No. 19 Military Mission, 19 June 1941: TNA FO 371/26347.
105. Spears Mission to War Office, 21 June 1941: TNA FO 371/26347.

Chapter Eleven: Asia, the Far East and Australia

1. *On Guerrilla Warfare* was translated by Samuel Griffiths, US Marine Corps, in 1940 and published in Griffiths (1961); 'CG's Comments on Foot's Book': Gubbins papers 3/2/57, IWM; Astley (2007), p. 20; Wilkinson and Astley (1993), p. 34. The cover of GS(R) Report No. 7: *Considerations from the wars in Spain and China with regard to certain aspects of Army Policy*, is found among the *Notes on the Sino-Japanese War* collated by the DMI: TNA WO 106/5572.
2. Hart-Davis (1987), p. 208.
3. Peter Fleming, 'Notes on the Possibilities of British Military Action in China,' August 1939: TNA HS 8/260. Emphasis in original.
4. Holland to MI1(a), 15 September 1939: TNA HS 8/257.
5. Hart-Davis (1987), p. 215; Correspondence between Cadogan and Beaumont-Nesbitt, September 1939: TNA FO 371/23552.
6. MI(R) War Diary for September 1939: TNA HS 8/263.
7. C-in-C Far East to War Office, 13 April 1941: TNA CAB 121/317.
8. C-in-C Far East to War Office, 13 August 1941: TNA WO 106/2629.
9. War Office to C-in-C Far East, 9 September 1941: TNA WO 106/2629.
10. 'Memorandum by SOE on their Proposed Organisation in India and the Far East': TNA HS 1/202; Note by Sir Frank Nelson on the above, in TNA CAB 121/317; Nelson to Keswick, 19 March 1942: TNA HS 1/164.

Chapter Twelve: MI(R) and SOE

1. Astley (2007), p. 30.
2. Summary of Secret Reports regarding internal conditions in Germany, Gladwyn Jebb, 30 May 1940: TNA PREM 3/193/6A.
3. Dalton Diary, 3 and 14 June 1940: Pimlott (1986), pp. 34, 40.
4. Beaumont-Nesbitt to Ismay, 3 March 1940: TNA CAB 21/1425; COS (40) 271, 21 March 1940: TNA CAB 80/9.
5. H.M. Barnard to Ismay, 8 March 1940: TNA CAB 21/1425.
6. Minutes of JIC, 12 March 1940: TNA CAB 81/87.
7. Minutes of JIC, 21 March 1940: TNA CAB 81/87.
8. 'Report on the organisation within the War Office for the conduct of para-military activities', Brigadier Wyndham, 25 August 1940: TNA HS 8/258.
9. British strategy in a certain eventuality, 25 May 1940 (Report by Chiefs of Staff), circulated to the War Cabinet as WP (40)168: TNA CAB 66/7.
10. Astley (2007), p. 30.
11. Draft Memo of Holland to Beaumont-Nesbitt, 4 June 1940; 'Comments by Colonel Holland on the DMO&P draft', J.C.F. Holland, 4 June 1940: TNA HS 8/263.
12. 'Comments by Col. Holland on DMO&P's draft', 4 June 1940: TNA HS 8/263; DMI to VCIGS, 5 June 1940: TNA HS 8/256.
13. Ismay to Beaumont-Nesbitt, 5 March 1940: TNA CAB 21/1425.
14. DMI to VCIGS, 5 June 1940: TNA HS 8/256.
15. Meeting of 13 June 1940: TNA HS 8/258 and CAB 63/132.
16. Medlicott (1952), pp. 44, 46.

17. Dalton (1957), p. 368.
18. Gladwyn, Baron (1972), p. 104.
19. Dalton diary for 21 June 1940: Pimlott (1986), p. 45.
20. Dalton diary for 25 June 1940: Pimlott (1986), p. 65.
21. Dalton diary for 29 June 1940: Pimlott (1986), p. 50.
22. Minute on D activities in the Middle East, 7 August 1940: TNA HS 5/60, HS 3/147 and HS 3/154.
23. Minutes of meeting of 1 July 1940: TNA FO 1093/193; Garnett (2002), p. 30.
24. Meeting of 1 July 1940 to discuss the direction of sabotage: TNA FO 1093/193; MI(R), *An aide-memoire on the co-ordination of subversive activities in the conquered territories*, 6 July 1940: TNA HS 8/259.
25. Minutes of meeting of 1 July 1940: TNA FO 1093/193.
26. Mackenzie (2000), p. 68.
27. Appendix C to secret memo by DMI, 18 July 1940: quoted in Foot (1966), p. 9; Pimlott (1986), p. 57.
28. Dalton diary for 10 July 1940: Pimlott (1986), p. 56.
29. Memorandum by the Lord President of the Council, 19 July 1940: TNA CAB 66/10.
30. Churchill to Dalton, 16 July 1940 quoted in Mackenzie (2000), p. 69.
31. Minutes of JIC, 17 July 1940: TNA CAB 81/8.
32. MI(R) War Diary for 22 July 1940: TNA HS 8/263.
33. MI(R) War Diary for 24 July 1940: TNA HS 8/263.
34. MI(R) War Diary for 29 July 1940: TNA HS 8/263.
35. Taylor to Goodwill, 2 August 1940: TNA HS 5/497.
36. 'Duties and Activities of MI(R)', 22 July 1940; 'List of current MI(R) activities' (undated): TNA HS 8/256.
37. DMI to DRO, 2 August 1940: TNA HS 8/258.
38. Astley (2007), p. 39; MI(R) War Diary for 15 August 1940: TNA HS 8/260.
39. Astley (2007), p. 39; MI(R) War Diary for 1 August 1940: TNA HS 8/263.
40. Hugh Dalton, 'The Fourth Arm', 19 August 1940: TNA HS 8/258; Annex I, Para 3, to paper on Subversion, October 1940: TNA HS 8/334.
41. Note on 'The Fourth Arm' in agenda for Chiefs of Staff Committee of 21 August 1940, compiled on 20 August: TNA HS 8/258.
42. Wyndham to Gladwyn Jebb, 26 August 1940: TNA HS 8/258.
43. COS(40) Minutes of a Chiefs of Staff Meeting (undated), August 1940: TNA CAB 84/17.
44. *Ibid.*
45. DDMI(R) to DMI, 26 August 1940: TNA HS 8/258; 'Report on the organization within the War Office for the conduct of para-military activities', Brigadier Wyndham, 25 August 1940: TNA HS 8/258.
46. 'Report on the organization within the War Office for the conduct of para-military activities', Brigadier Wyndham, 25 August 1940: TNA HS 8/258.
47. DMI to VCIGS, 'Reorganisation of MI(R)', 12 September 1940: TNA HS 8/258.
48. 'Quasi-Military organizations and Activities: an adjunct to political and military strategy', L.F.R. Kenyon, 19 September 1940: TNA HS 8/261.
49. MI(R) War Diary for 23 September 1940: TNA HS 8/263.
50. 'Irregular Tactics and Strategy', Holland to DMI, August 1940: TNA HS 8/256.
51. *Ibid.*
52. 'General Staff Research', Holland, 23 August 1940: TNA HS 8/258.
53. 'Irregular Tactics and Strategy', Holland to DMI, August 1940: TNA HS 8/256.
54. MI(R) War Diary for 23 September 1940: TNA HS 8/263.
55. Astley (2007), p. 41.

56. Dalton to Wavell, 11 June 1941: TNA HS 4/198.
57. Wavell to Dalton, 16 June 1941: TNA HS 4/198.
58. Wavell to War Office, 4 June 1941: TNA HS3/146; Wavell to War Office, 16 June 1941: TNA HS 3/146.
59. 'Future Strategy: appreciation by the Chiefs of Staff Committee', 4 September 1940: TNA CAB 66/11/42.
60. Philby (1968), p. 11.
61. Wilkinson and Astley (1993), p. 77.
62. Major G.M. Forty, 'History of the Training Section of SOE, 1940–1945', September 1945: TNA HS 7/51 and HS 8/435; Wilkinson and Astley (1993), pp. 77–8.
63. Wilkinson and Astley (1993), p. 76.
64. *Ibid.*, p. 77.

Conclusion

1. Astley (2007), p. 41; Dodds-Parker (1983), p. 39.
2. Hailsham (1990), p. 144.
3. 'Irregular Tactics and Strategy', Holland to DMI, August 1940: TNA 8/256.
4. TNA CAB 63/192, f.108.
5. Macrae (1972), p. 12.
6. Notably Malcolm Munthe, Andrew Croft, Millis Jefferis and F.T. Davies.
7. When Joan Bright returned to the more traditional War Office she complained she was neither 'fish nor fowl' and not easily accepted as an equal by junior officers of the Civil Service. See Astley (2007), p. 46. See also Atkin (2017), p. 17.
8. Foot (2001), p. 22; Linderman (2016), p. 106.
9. Gladwyn (1972), p. 101.
10. Astley (2007), p. 30.

Bibliography

Allen, W.E.D. (1943), *Guerrilla War in Abyssinia* (Penguin, London).

Amery, Julian (1973), *Approach March* (Hutchinson, London).

Anglim, Simon (2005), 'MI(R), G(R) and British covert operations, 1939–42', *Intelligence and National Security*, 20(4): 631–53.

Anglim, Simon (2010), *Orde Wingate and the British Army 1922–1944* (Pickering and Chatto, London).

Astley, Joan Bright (2007), *The Inner Circle: A View of War at the Top* (The Memoir Club, Stanhope).

Atkin, Malcolm (2015), *Fighting Nazi Occupation: British Resistance 1939–1945* (Pen & Sword, Barnsley).

Atkin, Malcolm (2017), *Section D for Destruction: forerunner of SOE* (Pen & Sword, Barnsley).

Atkin, Malcolm (2019), *To the Last Man: the Home Guard in War and Popular Culture* (Pen & Sword, Barnsley).

Belhaven, Lord (1955), *The Uneven Road* (John Murray, London).

Broomhall, W.M. (1957), 'Memoir', *The Royal Engineer's Journal*, LXXI (September 1957): 300–2.

Calvert, Michael (1954), *Prisoners of Hope* (Jonathan Cape, London).

Calvert, Michael (1964), *Fighting Mad* (Jarrold, Norwich).

Connell, John (1959), *Auchinleck* (Cassell, London).

Croft, Andrew (1991), *A Taste for Adventure* (SPA, London).

Dalton, Hugh (1957), *The Fateful Years: Memoirs 1931–1945* (Muller, London).

Davidson-Houston, J.V. (1949), *Armed Pilgrimage* (Robert Hale, London).

Deletant, David (2016), *British Clandestine Activities in Romania during the Second World War* (Palgrave Macmillan, Basingstoke).

Derry, T.K. (1952), *The Campaign in Norway* (HMSO, London).

de Wiart, Adrian Carton (2007), *Happy Odyssey* (Pen & Sword, Barnsley).

Dodds-Parker, Douglas (1983), *Setting Europe Ablaze* (Springwood Books, Surrey).

Dorril, Stephen (2000), *MI6* (Free Press, New York).

Dunsterville, Lionel (1920), *Adventures of Dunsterforce* (Edward Arnold, London).

Elliott, G. (1998), *I Spy: the secret life of a British agent* (St Ermin's Press, London).

Fell, W.R. (1966), *The Sea Our Shield* (Cassell, London).

Fergusson, Bernard (1961), *Wavell: Portrait of a Soldier* (Collins).

Fleming, Peter (1957), *Invasion 1940* (Hart-Davis, London).

Foot, M.R.D. (1966), *SOE in France* (HMSO, London).

Foot, M.R.D. (1970), 'Special Operations II' in Elliot-Bateman, Michael (ed.), *The Fourth Dimension of Warfare, vol. 1: Intelligence, Subversion, Resistance* (Manchester University Press), pp. 19–34.

Foot, M.R.D. (1999), *SOE: The Special Operations Executive 1940–1946* (Pimlico, London).

Foot, M.R.D. (2001), *SOE in the Low Countries* (St Ermin's Press, London).

Foot, M.R.D. and Langley, J.M. (1979), *MI9: Escape and Evasion 1939–45* (Book Club Associates, London).

Garner, Tom (2018), 'Norway Commando: an interview with Charles "Sonny" Wright', *History at War* (October 2018): 68–74.

Garnett, David (2002), *The Secret History of PWE* (St Ermin's Press, London).

Gladwyn, Baron (Gladwyn Jebb) (1972), *The Memoirs of Lord Gladwyn* (Weidenfeld & Nicolson, London).

Grehan, John and Mace, Martin (2015), *The Battle for Norway 1940–1942* (Pen & Sword, Barnsley).

Griffiths, Samuel (1961), *Mao Tse-Tung on Guerrilla Warfare* (Praeger, USA).

Gubbins, Colin (1948), 'Resistance Movements in the War', *Royal United Services Institution Journal*, 93(570): 210–23.

Hailsham, Lord (Quintin Hogg) (1990), *A Sparrow's Flight: the memoirs of Lord Hailsham* (Collins, London).

Hart-Davis, Duff (1987), *Peter Fleming* (Oxford University Press, Oxford).

Holland, J.C.F. (1935), 'The Military Possibilities of the Autogyro', *Royal United Services Institute Journal*, 80(518): 355–60.

Household, Geoffrey (1958), *Against the Wind* (Michael Joseph, London).

Kemp, Peter (1958), *No Colours or Crest* (Panther, London).

Kemp, Peter (1990), *The Thorns of Memory* (Sinclair-Stevenson, London).

Kiszely, John (2017), *Anatomy of a Campaign: The British Fiasco in Norway, 1940* (Cambridge University Press, Cambridge).

Kotakallio, Juho (2014), *Hänen majesteettinsa agentit. Brittitiedustelu Suomessa 1918–1941* (Atena, Finland).

Kyle, Keith (2011) [1991], *Suez: Britain's End of Empire* (I.B. Tauris, London, revised edn).

Lawrence, T.E. (1929), 'Guerrilla Warfare', *Encyclopaedia Britannica*.

Linderman, A.R.B. (2016), *Rediscovering Irregular Warfare: Colin Gubbins and the origins of Britain's Special Operations Executive* (University of Oklahoma Press, USA).

Lindsay, Donald (1987), *Forgotten General, a life of Andrew Thorne* (Michael Russell, London).

Lovat, Lord Simon (1978), *March Past* (Weidenfeld & Nicolson, London).

McKay, C.G. (1993), *From Information to Intrigue: Studies in Secret Service based on the Swedish experience 1939–1945* (Frank Cass, London).

Mackenzie, W. (2000), *The Secret History of SOE* (St Ermin's Press, London).

MacLaren, Roy (1976), *Canadians in Russia, 1918–19* (Macmillan, Toronto).

Macpherson, Sir Tommy, with Richard Bath (2010), *Behind Enemy Lines: the autobiography of Britain's Most Decorated Living War Hero* (Mainstream Publishing, Edinburgh).

Macrae, Stuart (1972), *Winston Churchill's Toyshop* (Walker Publishing, USA).

Maschwitz, Eric (1957), *No Chip On My Shoulder* (Herbert Jenkins, London).

Medlicott, W.N. (1952), *History of the Second World War Vol. 1: The Economic Blockade* (HMSO, London).

Melville, Michael (2004), *The Story of the Lovat Scouts 1900–1980* (Librario, Kinloss).

Messenger, Charles (1988), *The Middle East Commandos* (William Kimber & Co.).

Mockler, Anthony (1984), *Haile Selassie's War* (Oxford University Press, Oxford).

Munthe, Malcolm (1954), *Sweet is War* (Duckworth, London).

Ogden, Alan (2019), *Master of Deception: the wartime adventures of Peter Fleming* (Bloomsbury Academic, London).

Oxenden, Nigel (2012), *Auxiliary Units: History and Achievement 1940–1944* (BRO Museum, Parham).

Parker, John (2000), *Commandos: the inside story of Britain's most elite fighting force* (Headline Books, London).

Pearton, Maurice (2000), 'British Intelligence in Romania 1938–1941', in George Cipăinu and Virgiliu Țârău (eds), *Romanian & British Historians on the Contemporary History of Romania* (Cluj University Press, Romania), pp. 187–203.

Philby, Kim (1968), *My Silent War* (Macgibbon & Kee, London).

Pimlott, Ben (1986), *The Second World War Diary of Hugh Dalton 1940–45* (Jonathan Cape, London).

Playfair, I.S.O. (1954), *History of the Second World War: The Mediterranean and Middle East. Vol. I. (to May 1941)* (HMSO, London).

Prendergast, J. (1979), *Prender's Progress* (Cassell, London).

Pryce-Jones, David (1975), 'Britain's Secret Resistance Movement', in Richard Cox (ed.), *Operation Sealion* (Thornton Cox Ltd), pp. 177–86.

Riley, Jonathon (1998), *From Pole to Pole: the life of Quintin Riley 1905–1980* (Anthony Rowe Ltd, Chippenham, 2nd edn).

Riley, Jonathon (2006), *The Life & Campaigns of General Hughie Stockwell* (Pen & Sword, Barnsley).

Rodriguez, Helen (1983), *Helen of Burma* (Collins, London).

Schofield, Victoria (2007), *Wavell: Soldier and Statesman* (John Murray, London).

Shakespeare, Nicholas (2017), *Six Minutes in May: how Churchill unexpectedly became Prime Minister* (Harvill Secker, London).

Shirreff, David (2009), *Bare Feet and Bandoliers* (Pen & Sword, Barnsley).

Siemon, Rosamund (2005), *The Eccentric Mr Wienholt* (University of Queensland Press, Australia).

Skidmore, Ian (1981), *Marines Don't Hold Their Horses* (W.H. Allen, London).

Slessor, Sir John (1956), *The Central Blue* (Cassell, London).

Spencer-Chapman, Freddy (1949), *The Jungle Is Neutral* (Chatto & Windus, London).

Thesiger, Wilfrid (1987), *The Life of my Choice* (Collins, London).

Turner, Des (2011), *SOE's Secret Weapons Centre: Station XII* (The History Press, Stroud).

Vanderlinden, Jaxques (1988), *Le gouverneur et les militaires (1935–1940)*, Académie Royal des Sciences D'Outre Mer, Classe des Sciences Morales et Politiques Mémoires in-8°, Nouvelle Série, Tome 49, fase. 3, Bruxelles.

War Office and MOI (1942), *The Abyssinian Campaigns: the official story of the Conquest of Italian East Africa* (HMSO, London).

Ward, Arthur (1997), *Resisting the Nazi Invader* (Constable, London).

Ward, Arthur (2013), *Churchill's Secret Defence Army* (Pen & Sword, Barnsley).

Waterfield, G. (1944), *Morning Will Come* (John Murray, London).

West, Nigel and Tsarev, Oleg (2009), *Triplex: secrets from the Cambridge Spies* (Yale University Press).

Wilkinson, Peter (2002), *Foreign Fields* (I.B. Tauris, London).

Wilkinson, Peter and Astley, Joan [Bright] (1993), *Gubbins and SOE* (Pen & Sword, Barnsley).

Young, Kenneth (ed.) (1980), *The Diaries of Sir Robert Bruce Lockhart: Vol. 2: 1939–1965* (Macmillan, London).

Index